Dhobis of Delhi

"An illuminating contribution to the study of cities and margins world-wide, the anthropology of South Asia, caste, or class, this book is an eye-opening exploration of choices people make to identify themselves with particular social movements, advocacy groups, and political ideologies. The product of many years of ethnographic engagement, this work is both about Delhi and a small community in the city—a group of 'un-touchables' who have chosen not to join the Dalit movement or iden-tify as Dalit. How the modern city affects the Dhobi becomes clear in Channa's work, something both engrossing and humanistic. I can think of no one as knowledgeable and insightful as she is in this book."

— Virginia R. Dominguez, Edward William and Jane Marr Gutgsell Professor of Anthropology, University of Illinois at Urbana-Champaign; Consulting Director and Co-Founder, International Forum for U.S. Studies

"This book stands as an exemplary model of ethnography, showcasing breadth, depth, and a richness of prisms that delve into various faces of the lives and social structures of Dhobis in Delhi. Channa's profound rap-port with and insightful observation of the people over several decades have enabled the portrayal of Dhobis not merely as victims of the caste system, but as active agents who adeptly navigate their lives and assert their identities, striving for equality in the larger society. This book offers valuable insights not only for those seeking a better understanding of the contemporary life of Dalits in India but also for those interested in con-ducting fieldwork, holistic community observation, and coherent yet multi-perspective and nuanced ethnography."

—Yasuko Takezawa, Professor, Intercultural Research Institute, Kansai Gaidai University; Professor Emeritus, Kyoto University

"Channa's book is a much-needed contribution to the resurging debate on caste. Whether as an analogy for racial oppression or as an axis of dis-crimination and counter-discrimination in South Asia and diasporic contexts, there is a need for nuanced perspectives on community life, identities, and strategies for navigating the complex urban environment. This ethnography deconstructs the embodied experiences, practices, and meanings of caste, especially from the vantage of the particular urban sites that the Dhobis navigate. The book illuminates a heterogeneous field where untouchables' collective identities and strategies of resilience do not all align with the politics and subjectivities of the Dalit Movement and offers a cogent explanation as to why."

—Faye V. Harrison, Professor of African American Studies and
Anthropology, University of Illinois at Urbana-Champaig

"In a world where third-world cities are louder than ever, Channa's diachronic study of a marginal group that has made silence part of its survival strategies is hugely welcome. Her eyes elicit changes in the urban space that only her wit combined with forty years of field experience allow her to see, such as the 'air conditioning' of (poor) homes or the growing commodification of small liminal neighbourhood spaces where people could wander around doing nothing. Tragically, in this city, especially for such groups of poor, physical intra- or extra-group socialization is becoming less accessible, even as digital socialization within and between groups offers new horizons. Channa´s circumscribed and detailed Delhi story provides many insights into urban anthropology, making this book of universal value."

—Livio Sansone, Professor of Anthropology,
Federal University of Bahia

"Understanding how a community defines and locates itself through its experiential realities in a layered and diverse context is challenging. Unheard voices and invisible realities create a disconnect between the researcher and the research. In this commendable work, Channa, an eminent anthropologist, captures the community's lifeworld, aspirations, pain, and numerous explicit and implicit transitions with the changing city and how its embodiments in a self-reflective claim form a history. It delves deep to unravel the constructs ingrained in their collective memories and captures not just the voices but also the changes that have transpired. It is a must-read work to grasp how a community, with its resilience and viability against all odds, becomes a knowable entity in a larger framework of given space and time."

—Badri Narayan, Director, G B Pant Social Science Institute

Dhobis of Delhi

An Urban Ethnography from the Margins, 1974–2023

SUBHADRA MITRA CHANNA

OXFORD
UNIVERSITY PRESS

Great Clarendon Street, Oxford, OX2 6DP,
United Kingdom

Oxford University Press is a department of the University of Oxford.
It furthers the University's objective of excellence in research, scholarship,
and education by publishing worldwide. Oxford is a registered trade mark of
Oxford University Press in the UK and in certain other countries

Published in the United States of America by Oxford University Press
198 Madison Avenue, New York, NY 10016, United States of America

British Library Cataloguing in Publication Data

Data available

Library of Congress Control Number: 2024941344

ISBN 9780198926207

DOI: 10.1093/9780198926238.001.0001

Printed and bound in India by
Replika Press Pvt. Ltd.

This book is dedicated to my late husband,
Dr Vardesh Chander Channa,
who introduced me to the dhobis and
encouraged me to be an academic.

Acknowledgements

This book has taken a long time to evolve, and many persons who started this journey with me have left on the way. For accomplishing this work I wish to extend my deepest gratitude to the dhobis of Delhi, who have hosted me in their homes, fed me when I was hungry, unconditionally accepted me, and offered help in my project in every possible way. I am specifically thankful to the late Chaudhuri Bulakhi Ram, who was at the helm of the *biradari* when I began my fieldwork as a shy young woman, who had never had any experience of working or even walking in the lanes of Old Delhi. He welcomed me into his home, encouraged me, and paved the way for entry into the *biradari*. His son Suraj also passed away on the way, but his grandsons and daughters-in-law continue to welcome me into their homes. I must acknowledge Bishanlal, who has kept his house always open for me, where I can walk in anytime and ask any questions. The first woman to do a PhD from the *biradari*, Dr Sheetal Kanojia, and her husband and their extended family have again been like my own family and will remain like that. There have been so many others: Omi Pahlwan, his wife, sons, and extended family, the numbers of dhobi men and women with whom I have shared so much time, so many emotions and experiences; they remain alive in my writings and my mind forever. This book has benefited greatly from the excellent suggestions and comments given by the two anonymous reviewers and I am extremely grateful to them and to the entire production team of Oxford University Press for their efforts.

Contents

Introduction: Doing Urban Ethnography in the Present   1

1. The Dhobis of Old Delhi   27

2. The Social World of the Dhobis   56

3. Livelihood, Resources, and Strategies for Survival   88

4. Living Life as a Dhobi (Man and Woman)   120

5. Negotiating Power in the Realm of the Sacred   157

6. The Political Realm   193

7. Conclusion: Surviving in a Discriminatory World and
   the Future of the City   216

Bibliography   237
Author Index   247
Subject Index   251

Introduction

Doing Urban Ethnography in the Present

Ethnographies are the hallmark of a particular genre that began with colonial anthropological research but has now been accepted into several other disciplines. In its inception, this method led to the descriptive recording of some out-of-the-way remote and unknown groups, a community, a tribe, or even a person or category. In contemporary times, anthropological gaze has undergone much transformation, moving closer to home, studying the everyday lives of ordinary peoples using a methodology that no longer assumes that whatever is to be studied is within the grasp of the scholar, or that it has a boundary or can be located easily on a map or captured in an eternal time frame. Ethnographies are increasingly becoming impressionistic, bordering on the blurred line between fiction and fact and attempting to take account of a reality that seems fleeting at best. If that is so, then the most relevant question that can be asked is, why write one?

Does ethnography add to existing knowledge? And the answer is that it does. In the ethnographic moment there is a condensation of data that has situational relevance and is able to capture some portion of the real world given the anthropological training and skill of the scholar. Ethnography is not necessarily a record of relevant information as much as an intuitive insight, an understanding that comes through with deep association with what anthropologists call the field. What is actually seen and heard and recorded is also supplemented with history, mostly in the form of ethnohistory, a history constructed through the eyes of the people along with secondary information, partly quantitative and partly qualitative. This entire process is mediated by the subjective perception of the ethnographer, seen through her eyes, heard through her ears, and cognitively sifted through her perceptions. Yet, a combination of various sources is

Dhobis of Delhi. Subhadra Mitra Channa, Oxford University Press. © Subhadra Mitra Channa 2024.
DOI: 10.1093/9780198926238.003.0001

able, if the ethnographer is astute, to bring about a degree of illumination into the lives of the people being studied within the context of their existence. Ethnography is able to add to existing knowledge about what is happening in the world and act as an aid to understanding of the processes of political economy and historical transformation. It is relevant and significant primarily if it can highlight the plight of the marginalized, the dispossessed, where one is able to grasp at least some of the insidious processes of domination and inequality that are becoming pervasive in the modern world. At the same time, the microprocesses of practice observable through the ethnographic method enable the anthropologist to become aware of and disseminate the subversive and silent modes of protest and dissent that exist at the level of everyday life and which, although not overt, are nevertheless potent in their accumulative impact (Scott 1985).

It is only the ethnographic method that has ability to record and observe the minute and all that which is not overtly and loudly visible or audible. The value of such work is now recognized outside of the anthropological/sociological realms as economists like Gill (2010: 154) acknowledge that while the New Institutional Economics (NIE) acknowledges the social context of market exchange, 'there is a marked reluctance to engage with the actual fluid reality and complex nature of these social relations in any detail'. Anthropologists have recognized the power of the small and subservient, and only qualitative and in-depth sight can reveal the manoeuvring of the powerless and the power of the marginal. As de Certeau (1984: xvii) says, in writing about the simple, everyday process of cooking and eating, 'The tactics of consumption, the ingenious ways in which the weak make use of the strong, thus lend a political dimension to everyday practices.' Again, as de Certeau (1984: xvii) puts it, this marginality is no longer something that happens to a few; it is becoming universal, it is a silent majority which is composed of a variety of categories, but together they do compose the 99 percent. It is then only natural that anthropologists should devote themselves to studying this majority, and even if they study the dominant 1 percent, it will be to understand the processes of domination from another vantage location. It is imperative to acknowledge the political nature of ethnography, for it is only through the political—the path that illuminates the power plays of the ordinary, the mundane, and the largely unnoticed—that anthropological ethnography makes a claim for its continued relevance. *It no longer claims to be factual or objective but it does claim to make a point, to highlight a position, and to make visible what is mostly considered not worth looking at.*

Contemporary anthropologists have taken the question of 'positionality' (Rosaldo 1997:175, Harraway 1999) seriously, flowing naturally from the shift in perspective from objectivity to intersubjectivity. No longer is the anthropologist convinced of a preconceived research design, a methodical working out of predetermined research questions. I would agree with Engebretsen (2012:203) that 'Fieldwork is, if anything, a collaborative enterprise, more often than not, guided by serendipitous chances'. In my long interaction with my field, I have encountered many such serendipitous situations; in fact, these have added much more to my insights than the planned research that I had initially mapped out for my PhD that was completed by the end of the seventies, and I was able to claim my degree in 1982. The bias in this work is that it looks at the world from below or from the margins, and therefore it is only logical to follow the works of scholars such as Scott (1985) and de Certeau (1984) as well those like Bourdieu (1996[1984]) and most others engaged in identifying and understanding the processes of domination and subordination, as well as resultant countercurrents of protest, resistance, and survival. Several of these authors are mentioned and discussed in the text that follows.

In my work I have often used the collective, like 'dhobis do like this' or 'dhobis engage in such an activity', and it may be taken as a lapse. But here I refer to Sax (2009:94)—'If we define agency rather straightforwardly as the capacity to effect changes in the external world, then it is perfectly reasonable to ascribe it to groups, organizations, even to non-human entities'; in other words, if sometimes agency appears de-individualized, one can assume it is the group acting or even thinking as a collective. Sax (2009) refers to the theories of 'collective intention and distributive cognition. The former argue that group intentions have the first, a particular characteristic and are more than merely the sum of individual intentions, the latter that knowledge of the complex system is distributed among numerous agents, no single of them necessarily has knowledge of the complete system'. Keeping the second aspect in mind, an anthropologist having access to multiple sites of information may take the liberty of constructing a collective perception or attributing a holistic dimension to certain observations, collected from fragmented sources. Such constructions, although somewhat impressionistic, may still convey important information about the group in general.

I have described my positionality in detail elsewhere (Channa 2013b), but it is necessary to mention that this positionality has changed with changes in my own lifecycle, especially as this work spans more than forty years. A large part of the material used in this work has been collected through ethnographic fieldwork that I began around the year 1974, as a young research scholar collecting material for my PhD, and which I continued in bits and pieces till the end of the year 2019. From 2016, in fact, I began a kind of restudy, going back systematically to the households, informants, and neighbourhoods that I had visited in the earlier phase of my fieldwork that was carried out with an intensity only possible for a research student over a period of four years, from January 1974 to the middle of 1978. In between I kept in touch only to carry forward the personal relationships and to remain in contact with the community with whom I had formed fairly intimate contacts. I have been going back to the field right up to the time this manuscript went to press. I shall continue my association with the dhobis as the relations formed with them are now a part of my social world. Monge (2012: 14) has written that urban research can be a 'reflexive intermingling of the field dimension with the theoretical problematic of the spatial and temporal axis of both the city and the ethnographer who writes about the city'.

In spite of this long immersion, I agree with Bourdieu (1996[1984]: 4) that 'The "objectivity" of judgement always remains elusive and implicit'. Positionality comes up naturally as one is going through one's narrative about the field and gathering up the evidence to be presented. Ethnography is a construct around some moot questions that the narrator feels are central and which may, as in my case, change over time. Often and correctly so, this significance is not of the anthropologist's concerns only but also of the people who are finding their voices through this ethnography. These voices may also change over time and are an important indicator of social transformations.

The intimate relationships between the researcher and the field that anthropological fieldwork makes possible makes it also the tool par excellence for bringing forth the unheard voices from the peripheries, voices that are never articulated or foregrounded, even if they are ever spoken. Historians have rarely recorded the lives of the ordinary people as they go about obscurely doing their daily work. They have mostly picked up the kind of events and people that 'make headlines', so to say. As an example, in her otherwise excellent and detailed account of Delhi,Gupta (1981) makes hardly any mention of the ordinary people of the city, no doubt being limited by the lack of any kind of records or writings about them. With reference to India's past, Sarkar (1997) has described the nature of history as written in Mrityunjay Vidyalankar's *Rajabali* as mostly a chronicle of kings, real and mythical. Such history was more concerned with the maintenance of the moral order and the legitimacy of the king, in so far as he maintained or did not maintain it. Another moot point is the moral order itself. Did the one prescribed by a high-caste Brahmin such as Vidyalankar concur with the one acceptable to a lower-caste community? As I found out during my fieldwork, it did not; it varies significantly from that of the upper castes and classes but remains unnoticed and unrecorded. As pointed out by Pardo (2018), the moral universe of the masses does not always tally with formal laws and dictates from the top and is manifested only in conflict or revolution. Fiction has been more generous in bringing forth the voices of the marginal, but fiction, although capable of causing revolutions, is rarely quoted as real knowledge.

One then of necessity turns to anthropological writings, which carry the potential to make the people speak for themselves. Ethnography can identify power fields that constrain and subjugate people as well as their agency in contesting and pushing the boundaries of their existence, their resilience and viability in the face of all the odds. In this work I prefer to take both a critical and a reflexive position. This then calls for a specification of whose position I am interrogating and what form of subordination I wish to address. In the present study, unlike a class situation taken for granted in most studies with a political economic backdrop, I take a small caste group, located at the bottom of a society. The field is seen as layered and complex. Hannarez (2010:60) has described a certain kind of field study as studying 'sideways', where the anthropologist belongs more or less to the same or similar community that is being studied. It is only when the anthropologist is able to 'merge' with the field, be present without being noticed, that one may talk about 'surrendering to the field' (Hannarez 2010: 62). As my narration about my field study will clarify,

I did make an attempt to study sideways as well as to make my presence inconspicuous to the extent that, at least if not all the time but at some times, people did go about their lives as if I was not present. The commonality that I shared with my field is one of belonging to the same city, the ability to speak the same language and comprehend the same cognitive cultural map. I differed in my class position but was able to negotiate my position to a relative sense of equality that has persisted over the years, enabling me to continue my social relationships with those who are being represented in this work.

The ethnography presented here is situated in a city, namely Delhi, a busy mega-metropolis. Urbanization is a process to which a majority of the world's population is now subject. Very soon, most of the world's population is going to become urban. Yet, although located within democracies and to nation states overtly committed to the notions of social justice and equality, the urban scenario reflects the inequalities and marginalities stimulated by the ever-spreading market economy, the corporatization of the states, the growing chasm between the rich and poor, and all forms of exploitation of the majority on which the prosperity of the few thrives. The modern cities are increasingly reflecting the political economy of inequality and widening chasms, so characteristic of the body politic as of, now, a 'creeping urban apartheid' (Yiftachel 2009:92) that is becoming increasingly pervasive under conditions of neoliberalism. Most cities contain some given categories of marginality, like the informal sector, the immigrants, the minority, the illegal, and the unwanted. The lower castes in the Indian cities, especially the untouchables (known officially as Scheduled Castes as untouchability in considered illegal and is a cognizable offense), have always been part of this marginal category, whether in the rural or in the urban areas (Deliege 1999, Mendelsohn and Vicziany 1998).

The book proposes to trace the adaptation and survival of one particular dhobi community or *biradari*, as it is locally known in the city of Delhi, as it managed to survive as the city around it grew and expanded. But the ethnography is not centred only on the community, as the dhobis did not live in a capsule. They were, and still are, part and parcel of the city of Delhi, and have their fortunes tied to that of the city. According to their collective narrative, they have always been part of the city of Delhi, and their rural roots, if any, are so far back as to be forgotten. Because they have always been part of the city or *sheher*, they call themselves 'Sheheri' dhobis, a name that remains confined to their own community of dhobis, finding little resonance outside[1]. Some of the narrative about the past and the present comes though my own life in the city, a city in which I was born. Quite a bit of the narrative is collected from people, like my mother, who spent the greater part of their lives here, and who have been witness to the many events and happenings that the city has been a witness to. I have seen the city grow and change all around me, and my life is also interwoven with the life of this city. Oral traditions are increasingly being accepted as real history or acceptable history (Jackson 2009). Again, as Clifford (1990b: 115) puts it, 'ethnography brings experience and discourse into writing'. The ethnographer's agency involves the translation of life into text. In another way it is also a rediscovery of what is already being 'written' in that culture. Clifford quotes Derrida (1974) to say that '*all* human groups write—if they articulate, classify, possess an "oral literature" or inscribe their world into ritual acts' (Clifford 1990b: 117, emphasis in original text). In a later part of this volume, this 'writing' is discussed in greater detail with respect to the dhobis.

The relationship with the river Yamuna, and the trauma of separation from it, have become a narrative of pain, but otherwise the dhobis have found their niche in the new environment, and their story, although one of struggle, is not without hope and visions of a viable future. They are not the only ones, as the ethnographies of other similarly situated marginal groups have shown. Works such as that of Ahmad (2018), Gill (2010), and Prashad (2000) elaborate on the struggles and survival of similar untouchable communities located in the city of Delhi. I will refer to these works as and when it is relevant to do so.

Locating the Study: the Dhobi Community in the City

There has been much discourse regarding the prevalence of caste or class in modern India, especially in the cities of India. But as rightly shown by Parry (2012), this is more a matter of *which Indian city*, and, I would like to add, which part of a large metropolis like Delhi one is focusing on. Contemporary urban studies, especially those that focus on non-Western cities, have taken up a postcolonial theoretical stance;

for example, Robinson (2006) argues that one cannot use the same concepts and definitions that were developed by the study of Western urbanization to the cities of the South. She specifically emphasizes 'the strong sense of adaptability, originality and resilience that is said to characterize the urban in the non-western city' (Robinson 2006:4). In another place (Channa 2018b), I have argued in a similar way to show that community and interpersonal bonding are very strong in the cities of India, where the neighbourhood and community are important components of urban life. As Parry (2012) describes, there are different kinds of cities in India; one cannot lump a religious and ancient city like Benares together with a newly constructed, industrial city like Jamshedpur. However, moving beyond the structure and history of a city, if we visualize the city as a field of experience rather than simply a structural entity with a boundary, then this field of experience being socially constructed by its inhabitants (Cinnar and Bender 2007) is likely to vary according to the spatial, cultural, and social position of those whose experience is being documented.

Most studies on the lower castes have shown that they tend to occupy the bottom of Indian society (Channa and Mencher 2013), although some of them have been able to climb the social ladder through the channel of politics. In most of these cases, however, the gains are individual and not community-based. While individuals like Mayawati or Ramvilas Paswan may be held up as symbols of power of the lower castes, their gains have rarely been transferred to their communities in entirety or even partially. At the most, only immediate kin stand to gain; at times not even them. While choosing a low caste, it then becomes automatically a study of a relatively poor section of society, a socially, economically, and, as in this case, politically marginal section of the city. The last needs to be emphasized, as unlike the lower castes in other parts of India, specifically in Maharashtra and the south, the dhobis have not acquired the class consciousness that characterized the Dalit movement. In this work I will take this up as a moot question to be answered, as to when and why a caste becomes a class, and when it does not.

Since one is speaking in terms of caste, it is essential to keep the larger Hindu caste-based society as a wider frame of reference. Caste must be understood as it is at an abstract and pervasive level, diffused throughout South Asia, existing as an ideological backdrop but with innumerable situational manifestations, both spatially and temporarily. The caste, or the Jati and Varna system, as Srinivas (1962) had rightly pointed out, is a pervasive thought system embedded in the minds of the people of South Asia and particularly peninsular India. These ideas and perceptions exist at all levels and in all types of social groups—rural, urban, and among all classes. They are pervasive among all occupations, ranks, and military, bureaucratic, and educational institutions. We can in fact take it as a way of life that is here to stay, although its manifestations are multifarious and polysemic. As pointed out by Gill(2010:181), caste considerations are central to many forms of economic exchange and even market relations; as she points out, 'in the South Asian context, caste is one such "culturally specific" institution that continues to underwrite economic relations, especially in the unorganized sector, even in liberalized contemporary India'.

Therefore, keeping in mind the forces of globalization and the contemporariness of the study, I do not wish to put a boundary on the society or even on the web of social relations, but only understand it in terms of layered densities, from a 'core' where the study will be primarily located to the merging of the core with multiple connections to webs of signification of wider and wider ramifications, the outermost point of which it is best to leave unidentified. At no point are we looking at any real boundaries, except for those of kinship and marriage, which will remain as a central point of identification of the primary entity under study. My study of this small community (earlier localized but later spread across Delhi) reflects well Parry's observation based on his study of slums around the industrial town of Bhilai: 'A detailed knowledge of such localities is an invaluable check on the reality of our representations of the wider urban system' (2012:45). This observation also breaks down the artificial divide between anthropology *in the* city and anthropology *of the* city suggested by Fox (1977), who identified three ways of studying the urban phenomenon anthropologically—namely urbanism, meaning study of an entity within the city, poverty (as explicated by the culture of poverty school), and urbanization—that would involve studying the city itself. A study like the present one encompasses all these aspects, as did Parry's work on Bhilai. While studying within the city, it is not possible to keep the city out of the analysis, for whatever historical or contemporary changes, events, and forces, such as of global markets, wars, and violence, that the city witnesses are passed on to its inhabitants, at times changing the entire course of their lives. As we will examine in the chapter on world-view and religion, even ideological changes taking place at a higher level permeate down to the small communities, bringing about transformative states of thought and beliefs. However, while one may mention context, it is not so simple to contextualize, even if one is taking into account the history, both written and narrated, of the field, the information of various kinds obtained from newspapers, archives, and the internet. The context, like the field, is always available in shreds and patches, dissected by our perceptions and intercepted by the time frame, the location, and the interests of the researcher. It is, as Axel (2002:22) puts it, 'productive yet fragmentary' in character.

Again, as Raymond Williams (1973) pointed out in his work *The Country and the City*, in the post-industrial world it is difficult to iden-tify a 'knowable community'. There is no bounded and structured whole amenable to study, as was presumed, wrongly, by some earlier scholars, an assumption that most transcended in one way or the other. The ques-tion that Marcus (1990: 171) puts directly is, 'What is holism once the line between the local worlds of subjects and the global world of sys-tems becomes radically blurred?' However, one can still presume that a microcosm is a kind of reflector of the larger political economic contexts in which it is embedded. As Marcus suggests (1990:172), 'the ethnog-rapher constructs the text around a strategically selected locale, treating the system as a background, albeit without losing sight of the fact that it is integrally constitutive of cultural life within the bounded subject'. The group that I am focusing on is a small one taking its identity from its caste-based occupation of washing clothes. However, this is not its only identity, for then it would merge with large numbers of such groups, all over India, who are identified by their occupation of washing clothes and with regional versions of the label of washermen. In North India they are known as dhobi, in Bengal as dhopa, and by slight variations of these names elsewhere. Local divisions follow various criteria that are inclu-sive of regional identities, but not limited to it. In a subsequent chapter, I discuss the internal structures and divisions of this social category. At this point it is enough to say that this book focuses on a group using the criteria of caste or jati; therefore much of the analysis will draw upon the theories and perspectives generated by caste studies in India. In putting a conceptual boundary on the object of my research, I refer here to Sax

(2009:20): 'It is difficult to imagine how academic ethnology could proceed without an object of study, however loosely defined, because the dichotomy of subject and object is a condition for disciplinary knowledge.'

Doing Ethnography in the City

This is an urban study, related both to my interest in urbanization and to the fact that the urban is assuming great importance as a site for anthropological studies. Urban anthropology, or, as Pardo and Prato (2012:1) would prefer to designate it, 'anthropology in the city', is soon to encompass a majority of populations globally. Yet since it is anthropology, one goes with the 'tried and tested anthropological technique of long-term participant fieldwork' (Pardo and Prato 2012: 3). However, the definition of urban, as well as of the city, has not been resolved, as criteria such as demography, density of living, and urbanism as a way of life, as posited by early twentieth-century scholars such as Mumford (1961), were found lacking in terms of global application. The consensus hovers around the label of 'city'. However, whether urban ethnography is the study of the city in its entirety or any work with the city as a backdrop remains an issue. Since this study is both located in a city and includes the city within the analysis as a prime actor in informing and constraining the situations that have been studied, one may venture to accept Pardo and Prato's definition of urban anthropology as 'anthropological research carried out in urban areas' (2012: 8).

Again, referring back to the caste/class debate, it is prudent to mention that the predominance of either of these values is also dependent on the nature of the city. As Parry (2012) has discussed with dexterity, the nature of urbanism differs significantly in India, from city to city and town to town. There is definitely the difference between orthogenetic and heterogenetic cities (Redfield and Singer 1954); but in many cases, especially in modern times, as most cities are growing out of their original spatial and temporal locations, the phenomenon of a single city being divided into its orthogenetic and heterogenetic parts is increasingly observed. This is particularly true of Delhi; with its broad division into Old Delhi and New Delhi, as well its expansion into the NCR (National Capital Region) areas. The origin of this work is in the Old Delhi area, but with the demographic spread of the community under observation the study had to open up to include many other parts of the city, some of them of recent origin.

Analysing the city as an experiential reality is then diversified, even for the same community, as they spread to different parts of the city. The Old city continues to nurture the values of community and neighbourhood bonding, and the New city is becoming more and more impersonalized and compartmentalized into bounded entities of 'gated communities' and locked-in, air-conditioned apartments, what Kuldova (2017:17) has referred to as 'luxotopias'. To give a sense of the Old city, let me narrate a walk that I had taken on a winter morning, getting down from the metro train, and walking towards the interior of the Old city, into one of the densely populated *mohallas*, as the neighbourhoods are called in Hindi. I met an older gentleman, sitting out in the sun, looking quite happy and peaceful, and just sitting. I was trying to locate a dhobi whom I had known a long time back, and was looking here and there to see if I could ask someone about him. The gentleman looked at me and asked me if I was looking for someone, so I told him I was looking for Omi Pehlwan. He immediately replied that Omi had passed away but that other members of his family were sitting at his shop that was a few metres ahead. When I asked him as to who he was, he said that he was from the baniya caste and owned a cloth shop. But at present his sons look after it so he is leading a retired life. He sits at this place, outside of his house and facing the lane, and talks to passers-by, to entertain himself. As he was talking to me, he greeted several persons passing by, as if he was familiar with most people around him. He was well aware of the dhobis, and knew them personally, like he knew Omi, the person I came looking for.

He described to me the changes that had taken place in the Old city, how residential houses were being rapidly converted to commercial spaces, and how the earlier spacious residences were now being converted to high-rise apartment buildings, to accommodate the rising population. I could see several apartment complexes several storeys high replacing the traditional two-and-a-half storey, single houses that used to accommodate a single, often joint, family. The commercial activities in this particular neighbourhood were of the manufacture and supply of iron and steel parts for various industries. One could still feel the commercial and even manufacturing activities going in the interior of these houses. In this area housing the old residents of Delhi, gentrification and commercialization are pushing out the earlier inhabitants and livelihoods; even the leisure activities of the older residents are being affected. Earlier, all houses had a veranda and an extension in their front that was made like a flat slab, where anyone could come and sit. These flat sitting areas, known as *chabutra*, served multiple functions in earlier times (Gupta 1981:170) and were often the means by which a house expanded and encroached onto the road in front. Any pedlar or weary walker could sit and take rest, irrespective of his caste or community, as the *chabutra* were regarded as exterior to the main house and the norms of purity and pollution did not apply to this space. This space was also used by the men for their gossip sessions or for elderly men to sit and watch the neighbourhood life pass by, like the person I met that day. The elderly had the feeling of remaining within the social world, in spite not being physically active. At present, however, with land becoming a commodity and priced for every inch, these were being absorbed within the commercial spaces. Most people were converting their ground levels to shops, and demolishing these sitting places to add a few inches to commoditized space. With changes in the style of living, many families had completely enclosed all the living area and installed air conditioners, rather than leave open space for the breeze to come in or for people to sit.

The gentleman I was talking to lamented that in the present times very few people had time to talk, and therefore the public spaces reserved for gossip were being seen as redundant in the faster life of the urban city. Yet, he said, he felt much happier in the Old city, where there was still some community life left and people had time to at least greet each other. He told me that he could never think of living in one of those high-rise apartments where one could not even see who one's neighbour was, let alone talk to them. He pointed to a large temple just across the street and said that earlier it was a smaller temple and there was a small tailor shop next to it. The neighbourhood raised money to expand the temple and make it grand and, in the process, pushed the tailor to abandon his shop. In a similar manner, a house up the lane had a dhobi ironing clothes in their *chabutra*, but they too expanded their house and the dhobi had to leave that space. In the process of gentrification, the marginal were being continuously pushed out. In the earlier city, when land was meant for living and not seen purely as a commodity, there were many spaces that could be inhabited or used by the marginal, the weary, and the one who could eke out a small living from there. But as space is being equated with money, most of these spaces are absorbed as commercially viable and there is hardly any space for a tired pair of feet to find rest, without having to spend money, as in a tea shop or cafeteria. There is again no space for the informal meetings of the neighbourhood.

Yet the Old city retains some flavour of the intimacy of social life where people are aware of each other's existence. The person I was talking to talked extensively about the dhobis, once I told him about my research. Although he was from an upper caste, his knowledge about the people around him irrespective of caste and religion was quite impressive. He told me that the dhobis invited him often for their weddings but he didnot go as their functions went on for the entire night and they served dinner at 1a.m. and dida lot of drinking and merrymaking that appeared rowdy to him. In the Old city, jati identities live on. Every person is known by the identity of the caste (more appropriately, jati) to which he or she belongs, and there is no camouflaging of caste identity in these face-to-face neighbourhoods.

Caste in the City

The jati system, especially for the communities that are at its bottom, exists in the urban milieu with its own characteristics. These jatis, with their polluting yet necessary bodies, are strategically absorbed within the living social space. In the villages, they are usually located outside the main habitation area, but in the cities, they have to be accommodated, but in a specific way, keeping their pollution out of the way yet available for doing the necessary works. The city of Old Delhi has been designed in a way that the lower castes live inside but remain out of the way. Narayani Gupta (1981), in her elaborate description of the history of settlement in Delhi, does not mention the dhobis or how they came to occupy their *katras* (enclosures). The best information that can be gathered from Gupta's work is that by the early nineteenth century, when most of the city was rehabilitated after its evacuation by the British in 1857, the poor were settled away from the core towards what was then the outskirts of the walled city. Areas near Turkman Gate and Mori

Gate were inhabited 'mostly by the poor kumhars, butchers, dyers of cloth, chamars (this caste was alone in Delhi Muslim by religion) and telis' (Gupta 1981: 55). She does not mention the dhobis, as most other writers on the city of Delhi do not. The present-day dhobis do live at the places mentioned, but they are also located at more central places in Old Delhi, like Kucha Pati Ram (near Sita Ram Bazaar), Farashkhana (then forming the outer wall of the city), Billimaran, and so on. It is evident that even if they were earlier located towards the outskirts, with the expansion of the city—even Old Delhi—they have moved somewhat towards the central part. The areas of Daryaganj, Delhi Gate, Kashmiri Gate, and Civil Lines expanded, making the old part of the walled city more central. Ahmad (2018:25) mentions that Goodfriend (1983) had listed as many as twenty-two occupational *biradaris* in Delhi in 1980. It is interesting to note that the city plan was conceptualized according to named communities or *biradaris* associated with particular occupations and not by the occupation itself, indicating, as has been noted by the other scholars of Delhi (Ahmad 2018, Prashad 2000, Gill 2010), that most occupations tend to have an underlying social relational structure in the form of kinship-based communities.

As the city has been expanding, it has continued to absorb these caste communities, creating special 'colonies' (an Indian way of referring to neighbourhoods) for them, as these have spread out of the Old Delhi area. In accordance to implicit caste norms, these neighbourhoods in the New city are given names that give a clear signal that a low-caste community stays there, like 'Balmiki colony' near the busy intersection at Pusa Road in New Delhi, or the earlier named 'Bhangi Colony' and Reghar Pura in Karolbagh. But the stark visibility of the Balmikis along with the construction of a temple in their name in the heart of the city is linked to their political assertions, not visible in the case of other caste groups of similar ranking. The Balmikis, who built their residential complex around the Balmiki Temple built in 1937 (Prashad 2000: 106) have acquired a political identity that verges on class formation. But in the precolonial era, at the time when the city was newly built, the presence of low and untouchable castes was not marked but discreetly hidden away, in a kind of social invisibility made possible by physical cloistering. Reference would be made to such and such a *mohalla* (neighbourhood) or *katra* specific to an occupational jati within the city, but it would be considered too audacious for any prominent place to be named after a low caste.

There exist some outstanding ethnographies of the lower castes of Indian cities that highlight the salient social as well as political aspects of their life in an urban milieu. Some that must be mentioned include Owen Lynch's (1969) work on the Jatavs of Agra, Khare's(1985) work on the Chamars of Lucknow, Mary Searle-Chatterjee's (1981)work on the sweepers of Banaras, Prashad (2000) on the Balmikis of Delhi, Ahmad (2018) on the Muslim butchers of Delhi, Gill (2010) on the Khatiks (Hindu butchers and pig rearers) who made a transition to monopolizing the plastic recycling trade of Delhi, and Natarajan (2012) on the potters of Chattisgarh (there are others that may not have been noted). Each one of these has made a valuable contribution to the study of the city as well as that of the community. Khare brings out the character of an old city of India, which is not quite like the cities in the West, with their atomized and fragmented individualistic lifestyle, by describing the 'ghar-gali-mohalla' cluster that regulates life in the old city of Lucknow. The *ghar-gali-mohalla*, referring to the house, the lane, and the neighbourhood, is an apt description of social life in the old cities of India, where the architecture and planning ensured a smooth flow of social life, denying the privacy of closed apartments of the modern cities but ensuring that one remained in touch with people all around. The open nature of living and the continuity of life beyond the physical space of a single house onto the street and the adjoining areas also required a high level of caste-based segregation. While it is possible to live in a high-rise apartment in a modern city layout not knowing who lives in the apartment next to one and to even dying in anonymity—like the man described by Obama (1995) in his autobiography who remains unnamed and unknown even after his death—such a situation is impossible in cities in parts of the world like South Asia. Except perhaps in very modern and hyper-urbanized sectors like Gurgaon near Delhi, a city that grew up to accommodate mostly young people working in global corporate sectors, in most parts of India, even in megacities like Delhi and Mumbai, it is near impossible to live in social isolation. Gupta (1996), Ahmad (2018), Gill(2010), and Prashad (2000) have worked in Delhi, and each ethnography brings out some aspects of Delhi that give the background to a specific community as well as the distinct lifestyle and praxis of these groups.

Gill's work is particularly interesting, as she shows how a particular community (*biradari*) made a transition from one occupation to another and created a monopoly drawing upon the symbolic pollution of a similar kind attached to both occupations. From being pig rearers and butchers and sellers of goat and pig meat, they have captured the plastic recycling business at all its three levels—door-to-door scavenging and picking up garbage (wet and contaminated), door-to-door or wholesale dealing in scrap (dry but still garbage), and finally the plastic recycling factories which involve the separation of the scrap. Although plastic has only become an industry since1992, and the liberalization of the economy, the association of Khatiks with the work stems from their earlier status as untouchables engaged in a polluting task. The collection and recycling of waste are also viewed as polluting and demeaning, and therefore the Khatiks made a foothold by transitioning from their earlier work as scavengers and rag pickers, and blending in with the more viable occupation of recycling of garbage. Even though the high-end factories may be owned by upper castes, the actual work of segregation is seen as best done by Khatiks, as they are seen as proficient in it due to their historical association with dirt (*kuda* or garbage). The Delhi Khatiks involved in this trade at all levels have also established kinship and *biradari* ties among themselves to reinforce the economic with the social.

Doing Fieldwork in the Indian City

Caste-based notions of purity and pollution as well as the cultural characters of communities or jati, based on linguistic and regional characters, in addition to religion and caste, have led to the phenomenon of clustering in Indian cities (Beteille 1969). Chandravarkar (2009:208) has remarked that the 'rural-urban divide in India is really slippery'. He follows on the earlier work of Pocock, who in a seminal paper written in 1960 made the observation that in India many cities have existed from ancient times and there is no real difference in the social principles that govern life in the city and in the rural areas, concluding by saying that the most distinct character of an Indian city is that it is Indian before it is anything else. The ancient cities such as Delhi, Lucknow, and Banaras have deep roots going far back into antiquity. The past persists mostly in the form of a moral order, discordant with Western individualism and the legal rational framework expected of an urban city in the West. Urbanism here does not always mean alienation, and, if it does, its meaning is derived from a completely different source than the atomization envisaged by scholars of urbanism in the West, such as Cooley (1902), Wirth (1964), and Simmel (1903[1976]). The moral order of city life is dictated more by values of caste, religion, community, and social norms than by formal laws and the governance of the state. As I have discussed in an earlier paper (Channa 2018b), legitimacy (Pardo 1996) is located not in the formal legal-jural system of the laws of the land but in a moral order located in community, caste, and the social world. Therefore, the neighbourhood has a far greater control over one's actions than the state and its representatives in the police or courts of law. The *ghar-gali-mohalla* model (Khare 1985) is very much applicable to the Old city of Delhi, and to most of the new neighbourhoods as well, especially if they are not in the too elite part of the city. The middle-class localities are as much bound by social norms of propriety and moral order derived from caste and religion as any village or small town (Abraham 2017).

Clustering is therefore an essential aspect of urban living, for if one has to live one's life under close scrutiny as well as in cooperation with one's neighbours, it is best that they are the 'same kind of people' as oneself (see also Ahmad 2018:58). Therefore, while Old Delhi is definitely clustered by caste, religion, and traditional occupation, even New Delhi, comparatively recently built, shows a significant level of clustering, such as Bengali areas, South Indian areas, and Kashmiri and Muslim neighbourhoods. Even affluent Muslims—Bengalis and Kashmiris, for example—prefer to live in their own religious or regional clusters that take on the character of the community; for example, the Bengali neighbourhoods will have fish, groceries, and sweet shops, and even vegetable vendors catering to the cuisine and palate of the community in question. These neighbourhoods also become the centre for cultural activities like public rituals, cultural functions, and visits by celebrities belonging to that particular community or group. While such a phenomenon of 'clustering' is also seen globally in large cities of the world like New York, San Francisco, and Durban, in India they are an almost ubiquitous part of all cities, unless very recently built, like Chandigarh. While in the global cities the clustering is usually of the migrant populations, such as Chinatown and

Little Italy, in India it encompasses nearly the entire population. This is not to say that every neighbourhood has this character, but there is a tendency for people of one kind to move to a residential area that has more people like themselves, so that even newly built areas of the city tend to form clusters over a period of time.

Therefore, the point that I wish to emphasize is that any ethnography, like this one, needs to draw a conceptual boundary around this cluster that is not separate from, but yet can be discerned as, a denser web of relationships, and is of a different nature than the relations that bound any individual or household to the larger society. In other words, as far as India and also many non-Western societies are concerned, the individual and opposed-to-society model does not apply. Even at the most primary level, it is very difficult to isolate the individual from the social group or primary social identity within which he or she is embedded. It is towards this primary identity that we need to look in order to have a unit for basing our ethnography. *We may define it in terms of the densest web of relationships, from where if we extract the individual, the individual will lose all sense of self.*

In fact, the South Asian self is so used to being embedded that even if people transcend their primordial identities of caste, region, and religion, they find new identities in which to embed themselves. For example, in the newly built parts of the city there are now neighbourhoods based on modern professions like lawyers, doctors, and journalists; even people belonging to certain offices like the Life Insurance Corporation and the Planning Commission have their own housing societies. In other words, people need to connect and form a community that is their moral universe as well.

Therefore, to locate a universe dense enough for study, I located a small group with a caste-based traditional occupation in the Old City of Delhi. I use the term density so as not to use the concept of boundary, traditionally commonly used in anthropology to designate a particular universe of study, especially if it is a group with an identity. The community (again in this context, a better word than group) has a name by which its members identify themselves, 'Sheheridhobis'; the prefix '*Sheheri*' meaning 'belonging to *sheher* (city)', in this case the city of Delhi. They are, then, an urban group par excellence as they incorporate the city in their very name. As I explain in the later part of the book, this identity is not a strict social boundary, although it does designate the limits of their kinship and marriage circle. In this way one can use the concept of endogamy to strategically locate, as suggested by Marcus (1990), a universe of study—that is, a universe only to the extent that it allows the scholar to focus on a 'knowable' entity, while not losing sight of the larger context in which it is embedded, affirming 'the intimate reassertion of history and social theory' (1990:167).

In this study we are moving from a small endogamous community to the larger community of washermen (dhobi) in general, to the caste or jati/Varna system, itself embedded in the larger Indian society, economy, and polity. Indian society, locally, as in the life of the dhobis or in the markets of Old Delhi, is both exposed to and interactive with the global market network, in turn controlled by the global institutions of market and what Grove (2019) calls global geopolitics. All the linkages are porous, from top to bottom, but we can grasp as a ground-level reality the identity (self-designated) and a density of relationships based on kinship, marriage, and a community interactive and cooperating structure called the *biradari* (a local and self-designated label). Fieldwork in such a complex situation takes on the character of what Gusterton (1997) refers to as a 'polymorphous engagement' (cf. Hannerz 2010: 77). There are days which one may spend wandering around absorbing things generally, 'surrendering' to the environment, and on certain other occasions one may make it a point to attend an important event or celebration, visit a family or friend, or maybe search the internet.

Referring to the social, political, and economic context, I have limited my immediate attention to the city of Delhi, a physical and political entity, but again intrinsically enmeshed in the larger global presence of the market and, to some extent, geopolitics. However, since I have methodologically and strategically placed my analysis to a bottom-up view, whatever I write here about Delhi is filtered through my own eyes, and those of my informants, which is of course a limited view, but the only possible view for which I can claim any authenticity. The justification for this bottom-up view is informed by the works of the subaltern school of historians, led by Ranajit Guha (Chatterjee 2011),and that of anthropologists, especially of caste and society in India, such as Mencher (1974), Narayan (2001), Nanduram (2008), and others. Ranajit Guha had developed a questioning attitude towards the notion of economic rationality, as ideally controlling all social actions, a deviance from his earlier Marxist point of view. In my earlier study of the dhobis(Channa 1985), which was also my PhD thesis, I attempted to show how the dhobis were conditioned by the concept of social rationality in their day-to-day life more than by economic calculations. Economic anthropology of that time was dominated by the rationalist and substantivist debate (Leclair and Schneider 1968) as well as by the French Marxists, represented among others by Maurice Godelier (1972) and Claude Meillassoux (1981). I had intuitively come across the notion of social rationality from a combined reading of whatever was in the repertoire of economic anthropology in the seventies. I was able to show and defend my thesis that the dhobis prefer to invest in social relations rather than immediate economic gains, as it is their community that acts as a buffer in times of stress. It is the *biradari* that comes to the rescue, as they could never earn enough money to have a financial cushion for their troubles. The community therefore acts as a safety net for tiding over the crises in life. However, since most members were equally poor at that time, this tiding over was not always very successful. But the community stood by at least as moral support, if not fully successfully as an economic buffer. This idea was again more informed by the studies of foraging or hunter-gatherer societies (Leacock and Lee 1982: 8), where it is shown that cooperation is the key to survival, in a situation where, due to technological constraints, it is not possible to store up resources for future use.

The dhobis, being part of a monetary economy, did not have any logistical constraints, but there was a positive side to investing in the community relationships, for the security provided was multifaceted. I describe the *biradari* in detail in a later chapter, but what is important to note is that the strongly knit web of relationships that also coincide with the outermost limits of the kinship circle provides all kinds of resources, finance being only one among them.

The city and its urbanism are a key aspect of this work. By looking at the growth of the city of Delhi, from the eyes of the dhobis, I have been inspired by the work of Ranajit Guha and other subaltern scholars, but also by that of historical anthropologists (Axel 2002). Just as Scott (1985:27) pointed out the ordinariness of the poor peasants that he studied, there is nothing significant about the small group of washermen (dhobis) who have apparently stood in the same place as the city grew around them.

Almost none of them, as of now—and I am looking at a span of forty years or more—are participants in the glitzy lifestyle of the urban megacity, Delhi, of the twenty-first century. The women of the dhobi caste, standing at various corners of the city, ironing the clothes of the neighbourhood, look more or less the same as they have looked over years past. Changes have come about in their lifestyle, as I will be describing later, but it is a slow and minimal kind of change. There have been no big entrepreneurs, although there are a couple of small entrepreneurs. No one has attained a high status in politics or in any other field for that matter. Yet they have persisted with their own way of life in this rapidly transforming, globalizing city. They have found their own niche within the capitalist and now neoliberal economy. They have maintained their self-respect and dignity, are not averse to their jati identity, and have not become adjunct to any larger political movement or identity. They are content to be dhobis, whether or not they follow the traditional occupation.

Exploring the Dhobis: Identity, Resilience, and Survival

An important aspect of this book is also to analyse, from the point of view of the dhobis themselves, why they have not opted for the politically more vibrant and powerful Dalit identity. In light of the universal stereotyping of all untouchables as Dalits, it becomes relevant to enter into a discourse regarding the emergence of a Dalit identity and the absence of the stimulating conditions for the emergence of such an identity among the dhobis and similarly placed occupationally specialized jati groups in Delhi, such as the barbers, scavengers, vegetable sellers, and potters. A small community and its articulations within the larger society have the potential to stimulate discussions and debates with wide theoretical implications. The Dalit identity, as also pointed out by Deliège (1999:16), is not universally adopted by all untouchable communities. Instead of accepting any term at its face value, it is necessary to examine the historical roots of the emergence of these identities as well as the reasons for which they are acceptable to the communities. I have already mentioned that history has been silent about most of the small and nearly invisible communities, while recording the larger and more spectacular aspects of the life of a city or a region. Delhi, as the seat of power of a long lineage of rulers—from different dynasties, regions of the world, of different religions and ethnicity—has a spectacular history, yet very little is known about the small, inconspicuous, and banal communities that have occupied its nooks and lanes, the *ghar-gali-mohalla* clusters. Prominent historians of Delhi like Gupta (1981) have focused on the rich and powerful players, like the Hindu merchants, Muslim aristocrats, and British and precolonial power holders. Gupta (1981:44) has admitted to the lack of archival data on the marginal when she points out that chroniclers of Delhi like Bhola Nath Chunder, who came from Calcutta, 'chose to observe only the upper strata of inhabitants'. Gupta has given a rich description of the city's social organization, demography, and political and social life, detailing many dignitaries and eminent personalities by their names and deeds, but the lower strata remain conspicuously absent, relegated to the shadow category of the identity less masses. François Bernier (1916) describes the occupational distribution of castes in Old Delhi, and, while mentioning the butchers (Ahmad 2018: 57), fails to mention the dhobis. Even the written literature about the city, as pointed out by Dalmia (2017), has revolved around the lives of the middle-class, mostly literate, and well-to-do people. Dalmia discusses how in the cities of North India, including Delhi, Lucknow, and Allahabad, the Hindu novel had a role in 'partly creating, partly anticipating the story of middle class modernity and modernism' (2017:3). The novel developed in Bengal by the works of writers such as Bankim Chandra Chatterjee, Rabindranath Tagore, and Sarat Chandra Chatterjee. Both Sarat Chandra and Rabindranath have dealt with the lives of the poor in a sympathetic manner, but almost always set in the rural countryside. The urban poor appear only as house servants or as prostitutes and other lumpenproletariat. Similarly, Munshi Premchand, the doyen of Hindi literature of that period, gave us poignant tales of the countryside, creating unforgettable characters from among the peasants, but there is little description of the urban poor or the lower castes in the city, except for fleeting references, while describing middle-class life.

A community like the dhobis provides no romanticism, no adventure, like those provided by the early communities studied by the anthropologists located in exotic locales of islands, forests, and deserts. They provide no material for lilting romances or even tragedies or comedies to tickle anyone's imagination. It is left to the anthropologist, if they wish to make such a community visible. As Scott (1985) has pointed out, even the studies on peasants tend to focus on large-scale rebellions and movements with significant historical impact. At the same time, the dhobis too have a different world view and perception of history. The large-scale upheavals did affect them, but they understood them only from the perspective of their lived experience of them. The larger political contexts were of no consequence. How the events such as partition at the time of independence affected their livelihood and that of the other people of their communities was of deeper concern than those considered of national significance. In my long association with them, I have found that politics is something that concerns them very little, except again in ways that directly pertain to their livelihood and day-to-day life. Apart from the subsistence activities, what engages them is religion and rituals. If one has to understand the political changes, as reflected in their life ways, then the most important signifier is in the changes in their religious perceptions and ritual performances.

It is the expressive mode of their existence reflected in the religiosity and performance of ritual activities that one finds the most discursive aspects of both their resistance and their transformations. Changes in their religious worldview best reflect the subtle manner of their adjustment to the changing political scenario, and their adaptation to changing political ideologies.

Resilience and Adaptation

Macro-level decision-making by the elite in power affects the people on the ground. The tenuous linkage between macro-level decisions and the microprocesses that affect even the smallest and the most marginal is often the direct subject of anthropological analysis (Thiessen 2012). The processes of globalization have fired the imaginaries of power elites across the globe, in imagining 'world-class' cities and so-called smart cities; yet local conditions often make it impossible to attain the ideal of a shining first-world city. Most media had reported how, during mega world events, cities like those in Brazil and China tend to put up walls and barricades to hide the poverty and squalor of their cities, while they paint and glamorize only selected parts that are made visible to outsiders.

As the city grows and gentrifies, older portions of the city, and the people who represent the lag between actual and imagined modernity, are pushed outside or out of sight. A central theme of this book is to trace the struggle of a marginal community, essential yet marginalized, that has been struggling to maintain its foothold in a city that is increasingly trying to exclude it from the city landscape (Channa 2023a). Similar situations have been reported by other scholars such as Gill (2010: 180), who highlights the 'particularly middle-class and bourgeoisie view of environmental concerns' that both threatens and excludes low-caste and marginal workers, in her case the Khatiks involved in the plastic recycling business. The seemingly dirty piles of plastic and other discarded items waiting to be recycled are seen as a fire hazard and unseemly to the eyes, and the government has been pushing them further and further out from the core areas of Delhi. In most cases the areas thus freed up escalate in value and add to the monetary economy of commoditized urban space.[2]

At this point the concept of resilience comes in handy. As pointed out by Gotham and Powers (2017: 140), resilience is a multidimensional concept that has been used in many different ways. There is a distinct difference in viewing resilience as a movement back to the original state or a kind of stable equilibrium state or in an open-ended perspective where it describes a system's ability to withstand and adapt to changing situations and external trauma. From the last perspective the society responds in a way that it survives but maybe with internal changes and external adaptations. This view of resilience, as given by Picket et al. (2004: 373)—that is open-ended, is not clearly predictable, and does not ensure that there is a return to the status quo but, rather, examines the manner in which a group adapts and survives in its changing surroundings and overcomes trauma—is shared by (Folke 2006, Pike et al. 2010, and Redman 2005). I have traced the journey, often difficult and full of struggles, of a people, subject of 'urban apartheid', who have been kept at the fringes of society, tolerated only for the service that they provide but looked down upon culturally and socially by the dominant groups who benefit from their services. They have witnessed all the traumas that the city of Delhi has undergone and are still suffering, but have survived, kept their identity, to a large extent kept their traditional occupation intact, and have transformed and adapted to the ever changing circumstances of their lives. They have not been able to transcend social barriers, but have learnt to use that as a weapon to challenge the upper layers by the strength of their *biradari* ties and their active choice of staying together and being dhobis, by making attempts to make themselves acceptable *as dhobis* and not aspiring to a changed identity.

As I mentioned at the beginning, the anthropologist can only justify her 'use' of the time and emotional resources of the people she represents if she is able to highlight their concerns. In my long period of association with the dhobis, I found that most of them dreamt practically. There was always a concern with the here and now, with little and big problems of day-to-day life, rather than looking for esoteric and grandiose visions. It was always the daily struggle for survival, for getting small luxuries, which at times, and especially in the initial period of my fieldwork, often meant just some food to eat. Even today, what concerns most is the continuity of a livelihood; for some it is getting a son or daughter educated, but for most it is just the carrying on from one day to the next, what in a broader perspective Lefebvre (1967[1996]) has made famous by the phrase 'right to the city',[3] which for the dhobis means a right to work, to livelihood and a space to live in the city, from which they derive their identity and their name.

In the body of this work, I will be taking up these issues in much greater detail, one by one, in the various chapters that follow.

Notes

1. There are comparable communities, like the Sheheri Bhangis, Sheheri Khatiks, etc., who occupy spaces within the city and who also trace their names from their claims to be part of the original residents of the city. The upper castes with similar claims usually prefer the prefix Dilliwale.

2. Gill (2010: 196) reports from the narration of the Khatiks that the Bharatiya Janata Party had ulterior motives for relocating them out of Jwalapuri, a location from which they were pushed out. It was reported that the then Chief Minister Sahib Singh Verma, a Jat, had initiated the move to favour his Jat *biradari*, as many of them owned agricultural land around that area and reaped substantial economic benefits from the escalation of land prices as the so-called 'polluting industries' were moved out.

3. The multiple ways in which this phrase can be interpreted and understood can be seen in works such as King (2018).

1

The Dhobis of Old Delhi

Narratives from the Margin about a Community, a River, and a City

Delhi was built on the banks of the river Yamuna. Historians have identified several cities on the banks of this sacred river, right where the present city now stands (Allen 2012, Safvi 2019, Hearn 1905).[1] The ruins of some of these earlier settlements are still scattered at various places in the city's landscape, where they stand in all their majesty of red bricks, massive arches, and long walls amid the din of modern-day traffic and the hustle and bustle of a crowded and busy city. New Delhi is the capital city of the modern nation state of India, a democratic republic. But the real Delhi, as any *Delhiwallah* can tell, is Old Delhi, the original walled city, built in the seventeenth century by Emperor Shah Jehan, one of the great Moghuls, known for his famous buildings and love of lavish architecture. He built his city on the site of Firozabad, identified by Safvi (2019) as the fifth city of Delhi built by Sultan Feroz Shah Tuglaq. Keeping in mind the issues of security, Delhi was protected from the 'North-West by the Ridge, and was linked to the East by a bridge across the Jamuna. The city was double fortified by the Palace and the city Wall' (Gupta 1981: 1). Old Delhi contains within it a few relics of times earlier than Shah Jehan's city, most prominent being the shrine of a Sufi saint at Chitli Qabar as well as the forgotten grave of Delhi's only queen, Razia Sultana, both of which predate the Mughal Empire. The present-day Old Delhi is known for its market centre, Chandni Chowk (Liddle 2017), which still serves the masses of Delhi, its iconic Red Fort, the Qila-e-Mubarak of Shah Jehan, from where on every Independence Day the flag of India is hoisted by the Prime Minister of India, following the tradition set by the first Prime Minister, Jawaharlal Nehru, on 15 August 1947.

This area houses some of the oldest resident populations of Delhi, and is known for its iconic places of worship—Hindu, Sikh, Jain, Christian,

Dhobis of Delhi. Subhadra Mitra Channa, Oxford University Press. © Subhadra Mitra Channa 2024.
DOI: 10.1093/9780198926238.003.0002

and Muslim. The Sisganj Gurudwara, the Baptist Chapel, St Stephen's School, the Fatehpur Masjid, and the impressive Jain Temple were all built in the year 1870 (Gupta 1981: 50).The Old city was bound by thirteen Darwaza (gates) (Safvi 2019: 94), of which only a few remain: Delhi Gate, at the central part of the city, Ajmeri Gate, Turkman Gate, Kashmiri Gate marking the earlier boundary of the walled city, and Lahori Gate, which gives entrance to the Red Fort. The memorial to Mahatma Gandhi was made where the earlier Rajghat Darwaza existed, and the Nigambodh Darwaza marks the cremation ghat where Hindus burn their dead, on the banks of the river Yamuna. The majestic Jama Masjid stands at one end of this area, famous as the largest and most beautiful mosque in Asia. The multireligious nature and cultural diversity of the city are marked by the Lakshmi Narayan Temple of the Hindus, Sisganj Gurdwara of the Sikhs, where the sons of Guru Teg Bahadur were martyred by the Moghuls, and St James' Church, where many of those who governed the city lie buried. The area is dotted with several Sufi shrines, smaller temples, and mosques. The large Jain temple that stands at the entrance to Chandni Chowk is also famous as a bird sanctuary and hospital. It is still referred to as the Walled City by the older residents of Delhi, for many of whom the place has the nostalgia of whiffs of food smells, quaint sights, and sounds. At the same time, it is a most important commercial centre and houses a dense market network dealing in practically all kinds of goods with both wholesale and retail outlets, including a reputed jewellery street, a food street, a street of fancy gold embroidery and trinkets, a wholesale cloth market, a market for paper merchandise and bookbinding, and specialized markets for practically everything under the sun. Most households with a middle range of income still do their shopping here, especially for bulk goods for special occasions like weddings and religious functions.

In addition to the historic architecture, what is most special about this area is that it still houses some of the original populations of Delhi. One can easily surmise that, since it was first built by a Muslim emperor, the initial dominant population must have been of the Muslims. But there were several Hindu caste groups as well; prominent among them were the Gaur Brahmins, Aggarwals (Channa 1979), a trading caste, Khandelwals, another trading caste, Kayast has (originally scribes at the courts of the kings), Zardoz, or gold-thread embroiderers (Gupta 1996), the Khattris, another merchant class of Northern India, and a plethora of service castes, such as barbers (Nai), launderers (Dhobis), butchers (Khatiks), household cleaners (Kahars), scavengers (Bhangi), and several others. Interestingly, several of the service caste groups have their Hindu as well as Muslim counterparts. Gupta (1981: 55) has mentioned that the Chamars of Delhi were alone in being Muslim by religion; everywhere else they are not. Ahmad (2018:25) writes, 'The names of the *mohallas* (localities) and oral histories of the people indicate that the walled city (formerly Shahjahanabad) was planned so that people of certain trades and occupational groups lived and worked in specific pockets – Gali Dhobiyan (washermen), Phaatak Teliyan (oil pressers), Qasabpura (butchers) and Churiwalan (banglemakers).' To these one may add Gali Prathewali, Kinari Bazar, Gali Batashe Bali, and so on. While there have been significant demographic changes among the dominant groups, especially by the replacement of Muslims by the Hindus, these caste groups have continued more or less as they were over the past three centuries or more. Since these marginal castes have been ignored by historians and all kinds of writers of fiction and literature, it is impossible to know how they survived and managed to continue their existence up to the present time. As mentioned in the Introduction, this book tells the story of the dhobis, a caste group ubiquitous all over India, as the washing of clothes has been an essential service to take the pollution off the bodies of the upper castes. The dhobi was not a mere launderer; he, as well as she (the dhoban or female counterpart of the male dhobi), essentially absorbed the pollution created by the bodies of the upper-caste men and women, through sweat, semen, blood, and by menstruation and childbirth. Anthropologists have debated the correspondence between pollution and auspiciousness and, as argued by Das (1982), some acts are auspicious but impure, such as childbirth; and, as pointed out by Raheja (1988: 24–36), the service castes have the function of removing inauspiciousness from the dominant castes within the jajmani system. Yagi (1999: 271) has also brought in the factor of danger (from evil spirits and evil eye) to which people become vulnerable at certain times of their lives, especially during life-cycle events such as childbirth and marriage. The service castes, especially the women like the *dhoban* and the *naun* (the wife of the barber) play protective roles in warding off evil at the same time as they remove the inauspiciousness. With respect to her field in a village near Varanasi, Yagi writes that the washerwoman washes the clothes of a woman who has given birth and also the clothes of women mourners at a death. Likewise, the dhobi men 'wash the clothes of the male relatives, thereby removing their impurity'.[2] Thus the washing of clothes by the dhobi was not just an act of physical cleaning but also one of ritual cleaning. But it is not simply impurity but also danger that is removed by them, and Yagi writes (1999: 272) that, although considered impure, the dhobi woman is also considered auspicious and is allowed to participate in marriage rites with women of the upper castes. It is also considered a good omen to meet a dhobi woman when one is going out, even if she is carrying dirty clothes. Therefore, as rightly pointed out by Das (1982), the relation between impurity and inauspiciousness is not a linear one, and a person can be impure and auspicious at the same time, as can a particular life-cycle event such as childbirth. For example, while a dhobi woman is considered auspicious, the highest Brahmin, the Maha Patra, who performs funerary rites, is considered inauspicious and to meet one is seen as a bad omen (Yagi 1999: 270). In the urban setting where this work is situated, the concepts of auspiciousness and inauspiciousness may not be on the surface, but they continue to linger in the minds of people belonging to all caste groups, especially in the more conservative parts of the city such as Old Delhi.

This book is a study of an urban landscape, a landscape that has been shaped by historical events, such as have created major crisis and also caused much social and political upheaval.[3] The dhobis have been through it all, watching from the sidelines, even as dynasties fell and power changed hands, as blood flowed in the streets or the city celebrated joyous events. The river Yamuna in the meantime flows silently at the back of the events, ordinary as well as spectacular, that the city and its inhabitants have seen and experienced. The river is one entity with which the dhobis have an intrinsic relationship. The river has always flowed, not only providing a backdrop but also being an active participant in the lives of the people who live here.

The ethnographic present of the book stretches from 1974 to 2023, but its historical backdrop stretches out much more into the past, back to the time of the First War of Independence in 1857. While the events of 1857 have been sourced from literature and secondary historical sources (Gupta 1981, Oldenburg 1984, Dalmia 2017), the events of 1947—that is, the second traumatic event that led to considerable demographic and social transformation—have been reconstructed from family narratives and memory reconstructs of the dhobis. These events have been extensively recorded by both academic and literary sources, including movies made about them such as Deepa Mehta's *Earth*, but here they are narrated from the viewing platform of the dhobis.

Writing of an ethnography is never a complete project: 'Ethnographic truths are thus inherently partial-committed and incomplete' (Clifford 1990a: 7). Every ethnography is a temporal interception into an ongoing process of life, the ethnographic present, where one artificially puts, as it were, a dam to stop the flow of social life and understand it in a somewhat timeless fashion. In this book I have strung together encounters, conversations, observations, narratives, and impressions collected over a period of forty years. Like all ethnographies, it is a construction and the judgement is entirely mine, but what is important is the overall impression of a lifestyle or form of life (Grove 2019: 3), if we may put it that way. The dhobis represent a way of living that had its own aesthetics, its reason to be, and in some ways it was a way of life that was cherished and is still cherished by a group of people, to whom it is what they identify themselves with. There are critics of this impressionist way of writing, who may settle for more rigour as expressed by quantified figures and graphs and so on. But nowhere do figures bring to life the people, the essence of their existence, their aspirations, their voices, and the whiff of something that is not quite describable but that exists outside of figures and tables. Some scholars at least may feel that this mode of representation has a purpose and a touch of the real: 'Concept creation when established with historical analysis and field research can produce scholarship that is insightful beyond our ability "to prove" that it is insightful' (Grove 2019: 11). Whatever is written down here may not be subject to proof, but it is a derivative, maybe a construction, from the association with real people—from a relationship nurtured and built up over several decades. It is a piece of history of a people who are not marginalized in the sense of being oppressed but subject to invisibility by being an obscure part of everyday life that everyone takes for granted. Usually, the ones being written about are either important or exotic. The dhobis are neither. They are just part of the everyday humdrum of life, who lurk behind heaps of dirty clothes and washed and ironed heaps, whose routine reality is just another of the uninteresting, unimportant, and yet essential aspect of life's routine existence. In this sense, 'Anthropology can be useful in ameliorating the power differences between local communities and hegemonic institutional structures that have the power to (de)legitimize certain narratives over others' (Hosbey 2016: 307).

I remember, when I had expressed interest in working among the dhobis for my PhD, the almost universal response from colleagues and family, including my teachers, was: 'Why dhobis?'; 'What is interesting about them?'; 'Could you not find a more important group to work on?' Unlike the picture most people have about anthropologists, my work among them did not bring me to any spectacular locales, to any 'exotic' community, nor did it expose me to any dramatic event or ritual. The dhobis were not even particularly interesting from the point of view of the government, like the tribes and more vulnerable groups like forest dwellers. But still they, in themselves, are a people; they have an identity and they are in many ways unique in that. Through them I learnt a different way of looking at the world, at the city of Delhi, that I had known from a very different platform.

Let us first take a brief overview of the history of the city, not perhaps as chronicled by historians but as it appears to the dhobis and to local residents.

Two Major Traumas and the Dhobis in the City

Till the year 1857, most parts of India were being ruled by the East India Company (or John Company as known to the locals). It had its headquarters in Calcutta, a city that was lovingly built by them for their own use and from where they ventured as traders and conquerors, initially for the overt purpose of commercial interests but, as the wealth of the subcontinent proved too tempting, as political occupiers. The revolt of 1857, called a 'mutiny' by the British (Hearn 1905), now described in school textbooks as the First War of Independence, had as its symbolic head the Mughal emperor, who was reinstated on the Delhi throne by the rebels. The uprising was suppressed, bringing to an end the Mughal Empire in Delhi. The throne of Delhi was vacated by sending the then ruler, Bahadur Shah Zafar, into exile to Rangoon (a part of British India at that time), and India became British territory under the rule of Queen Victoria.

As described by historians, the British, smarting from the audacity displayed by their own troops by turning their weapons against them, considered it legitimate to take exemplary revenge against the Indians, especially the Muslims, as they equated the throne of Delhi with them (Gupta 1981). According to folk history, all the young heirs to the throne of Delhi were massacred and hung up at what came to be known for posterity as the Khooni Darwaza (meaning the 'Bloody Gate'), a central landmark in the heart of Delhi near Delhi Gate, one of the thirteen gates that surrounded the walled city. The British eliminated as much as possible of the symbols of Mughal rule from the city. The palace that the emperor occupied was converted into barracks for their troops and later renamed Red Fort. They dynamited many beautiful pieces of architecture such as Jahanara's palace, which was razed and replaced with the Town Hall (a staid piece of architecture), and a statue of Queen Victoria was placed in front of it. The addition of a fountain led to the place being known forever as The Fountain. 'At one sweep the face of the city, so lovingly built by Shahjehan, was transformed. What the government decided was necessary for security led to some of the loveliest buildings of the city being destroyed' (Gupta 1981: 26). They built roads and railway tracks right through the city, breaking and destroying many houses and structures, including places of worship. One such road was Hamilton Road near Kashmiri Gate, near which St James' Church was built after 1857, and where many British killed in that war now lie buried. The majestic Jama Masjid was vacated and occupied by British troops in 1857 and made into a barracks, but later, once formal British rule was consolidated, it was handed back for worship to the Muslims.

Dalmia (2017: 25) describes a complete demographic transition of Delhi from a dominantly Muslim to a dominantly Hindu city after the takeover of the city in 1857. Following the evacuation of the city, the British began a process of resettlement from 1860 onwards that carefully transformed the character of the inner city. They took special care to screen the Muslims who were trying to come back, allowing entry only to those who had been loyal to the British and had not joined the uprising. The new power-holders particularly favoured the Hindu merchant castes, the Baniyas, who had remained out of the skirmishes, being non-violent and compliant as traders and merchants. Many of the big *havelis* of the Muslims were handed over to such loyal subjects, and within a span of a year or two the entire demographic structure of the city changed to one heavily favouring the Hindus: 'Thus a Muslim dominated Delhi changed character and became Hindu merchant-dominant'(Dalmia 2017: 26). The new rulers also occupied a large part of the city space, leaving very little for the native inhabitants: 'Two-thirds of Mughal Shahjahanabad came to be remodelled, the inhabitants squeezed into two-thirds of the walled city and its poorer suburbs' (Dalmia 2017: 25).

However, although the Muslim elite were pushed out, no one paid much heed to the sizeable numbers of Muslim service castes and craft specialists, notably the craftspersons like Zardoz, the carpenters, carvers, and the service providers like washermen and barbers, who continued their ordinary life in the city. Some of the dhobi informants had stories from their elders about looting and arson that was witnessed during 1857, but there were almost none about attacks on them. Squeezed into their cramped quarters, nearly invisible from the invading regime, they survived and kept performing their tasks even as the world collapsed around them. Their untouchable and marginal status probably made them an unattractive target anyway. The British, while cleansing the city of the 'dissidents', would have looked the other way as far as the service castes were concerned. For one, they too needed the performance of tasks such as scavenging, haircutting, and laundry, and there was no one to do them except those specified by caste to do so. This forced dependence had also led to the caste occupations being fostered during the colonial period.

After 1860, the British set up their own municipality in the Civil Lines area, and the British officers moved out to occupy the luxurious bungalows built for them there, while the Indians were squeezed into cramped lanes of the Old City. My mother told me that when she was young, that is around the 1930s and 1940s, the paths on the Delhi Ridge were covered with bark from the trees to enable the British men and women to go horse riding there.[4] The Old Secretariat Building was built to house the municipality and the revenue offices. In 1911, the government shifted its capital from Calcutta to Delhi. The Viceregal Lodge was adjoining the Civil Lines and the Ridge area and, with its regal ballroom and beautiful colonial architecture, temporarily housed the power elite before they moved to New Delhi. At present it is the main office of the University of Delhi, from where the Vice-Chancellor and other office-bearers carry out their administrative duties. The Central Ballroom has now been converted into a magnificent Convention Hall for the university.

The British maintained Calcutta as the capital of British India from 1858 to 1911, as they did not wish to be close to the seat of the Mughal power that they were replacing. They deliberately neglected Delhi and instead built and encouraged the other North Indian cities like Lucknow and Allahabad, where they built institutions of learning and judiciary to rival Delhi. As the colonial period set in, other kinds of changes began affecting the cities. Although Delhi became the capital in 1911 and continues till today to hold that prestigious status, it was the port cities and trading centres like Bombay, Calcutta, and Madras that developed more quickly under the forces of industrialization and commercial activities. Delhi remained an administrative centre rather than an economic hub for a long time to come and maintained its relatively conservative lifestyle, as a result retaining till the 1970s its tag of being a 'village'. It was primarily known for its old-world charm and its *galis* (lanes) of the Old City, made famous by the couplet from Ghalib.[5] When I began to do fieldwork among the dhobis in Old Delhi, the society that I interacted with was still conservative; the dhobis were still household servers, with long-time hereditary relationships with their clients. The political identity of the dhobis has also been influenced by the conservative character of Delhi, which did not modernize as early and in the manner of the commercial cities of Bombay and Ahmedabad.

After 1857, the city suffered another major trauma in 1947, when, following freedom from British rule, the country was divided into India and Pakistan, in a process inscribed in history as The Partition. The bloody exchange of population and its aftermath have been both recorded and written about by many reputed authors (Singh1956, Sahani 2008[1972]), also filmed (*Garam Hawa*),[6] and remains a part of the oral history of most families of North and East India, where the partition had actualized. After 1947, almost none of the aristocratic Muslim families remained in Old Delhi, thus nearly completing the transition that had begun in 1860. The final demographic transition reduced the Muslim population in Old Delhi to a minority in terms of both numbers and social profile.[7] A family narrative illustrates well the demographic transition of Delhi from the time of the Mughals to the post-independence era. When my mother went to school in the 1930s, she was the only Hindu girl in class and the only one who was middle-class, the rest being the daughters of the Muslim upper class, who came to school accompanied by servants and ayahs who carried their food and looked after them. When I went to the same school as my mother did, but in the 1960s, all the students were Hindus, with just a smattering of Muslim girls. The demographic transition was complete and so was the school culture, where everyone was subjected to strict discipline and food was served in the dining hall; no more ayahs and servants!

Most of the Muslim population that remained in Delhi were artisans, craftspersons, service castes, and those involved in the food business—like eateries, meat and fish shop owners—largely involved in the informal sector of the economy. They still have a viable and thriving economic niche located mostly around the vicinity of the Jama Masjid and the Old Delhi area. Foodies looking for gourmet Mughal dishes throng this neighbourhood, which also specializes in several crafts like zardozi and woodcarving. Ahmad (2018) has aptly described the meat and food industry dominated by the Muslim Qurashis of Delhi. At present upper- and middle-class Muslims are distributed all over Delhi but have a cluster known as Jamia Nagar near the Jamia Millia Islamia University.

The exodus of elite Muslims left the Muslim dhobis in distress. As narrated by an elderly dhobi, 'They [Muslim dhobis] were left with no work. They came begging to us and we shared some of our clients with them.' At the present time the number of Muslim dhobis is less than the Hindus, but they are still considered part of the larger Sheheri dhobi *biradari* and share the ghats (washing platforms) along with the Hindus. Their living quarters are, however, different. In my several visits to their *katra*, there has always been a little hesitation in engaging in conversation. Especially under the present Hindutva regime (Narayan 2021), they feel a bit threatened but are secure in their work. There is no feeling of alienation from their dhobi *biradari* and till the present time workplace sharing and easy social interactions are prevalent. This is in contrast to the attitude of the Muslim Qurashis (butchers) who, as Ahmad (2018: 55, 59) has noted, distance themselves from the Hindu Khatiks, who they say are from the lower castes, while they trace their lineage from the Qurashi tribe of Arabia—from the homeland of the Muslims—and prefer to project themselves as migrants and not local to India. The Qurashi have their separate *biradari* and have no social links with the Hindu Khatiks. Anyway, as described by Gill (2010), the Hindu Khatiks have moved away from their traditional occupations to that of the plastic recycling industry.

Most of the data collected from my informants were in the form of memory reconstructs about the period from 1947 onwards. The dhobis never had a literate tradition, and they were rarely written about by anyone. Here again there is a significant difference from the Muslim Qurashis, who have a strong written tradition and, as described by Ahmad, have constructed several narratives of their own history in written form. Dalmia (2017), in writing about the Hindi novel as it emerged in the cities of Northern India, after 1857, when a Hindu upper-caste middle class emerged, mentions that all the novels were about this class alone. With the spread of English education and modernity in terms of westernization, after 1870, an educated middle class emerged: 'And it is from these higher castes-Brahmin, Khattri, Kayastha, and Vaishya-that our novels largely draw their characters' (Dalmia 2017: 32). Did anyone at all write about the dhobis? They lurked in the background, perhaps coming in once with a bundle of clothes, but no one wrote about them, talked about them, or showed any interest in their lives. Therefore, it is difficult to say what they did from the time they settled in the Shahjahanabad to the time the city was remapped after 1857. The period after 1947 was reconstructed from the narratives of elderly people, who still had memories of them, in the 1970s, when I first began to do my fieldwork.

In 1947, once the British left the city, another demographic and cultural transition took place—a major one, as India transformed from a colonized to a postcolonial nation, and New Delhi was developed as its capital.

The River

Shah Jehan reportedly chose to build his capital in Delhi because of the river Yamuna. Describing the relationship between the Qila, or fort, and the river, Safvi (2019: 12) writes that the river flowed from its eastern side and was raised on a plinth of 12 yards. The other three sides were protected by a moat 3,600 yards long, 25 yards wide, and 10 yards deep, filled with water from the river. In other words the Qila was alongside the river. When the city was built, the Yamuna was a wide and flowing, navigable river; boats connected the city of Delhi to the hinterland of the Gangetic plains for food supply, and merchants came from far-off places, often by river, to buy and sell a variety of goods (Ahmad 2018: 24). But over the years the course of the river shifted, and instead of beside the river the Red Fort now stands on the Mahatma Gandhi Road, the name given to the popularly known ring road that circles Delhi. The river, although it shifted away was still a wide and rapidly flowing river, the site of many sacred places along its banks. One of the most ancient temples on its banks is near the fort, known as the Neeli Chhatri temple, believed to be a remnant of the first city built on the banks of the river, Indraprastha, by the Pandavas of the Mahabharata epic. This temple is attributed to Yudhistira, the eldest Pandava brother. The other site that predates the Islamic culture of Delhi is the Nigambodh ghat, the oldest and most revered cremation ghat of Delhi, where a succession of power-holders and luminaries have been cremated. The legend associated with it narrates that Brahma, the supreme god, had forgotten the Vedas in the Dwapar Yuga, but when he took a bath at this ghat on the river Yamuna, his knowledge came back to him. The names Nigam (Vedas) and Bodh (knowledge) are combined in this name. When the city of Shahjahanabad was built, a gate was built there, known as Nigambodh Darwaza, which no longer exists as all the gates on the river disappeared when it changed its course. Now the cremation ground lies on the other side of the ring road, away from the Fort. Apart from the Neeli Chatri temple, there are several temples on the riverside as the Yamuna is a holy river of the Hindus.

For the dhobis, the riverbanks were for the performance of their occupational tasks, and they have a pragmatic rather than a religious relation with the river; but they were also seen as inseparable from the river. The relationship of the dhobi with the river is embedded in folklore and collective ethnohistory. In many films and literary narratives the dhobi often forms a part of the river background. In the seventies, when I began my fieldwork, a large part of my time would be spent on the riverbank that used to be dotted with large vessels and *bhattis* (ovens for steaming clothes). Dhobis, both men and women, dotted the riverside and could be seen either thrashing clothes on the stone slabs or drying clothes on the grass. As told to me by many dhobis, they are impervious to the water animals and dangers, including from bites by water snakes. No one can harm a dhobi while he is washing clothes in the river. It is interesting to note that dhobis hang their clothes out to dry on typical makeshift bamboo stands, but they also spread them anywhere and everywhere. It is said in folklore that the dhobis have a boon that they can dry clothes in any place and they will remain clean. The boon appears to be true, as one finds clothes drying over railings by the roadside, on bridges, over hedges, and practically anywhere at all. Yet when the dhobi delivers these clothes, they are always clean.

From the mid-eighties onwards, the dhobis were gradually shifted away from the river. With increasing urbanization and density of population, the river began to get more and more polluted. In my childhood, I remember a river that flowed, and boating on the river was a popular form of recreation in a city that till then had no television. In the fifties, as a small child, I remember a riverbank of clean sand, where I would make sand castles and draw on the sand. There were artists who made sand sculptures and long summer evenings found many people sitting by the riverside, with the usual paraphernalia of peanut sellers, divers, boatmen, and the sellers of delectable *papad* who carried high metal grills on their heads. There are still beautiful memories of the moon shining on the flowing river and the sands glimmering in the moonlight. Those were the days when people slept out in the summer, when one could see a sky full of glittering stars as one drifted off to sleep. Since we lived very close to the Delhi Ridge, which still resembled a forest and not a cultivated garden, one could hear the shrill calls of the numerous jackals and an occasional hyena.

By the eighties, these were slowly passing into memory. The blue sky disappeared from Delhi; so did the stars and the moonlit nights by the river. The dhobis told tales about waking up entire nights by the riverside, and even seeing and hearing ghosts. Today the riverfront has been developed into manicured gardens, and where the dhobis spread their clothes out to dry memorials to prime ministers stand, Shakti Sthal for Indira Gandhi and next to her the memorial to her son Rajiv Gandhi. The riverfront is now green instead of being sandy, but it is out of bounds for the day-to-day activities that used to be carried on there. There is just some muddy sand left, where one can still access the river, which has stopped flowing and appears like a stagnant pool of cess. I am, however, only describing that stretch of the Yamuna and its banks that were used by the

Sheheri dhobis, the stretch adjoining the Red Fort and Old Delhi. Even till the early part of the last century, the river used to flow in full glory and would often break its banks, causing floods, which were a regular feature of the city in those days. My parents also lived in Old Delhi at Dariba Kalan, the only area of Delhi where most middle-class residents lived at that time, as Delhi had not expanded its boundaries. My mother told me that whenever the river flooded periodically, people from Old Delhi used to stand on the bridge (the old Yamuna bridge) and throw long ropes down into the river. There were many people floating by in the river, and a lucky few were able to hold on to the ropes and be hauled up. My mother recalled a family that managed to rescue a pair of twin girls who were adopted, brought up by them, and given the names Ganga and Yamuna. There were others also, especially rescued children, who were adopted by their rescuers. She never mentioned that people were ever concerned about the jati or religious identity of the people they were rescuing. It was seen as an act of dharma, a good deed that would bring them merit. An additional mouth to feed was not a burden in those days.

The women of Old Delhi also had an intimate relationship with the river. Women of traditional Hindu households would get up early in the morning and go to bathe in the river in groups, singing devotional songs. This was a daily routine and was followed by the women grinding wheat for making the daily meals. These women were from the upper castes; the dhobi women did not have any time for rituals. They went to toil on the riverfront, carrying food for the men, helping in drying and spreading the clothes, and generally lending a helping hand to the men who also toiled, come sun and rain, beating heavy clothes on stone slabs, washing them in the large vessels, and steaming them in the *bhattis*.

By the middle of the eighties, most of these activities had been forcibly curtailed by the state. There were two main goals facing the state—cleaning the river and developing the riverfront to resemble that of a developed country. Dhobis washing clothes in the river was not exactly the kind of view that the aspiring state had as its vision of a modern city. The so-called cleaning of the riverfront was a part of the larger project of the then Congress government, of modernizing and beautifying the city of Delhi, that included the clearing of slums and relocating the poor and the marginal on the outskirts of the city. Gill cites Baviskar (2002), who has referred to the judicial orders with respect to slum and industrial relocations as 'bourgeoisie environmentalism', 'where middle and upper classes push their concerns with visual beauty, entertainment, cleanliness, and safety in an organized way to shape a metropolitan space in their own vision, while the urban poor are unable to articulate their own agenda for the city' (Gill 2010: 191). The same goal has been carried forward by successive regimes, but the cleaning of the river still remains an unattainable dream. The dhobis realize this and often verbalize it, saying that *they* were not the people polluting the river but that it was being degraded by industrial and urban sewage wastes. The Delhi segment of the river stretches a distance of 22 kilometres, from Wazirabad to Okhla, and the waste from twenty-two drains falls directly into it. In November 2021, the Chief Minister of Delhi, Arvind Kejriwal, made a promise that he would clean Yamuna by February 2025. Large-scale projects for treatment and redirection of sewage are being planned. In 2023, the riverbanks and floodplains were cleared of most of the so-called slum encroachments, mostly poor people who had made their hutments and small kitchen gardens and some who were growing flowers, plants, and vegetables to sell on the riverbanks. The riverfront is being beautified by making lakes and gardens. There is little concern for those who have been displaced or for their livelihoods. The links of the dhobis with the river are broken forever. The only places that they can still wash are down the river, away from the main city.

The dhobis have a mixed reaction to the severance of the relationship with the river, as many of them feel that having the ghats in the vicinity of their homes is a matter of convenience and comfort. The women specially feel delighted that they no longer have to walk to the river two or three times a day, in addition to all their household work. In the seventies, one of the main reasons that young men at that time cited for their dislike of dhobi work was regarding the back-breaking work they had to do at the river. As one of them narrated, 'when the wind comes, we are hanging onto the clothes, when the sun comes, we are burning, when the rain comes we are getting drenched, it is never an easy situation for us'. But at present, when they are washing clothes either at their own homes or in the designated ghats around the city, they complain less about their work. The comforts of advanced technology, like washing and drying machines as well as clean running water, are available to them at or near their homes. Some of them, however, are nostalgic about the availability of free water as well as the social life on the riverbanks. There is also a generational factor, as the older generation is nostalgic about life at the riverbanks and the younger is happier with the modern facilities at the new ghats. While looking at some archival photographs of Delhi, I found one which showed the dhobis organizing bullfights on the Yamuna riverbank. From the time that I have known the dhobis, there have been few bulls and no fights. At present most of them have switched to two-wheelers for transport, while a few continue with the bicycle; but the *thela* (cart) and bull have disappeared in the urban milieu.

What is most missed or reminisced about, and most often mentioned, is the monthly meet of the Sheheri dhobi panchayat that used to take place on the riverbank on a new moon night. The loss of access to a free public space has dealt a severe blow to their social life. At present the panchayat is held in some *katra* or other, but since all dhobis may not feel comfortable visiting another *katra*, and is never enough space in the cramped *katra* for many people to gather, the gatherings have lost their earlier significance. The riverbank was a space with which every dhobi identified and it was a space of free access. The delinking of their life from the river has thus directly affected their community organization, more than their livelihood or cultural life.

The Cityscape: Caste and Geography

The dhobis claim that their particular community had been in the city ever since the city was established as Shahjahanabad, in the seventeenth century. All their social relationships, including those of marriage and kinship, were located within the walls of the Old City. But they were not the only ones; there were other occupational castes as well (Ahmad 2018, Gill 2010, Prashad 2000), although I did not interact with any of them except the Muslim dhobis, who too had been part of the same city. As described by Bayly (1999), when the cities began to grow during the colonial period, instead of getting modernized, in terms of emerging as caste-free societies, and developing cosmopolitan attitudes, the social order of the cities turned even more regressive and conservative, and the merchant castes that mostly dominated the cities turned to renewed conservatism to assert their superior social status.

As noted and described by historians and anthropologists, caste was never a static phenomenon, and new castes would emerge and establish themselves as endogamous groups (Seneviratne 1997, Dirks 2001). The Zardoz (craftspersons engaged in making gold-embroidered cloth in the Mughal courts), for example, slowly turned into an endogamous caste group as their work, being household based, caused them to prefer to marry a woman from a similar household who would be able to help in the family craft (Gupta and Channa 1996). Vijay Prashad, in writing about the Balmikis of Delhi, has written that many so-called occupational castes were locked into specific occupations more by the stereotypes held by the colonial authorities than by their work history: 'For the Balmikis, for instance, most worked as general landless field hands, but by 1880s those who moved into the cities entered the sanitation work force and all Balmikis began to bear the brunt of being sweepers *in perpetuum*' (Prashad 2000: xvi). Further, writing about the present-day Balmikis, Prashad writes that 'The dregs of all caste communities such as Khatiks, Sansis, Chamars, Churhas, Reghars, Lodhas, among others, formed the community of sweepers' (Prashad 2000: 21). In this sense Prashad prefers to call them a community more than a caste. This is not the place to go into the debate about defining caste, but what is clear is that, although seemingly caste and occupation appear to go hand in hand, especially at the lower end of the ladder, the relation is not a simple or linear one.

At times, however, a caste group may make a transition to their own advantage and monopolize an occupation that had not existed before but which resembles or has the same social status as their original occupation, like the monopoly by the Khatiks of Delhi of the plastic and waste recycling trade (Gill 2010). There is no work history as of now of the dhobis, who also show little concern about their past. As far as their memory reconstructs go, they were all dhobis, at least from the time of their settlement in Delhi. But the link between caste (or *biradari*) and occupation has a political potential as indicated in the works of Lynch (1969), Ahmad (2018), Gill (2010), and Prashad (2000), each of whom has recorded some kind of political mobilization based on the link between caste and occupation. In comparison to these communities the dhobis have shown least potential as a political entity, a fact to which I will return towards the end of this book.

The occupational basis of caste has not been emphasized in recent times, primarily for political reasons, either from the constitutional point of view or from point of view of those who wish for the equal status of all caste groups. Yet at the ground level it remains one of the most salient aspects of caste and a major reason for the survival of caste groups who bond on the basis of horizontal solidarity (Gupta 1991). As I have indicated elsewhere, the horizontal groupings are indicative of praxis and the vertical ones of ideology (Channa 2018a: 30). Occupational solidarity overrides religious ideology as the formation of occupational castes among the Muslims in India show. Historian Irfan Habib (2007: 173) has also pointed out that the Muslim rule in India did nothing to dilute caste; on the contrary, many Muslim occupation-based castes were created as the Muslims coming in from Central Asia and West Asia had many requirements of services and products that they initially fulfilled by enslaving certain people, converting them to Islam, and teaching them skills and crafts. Later, when these slaves were manumitted, they formed the Muslim service caste groups that also had a tendency, like Hindu caste groups, to perpetuate themselves through endogamy. Falling into the existing jajmani system, 'The menial castes duplicated themselves as *kamin* communities among the Muslims, not untouchable but still kept in contempt' (Habib 2007: 174, italics in original).

Bhatty (2016: 32) writes in her autobiography: '*Zaat* or *Jaati* played an important role in social relationships among Indian Muslims. The Indian Muslim society never followed the Islamic ideal and an elaborate system of socio-economic differentiation still exists among Indian Muslims on the model of the Hindu caste system.' She identifies two major Muslim groups in North India; Ashraf or Shairaf and Non-Ashraf or Kameen. The former are divided into four subgroups or castes: the Sayyids claiming highest rank as they claim direct descent from the Prophet Mohammed; Sheikhs, supposedly descended from the four caliphs who followed the Prophet; and the Mughals and Pathans, the former descended from Mughal rulers and the latter from their chieftains. According to her the Kameen (Kamin) were converts from the local service castes, who continued to follow their original occupations and were regarded by the Ashraf, exactly in the same way as the Hindu upper castes looked upon the lower castes, except that the Muslims did not practise ritual untouchability like the Hindus. Nevertheless, there was no intermarriage between

Ashraf and non-Ashraf and as far as possible between the sub-castes of the Ashraf. The Kameen were kept at a social distance and looked down upon. As described by her, the Kameen adopted a few Islamic practices like Nikah, but retained their caste panchayats. Interestingly, the dhobi caste panchayat in Old Delhi, at least till the 1970s, recognized five constituent groups, of which the Muslims were one.

Bhatty also writes about the divisions among the city-based Muslims, namely Qasbati versus Sheheri—the landowning gentry versus the migrants who live in the city: 'The former are distinguished by genteel lifestyle – takalluf or tehzeeb' (Bhatty 2016: 34). The elite Muslims also practised jajmani relationships with the service castes.

Bayly (1999: 226–7) has described how the caste system reinvented itself during the colonial period, when cities like Delhi, Calcutta, and Bombay were being populated by migrants from the villages in a process of rapid urbanization. Even when many of the occupations, like those of clerks and workers in the dockyards, industries, offices, and factories, were caste-free, the caste labels were never shed—quite the contrary. 'Paradoxically, when they entered the industrial work place, such people as the Bhangi, Chamar and Mahars became subject to caste conventions which were often more potent and "essentialising" than the norms of "traditional" village' (Bayly 1999: 226). It is possible that part of it was due to the formation of horizontal solidarity bonds as people sought to find solace in closer kinship and family in unfamiliar environments— bonds that inevitable coincided with caste or more appropriately the jati.

Bayly (1999) has described the greater absorption of caste norms among rural landowners of unspecified caste ranking that took place by the mid nineteenth century. Practices such as the remarriage of widows were practised by the lower castes and not by their jajmans, yet there was a subtle shading off of rank rather than any clear dichotomies. But as the British pressure on the landed gentry intensified, in terms of extraction of rent and general oppression, they began to contest their identity and asserted their superiority in the only way known to them—by improving upon their ritual rank. There was 'a widespread assimilation of sober bania-merchant or Brahman centred norms and values among landed people who had not previously embraced them' (Bayly 1999: 200). These upper-class landowners moving to the fast-developing urban centres carried this desire for high-caste respectability, necessitating the settlement of large numbers of service castes in the cities. Baniyas and Kayasthas were the dominant Hindu groups in Old Delhi, after 1857, and they continued to dominate society along with the elite Muslims; and all groups practised jajmani and relied on the services of the lower and untouchable castes: 'the functioning of the "modern" city's affluent clean-caste households – indeed their very viability as domains of order and respectability – had become dependent on the enactment of ever more elaborate acts of ablution and purification' (Bayly1999: 227).

The British found this ready-available coterie of service providers, neatly labelled and skilled, a good resource to make use of. As Bayly (1999: 228) informs us, manuals on home management were careful to instruct wives of British officers serving in India to choose servants according to proper caste specializations. Further, the British army needed its retinue of servers such as barbers, cleaners, and launderers and carried their load of these caste-specific attendants. Among the various sub-groups of the Sheheri dhobis is one known as Campowale, who derived their name from the British army cantonments where they served during the colonial period.

The city of Shahjahanabad, even when it underwent metamorphosis as a British-ruled colonized city, carried the caste organization as integral to its functioning, architecture, and day-to-day functioning of life. The city was sectorized into people of different castes and classes. There were large *havelis* of the rich, both Hindus and Muslims; the middle classes lived in apartments that were owned or rented. The lanes and bylanes of the Old city were narrow and appeared very congested and crowded, but once one entered the *haveli*, there was a surprising feel of open space. Most of the elite houses had an inner spacious courtyard and large rooms surrounding it. The richer households often had fair-sized gardens inside, with large trees and fragrant flowers. The apartments were not so luxurious but usually had long open verandas—a pattern typical of this part of the world—and were made keeping both environmental and social conditions in mind. Basham (1967) has mentioned that such house types were found even in the ancient city of Harappa, and I remember growing up in exactly this kind of a house. The courtyard in the centre provides space for the women to sit and enjoy some open space, as women of the upper classes were not allowed to go out on the streets, irrespective of whether they were Hindus or Muslims. The rooms were arranged around this courtyard, but did not open directly onto the streets, being protected by a running veranda. A veranda also ran around the courtyard inside. Each room was therefore protected from direct sunlight and exposure by a veranda running on both sides of it. Windows could be opened onto the veranda, thereby protecting the privacy of the occupants. The kitchen and toilets were towards the rear—that is, on the opposite side to the entrance. Most houses had one or at the most two toilets, with a separate room for a bath. The sizes depended on the total size of the house. The toilet was cleaned by a sweeper, and till the middle of the last century most toilets were the dry kind, where the night soil was picked up by a scavenger. Many houses therefore had toilets on the landings of the staircases, facilitating the removal of the night soil and cleaning of the toilet. Most people ate food in the kitchen, and separate dining space was unknown except in very elite homes, again till about the middle of twentieth century. The servants and other service castes entered through the back door, including the dhobi or dhoban. The back part of the house belonged to the women, as the kitchen was also situated there. The drawing room or the room for entertaining guests was always in the front. Women rarely used the front door. Most women only went out in the neighbourhood, if at all, and then they would visit each other from the back of the houses. The front was for formal visitors.

Most homes were built in such a way that the untouchable sweeper, man or woman, could enter the house from the back without polluting the main house. Till late into my adult life, I lived in a house where the toilet was located at the back of the house, with a separate entrance for the person who came in to clean it. With the switchover to modern Western-style flush toilets and commercial toilet cleaners, many households dispensed with the services of the toilet cleaners. In those homes where they are still employed, the work is restricted to sweeping yards, where they exist, and picking up garbage. The garbage was always left outside so that the cleaner did not have to come in. In two-storey houses there was always a winding wrought-iron staircase at the back, used by lower castes and servants. Even today, in Connaught Place a few buildings remain with a spiral staircase at the back, originally meant for this purpose. Irrespective of variations in architecture, having a veranda in front, and the toilets and kitchen at the back, was prevalent till recent times. Having attached bathrooms to bedrooms is something that is very recent and still found only in very modern houses, not in those built before the 1970s. As for other untouchable castes, barbers either sat by the roadside or had small kiosks, again at the roadside. They would also come home to cut hair, but it had to be done in the outer part of the house. All houses, big or small, apartments or bungalows, were built in a way so that caste distances and pollution norms could be maintained.

Such an architectural style was discarded only in the past couple of decades or so, after the economic liberalization in 1992, when foreign builders like Emaar Properties and others were entrusted with the development of a postmodern India. But this modernity is as of now still limited.

The *haveli* kind of housing pattern is very suitable for hot weather and dust, common to the Indo-Gangetic plains. In summer the verandas would be hung with *chiks* or curtains made of *khus,* an aromatic grass, which had a very cooling effect. Even government offices and public spaces were similarly protected from the heat. It is also adapted to caste-based notions of purity and pollution and norms of feminine seclusion. Although now *purdah* or seclusion is regarded primarily as a character of Muslim culture, it was widely prevalent in Delhi till the 1960s among the upper castes and classes of the old part of the city that housed the more conservative sections of society. Only very liberal women were seen in public, but not on the streets generally. They travelled by private modes and, till recent times, women of respectable families were not expected to take a public mode of transport (see Channa 2004 and Channa 2013c for more details). The women of the lower castes and classes were, on the other hand, commonly in the streets, performing various designated tasks.

In spite of the important services provided by them, the lower castes were always cramped into what are known as *katras*. These were usually separated from the houses of the elite and upper castes by being enclosed and accessed only through a very narrow opening that one could also easily avoid if one did not wish to pass that way. They were therefore a part of the city, yet made invisible in a way that one would never have to encounter them in the ordinary day-to-day activities around the neighbourhoods. In other words, the untouchability and low status of their occupants was amply made clear by keeping them, as one might put it, 'out of contact' and 'out of sight'. Such *katras* are to be found even today, and have been part of the city's landscape from the seventeenth century to the present. As Gupta (1981: 55) has described, when the British took over Old Delhi, the rich, especially the baniyas and few aristocratic Muslim families, ransomed their protection by paying huge amounts to the colonial rulers and had their majestic *havelis* preserved. Even at that time the poor were thrown towards the outer rim of the city, away from the Fort and the central part of Chandni Chowk towards Turkman Gate, Mori Gate, and Farash Khana.

As we can see, the three forces one could have expected to dilute caste norms in the city—namely the dominance of Islam, British colonial rule, and economic modernization—worked instead to reinforce caste norms and values and buttress the caste-based occupational specializations. The next section will describe the growth of Delhi in the postcolonial period to the period just before economic liberalization in the early nineties.

The Making of New Delhi: Expansion and Gentrification

In January 1974 I began my fieldwork in real earnest. At that time, the majority of dhobis were confined to the various *katras* inside the walled city and in the adjunct areas like Kashmiri Gate and Hamilton Road. They were also dispersed at strategic locations to be available for the gentry that were populating the city when it became established as the capital of British India. Specially designated ghats were built for them in the newly constructed New Delhi area near Minto Bridge, with eight numbered ghats, and adjacent to the Railway Quarters at ITO (deriving its name from the Income Tax Office situated there). Most of these locations were still close to the river Yamuna.

The expanding city in the postcolonial period, with its clubs, cinema halls, market centres, schools, hospitals, and hotels, was still bound by caste norms and ideology. It was imperative that clothes be sent to the dhobi, hair be cut by the *nai* (barber) and scavengers (*bhangis*) clean the lavatories at home.

During the seventies, when my association with the dhobis began, things were not yet transformed very much from the time of the initial development of New Delhi. Most of Old Delhi, although congested through a process of involution rather than development, was more or less the same as it was when Lutyens' Delhi, or New Delhi, was established. The latter is specially known for the spacious bungalows, powerful politicians, very senior government officials, and the super-rich. Lurking behind all that glamour there is the invisible retinue of servants, dhobis, and other service providers, lodged in the servants' quarters, who, as always, remain in the shadow of history.

Most of the dhobis of the Sheheri group still lived in Old Delhi, mostly in their original *katra*. Some lived in the backyards of the spacious bungalows of Lutyens' Delhi serving the important government officials, like in the Railway Quarters at ITO. By the mid-seventies, when massive relocation work was going on in Delhi under the leadership of Sanjay Gandhi, who took drastic steps to gentrify and improve the face of Delhi prior to the Asian Games to be held in 1982, a number of slums were cleared and a large number of new settlements known as resettlement colonies were built outside of what was then recognized as the core areas of Delhi and New Delhi. Although Mrs Gandhi and Sanjay Gandhi came under severe criticism for their reportedly heavy-handed treatment of people, and political opponents in particular, the dhobis are all praises for her. Indira Gandhi had made about twenty-two resettlement colonies and each one of them had a dhobi ghat.[8] Many dhobis dispersed into these colonies. One was built near Delhi University, near the Delhi Ridge, where several families settled, and this ghat is operational even today. Another one was built in a prime location in New Delhi, at Hailey Road, which houses prime buildings like the West Bengal State House and Fulbright House, among others. The dhobis not only have a ghat in this area but have four-storey apartment buildings as well. When I began my fieldwork in the mid-1970s, they had just begun to move into these apartments. While not all dhobis here are of the Sheheri *biradari*, many of them are. This ghat at Hailey Road was built by Chaudhary Brahm Prakash Yadav (1918–93), a stalwart of the then Congress regime. He was the first Chief Minister of Delhi, in 1952, at the age of 22. Being of a lower-status caste (Other Backward Class, OBC), he had sympathies for the downtrodden and gave the dhobis a place in the heart of New Delhi. Till the seventies, the dhobis were occupying prime positions in Delhi, and although they were still poor, they were surviving.

The dhobi ghats eventually became victims of gentrification and expansion of the city of Delhi, as it grew and modernized as the capital of a developing country. At present the regime in power claims India is now a regional superpower, and the face of the city has begun to reflect some of this assumed glory. But by the 1980s the then prime minister, Indira Gandhi, also had many plans. Major transformations were planned under her twenty-point programme. A person I have known for a period of time as an associate of my research, whom I had known as a young man in the seventies, Bishanlal, moved with his extended family from Kucha Pati Ram, a *katra* inside the walled city, to a newly built housing complex near Delhi University. An earlier slum colony known as Daya Basti had been converted into an apartment complex with adjoining ghats for the dhobis, called Subhadra Colony, and is part of a larger complex known as Shashtri Nagar. These were the resettlement colonies under the twenty-point programme and, to safeguard their traditional livelihood, the Congress regime built dhobi ghats in all these colonies. The dhobis who moved to this place continued with their traditional occupation.

The largest cluster of ghats was at Minto Road, near the centre of Delhi, adjacent to Connaught Place, popularly referred to as CP, regarded as the core of New Delhi. It was built as a circular market cum residential area, surrounding a large circular park, which is called Connaught Circus, although most people now refer to it just as CP. The market has a running veranda, or closed corridor, favoured by the British for the hot climate, to protect the shoppers from direct sun. Before the present expansion of Delhi, till the 1960s, it was the premier market of Delhi, with shops at street level and residential apartments on the first floor. It contained some of the iconic eating places of Delhi as well as premier cinema halls. In conformation to the style of most of Lutyens' Delhi, the entire complex was only two storeys high. The master plan of Delhi does not allow for high-rise building in Lutyens' Delhi, a norm that has protected much of Delhi's foliage and greenery. Later some high-rise buildings were added towards the outer rings, but the inner rings remain as they were as a protected heritage site. Significant changes were made when the Delhi Metro made its appearance, and the central park was redefined to accommodate the underground metro station. Earlier it was a shady garden full of very old and massive shade-giving trees, but now it is more ornate and developed like a multi-use park where public entertainment is often performed.

With land prices in Delhi spiralling, the Connaught Place area has become almost fully commercialized, with practically every residential apartment converted to some commercial use and the spacious bungalows of Barakhambha Road, a radial road leading out from Connaught Circus, all pulled down to make way for high-rise multistorey commercial complexes. Restaurants, hotels, and shops have proliferated in this space. The dhobis had their ghats at a stone's throw from this mushrooming commercial centre, but by 2019 they have been almost removed, their ghats broken and replaced by modern buildings. By 2023, only two ghats were remaining; the dhobis bravely continued their occupation in these two ghats, and visitors to this area could see clothes hanging in rows to dry. This area now provides housing for the higher echelons of people serving in the government and as a jewel in the crown, the ruling BJP (Bharatiya Janata Party) has built its shining new party office near to where the dhobi ghats were. I visited this area when the demolitions were being carried out, and a few ghats were still left. Many dhobis were still living there, but they were despondent. 'This is the last blow. Now we have no hopes as the BJP bosses will never tolerate the dhobi *ghats* near their headquarters' ('*Ab koi ummeed nahi hai*').

The pattern followed in the modernization of Connaught Place reflects the nature of transformation around most of New Delhi. While the portions protected by heritage laws remain more or less as they were, with cosmetic changes only, every other part is being refurbished to provide a maximum of space utilization. Many areas that were considered to be on the outskirts of Delhi, remote and faraway, are now considered as 'within' the city, as it keeps expanding beyond its earlier boundaries. Almost all the villages around Delhi have been sucked into it, and some of them, retaining the earlier rural architecture, provide an 'exotic' setting for high-end shops and marketing areas such as Shapur Jat village. Vasant Kunj, for example, had a rural setting even in the late seventies, with mud roads and a barren landscape spotted with rural houses and small markets. Today it is a upscale neighbourhood, surrounded by malls and high-end hospitals, with extensive landscaping of its once barren landscape. The apartments, once sold at affordable prices for middle-income groups by the Delhi Development Authority (DDA), are now sold at very high prices (an apartment for which the DDA had originally charged three lakhs is now being sold at three crores) and house the upper-middle rather than the lower-middle classes as it did earlier. With the gentrification of the city and rising property prices, most persons who are no longer in the high income bracket have been moving to the satellite areas, in the adjoining states of Uttar Pradesh and Haryana, which are considered extensions of Delhi and included in the more recently formed National Capital Region (NCR) that is given the status of a state but not fully so. This means that Delhi remains under both the central government and the state government. This has not brought much comfort to the people of this region, as a divided administration often proves non-productive.

During the last couple of decades, the Delhi Metro and the 2010 Commonwealth Games have been singularly responsible for bringing about radical transformations in the face of Delhi. The Delhi Metro finds its way deep into the heart of Old Delhi, with stations at Chandni Chowk, Red Fort, and Chawri Bazar, penetrating into the market and residential areas. In deference to the fact that this region contains some of the most iconic heritage structures, as well as it being a very densely populated locality, the metro stations here are built deep inside the earth, with an attempt to least disturb the character of the region. They have succeeded to an extent, as most of the area still wears the same look as it did before, yet major changes have crept in over the years.

The newly developed satellite areas such as Gurgaon in Haryana and Noida in Uttar Pradesh, however, have a different cultural setting, inhabited mostly by younger persons working in the corporate sectors that have flourished with the liberalization of the Indian economy. A detailed account of those sectors are beyond the scope of this volume, but as far as the community that is under study is concerned, they have neither migrated nor wish to migrate to these newly developed areas, where laundromats are likely to be more popular than the dhobi.

The dhobis who continue to live in Old Delhi and the more conservative areas of New Delhi have plenty of clients from the hotels, restaurants, hospitals, garment-manufacturing units, and similar institutions that need to get their laundry done in bulk and find it convenient to hand it over to the dhobi. Although very big five-star hotels and very high-end hospitals have their own in-house laundry, most others that are somewhat down the ladder in terms of scale and resources still outsource the laundry work. Since as of today, only those belonging to the community of dhobis do this work; it comes to them, keeping them economically viable. The dhobis displaced from Minto Road had a lucrative clientele in the nearby commercial complex of Connaught Place and adjoining areas and are highly aggrieved that, in return for their displacement, all that they have been offered are residential houses in Dwarka. This is a place at a far distance from the main city, and although it has a large residential complex, the displaced dhobis, who have been living and working in the core areas of Delhi, will not find work in the new location easily. Even if they find some work, there being no ghats in Dwarka, they will not be able to wash clothes in bulk, an activity that is the main source of their income.

Even more important than income and getting work is the question of the community, the deeply engaged social relationships into which the dhobis invest most of their energies and their emotions. When I began to work among them in the seventies, the most important of my findings was the importance of the *biradari*, as they call their community. The word *biradari* is used in different ways and for different levels of social formations, but in a nutshell it refers to the social world of the dhobis (and other jati groups) in Northern India. It has a caste-based, a spatial, and an occupational connotation. As Atkinson (2017: 22) points out, the community like that of the Sheheri dhobi may be a construct, but 'constructs have history, they are embedded in traditions and collective memories. The fact that they are "constructions" should alert us to the fact that they require collective work to create or sustain them.' The next chapter will take up these concepts as well as the process of their 'construction' in greater detail, as they form the crux of our understanding of the community's relationship to its environment—economic, social, and political. It is the network through which they negotiate their way around in the world in which they live.

Notes

1. Zarin Ahmad has listed the seven cities of Delhi as '(1) Qila Rai Pithora and Lal Kot (1052); (2) Siri (1303); (3) Tughlakabad (1321); (4) Jahapanahbad (1334); (5) Ferozabad and Kotla (1354); (6) Dinapanah (1530, 1540); and (7) Shahjahanabad (1648)' (Ahmad 2018:23).

2. It is to be noted that this field area is culturally similar to the Old City of Delhi and therefore one may easily transcribe from one to the other.

3. Narayani Gupta has mentioned three major crises in the life of the city—those of 1857–8, 1911–12, and 1947 (Gupta 1981:1). The first refers to the aftermath of the 1857 War of Independence, the second to the formation of the British colonial capital city of Delhi, and the third to the partition that also marked the independence of the country.

4. The Delhi Ridge is part of the Aravalli Range that runs through this region. Originally a part of the ancient forests, it is now much degraded and encroached upon, its biodiversity and forest having been lost forever.

5. '*Kaun jata hai Ghalib Dilli ki galiyan chod kar?*' ('Who wants to leave Ghalib, the lanes of Delhi?').

6. *Garam Hawa*, made in 1974, is considered a classic film on the partition, adapted from a story by Ismat Chughtai, directed by M.S. Sathyu, and scripted by Kaifi Azmi.

7. Ahmad (2018:26) writes that 'Overall, 32,900 Muslims left the city and 495,000 Hindus and Sikhs migrated to Delhi.'

8. Gill (2010:194) writes that 'Participants to the plastic recycling trade have always been loyal to the Congress Party. At the lower levels of labour working in the market and living in slum settlements, the support echoes a more general trend which views the Congress as a party that has done much for the urban poor in contemporary times by legalizing resettlement colonies'. This directly supports the sentiments of the dhobis.

2

The Social World of the Dhobis

Jati and *Biradari*

A community like the dhobis is usually referred to in social science, including anthropological literature, as a caste group. Some also refer to the internal divisions of a larger category like dhobi as sub-castes. Since most such literature begins the division at the level of the larger Varna categories, they construct the typology as if a larger body is undergoing divisions and subdivisions. The imposition of the external category caste also precludes the complexity and true character of the Indian social reality, 'an unhappy rendering' (Sen 1961:14). As rightly pointed out by eminent Indian scholar M.N. Srinivas (1962), the indigenous terms used are Varna and jati, whose meanings are diffuse and polysemic and not in the nature of rigid categories or smooth classifications as supposed by the Western scholars who initially wished to make sense of the Indian social scenario. In real life, in short, there are no sharply delineated, naturally bounded, genealogical communities. Families, nations, races, and even species are ultimately products of social traditions of classifying organisms. As such, they exist only in our imagination (Zerubavel 2012:75).

Numerous scholars have described these terms even while they used the terminology of caste to do so. But while Varna may to some extent be constricted to a more limited and generalized use, jati is a polysemic word that cannot be so confined (Hocart 1950). Even Varna has been given a much wider scope of meaning by scholars such as Smith (1994), although most still restrict it to its meaning as a derivative of the Rig Vedic hymn of Purusha Sukta (Channa 2018a:3).

Jati on the other hand is not a derivative of the scriptures or even an essentially religiously derived term. In its common usage jati or jaat, as is used almost all over India, is something that describes a person's very core identity, who she or he is and how the person is placed with respect not only to others but within the entire universe. As already described

Dhobis of Delhi. Subhadra Mitra Channa, Oxford University Press. © Subhadra Mitra Channa 2024.
DOI: 10.1093/9780198926238.003.0003

in the previous chapter, these terms are used by Muslims (Bhatty 2016) as well as other non-Hindus. Jati is not confined to one's Varna-derived or caste identity alone; it refers to one's gender, one's religion, one's history, and one's spatial location, and many other aspects of a person's existence. It defines one's species and location in the cosmos. For example, humans are *manusyajati* as against, say, *pashujati* (animals). Women are *strijati* as against *purusajati* (men). People who speak the same language are one jati; a Gujarati will refer to another Gujarati as his own jati, and a Muslim is the same jati as another Muslim. But jatis are not exclusive; one can be of a linguistic jati, a regional jati, and a specific gender jati. One can say that as a Gujarati Muslim is closer to one of his own jati than, say, to a Kashmiri Muslim. One can also say that a Gujarati Hindu and a Gujarati Muslim are closer than, say, a Kashmiri Pandit and a Kashmiri Muslim, respectively. But again, these are situational. One can say the opposite also, and state that as a Hindu one is closer to another Hindu, even someone of another region andspeaking another language, than to a Muslim from the same region and speaking the same language. One can be magnanimous and say that everyone who is human belongs to the same *manusya* jati. One can be very restrictive and consider only one's very close kinship network and one's endogamous circle only as one's jati. It is the last category, the circle of endogamy, that is the core of defining what has been projected as a caste-based identity. A caste group is largely defined as a circle of extended kin that includes one's relations by marriage and those who are potentially marriageable. This is quite contrary to the way David Schneider (1968) describes American kinship that is rooted in the concept of blood and biological relationships. In India, blood relations have wider connotations and include the notion of putative kinship, village-based, jati-based, or even religion-based. In North India, villages are exogamous because all born in the same village are considered as siblings. At the minimal and practical level, a jati is a group into which marriage is permissible.

Scholars such as Srinivas (1952) and Inden (1976) have used the notion of endogamy as the defining criterion of jatis. According to Srinivas, jatis refer to local, territorial, and linguistic caste groups that marry among themselves. Srinivas therefore clearly indicated that what is known as the Indian caste system does not have a pan-Indian character but is more of a regional phenomenon of local rankings and social and economic interactions. He even refuted the universal social superiority of the Brahmin, replacing it by the concept of dominant caste (1959). However, in the cities the jati rankings usually follow the more textual rankings than the land-based rankings that are found in the rural areas. For example, although Delhi is close to the Haryana region, where Jats are the dominant caste, Delhi itself does not have any dominant caste group, although in those areas of the NCR that are now carved out of Haryana the Jats may appear as dominant in terms of ownership of land and property. In Old Delhi the Aggarwals and other trading castes like the Khandelwals had dominated, but Delhi was also flooded with Punjabi refugees after 1947, and many of them rose to high positions and made considerable economic progress. Delhi reflects India in a way that, rather than the entire city being dominated by any one group, there are distinct neighbourhoods that reflect the historical past of their existence and evolution into recent times, by having a larger concentration of people from one region of India.

In the ancient Hindu texts there is a hierarchy of Varna categories, but, as explained in the Sanatana Dharma (1916), it is deeds and qualities that determine the actual Varna status of a person. Although the jati system historically reflects a great deal of flexibility, by the medieval period many of the community boundaries had hardened, especially because of endogamy. As per Tambs-Lyche (2017, 2021), the term jati came to designate a caste by the beginning of the Common Era, when the Gupta dynasty was established in India. The term Varna is found in the later Vedic times, and Brahmins became identified in the late Vedic period (c.1000 BCE). The Manusmriti (100BCE–200 CE) indicates the time period when the jati system was consolidated as a ranked hierarchy, as clearly postulated in that text. The closing of boundaries of the jati system can be attributed to the nature of kingship as developed in the South Asian region. In the west, the sovereign interacted with his subjects as individuals; in this region the king consolidated his power through the collectives of the jatis (Tambs-Lyche 2021: 2). We can see that even today Indian democracy has not been able to transform this collective, jati-based identity of its citizens. Although Manusmriti consolidated hierarchy, the practice of untouchability has not been properly located in any text, leading to the doubt in the minds of many Hindu scholars and social leaders, including Mahatma Gandhi, that it was never an integral part of the Sanatana Dharma. For this text, therefore, I will use the term jati rather than caste as far as possible. What sets jati apart from a more essentialized form of discrimination like race is its ambiguity and flexibility. This ambiguity and flexibility also increase the competitiveness between groups, as has been noted by scholars of Indian society (Dumont 1970, Srinivas 1962). Here social mobility is as a jati more than as an individual. Most political movements to support jati status one way or the other form at the collective level, be it the demand by the Jats of Haryana for OBC (Other backward class) status or of the Muslim Quarashis for establishing a respectable lineage connecting them to the Arab clans. However, from the period that the jati system becomes consolidated as inherited ranking, it has been difficult or near impossible for those at the bottom to come up to the top, mobility being restricted mostly to the middle-ranking castes as pointed out by Srinivas and Béteille. In describing the efforts towards upward mobility by the Muslim Quarash, Ahmad writes, 'Ascribing an occupational title has limited success in raising *biradari* status among others. However, taking on a common upgraded title strengthens solidarity and raises self-confidence among members' (2018:63).

As rightly pointed out by Tambs-Lyche, 'High and powerful castes build their identity upon a pride of achievement: some of the lower castes are united rather by their exclusion and stigma' (2021: 3). The lower castes have therefore found both security and identity in consolidation into smaller groups like the dhobi *biradari*, as in spite of its uncertain textual legitimacy untouchability is widely prevalent even now in India and in many rural areas and smaller towns. It is also practised in the urban areas, where people know about the jati status of a person. While doing fieldwork among the dhobis, I became painfully aware of these practices (Channa 2013b), as the dhobis are considered untouchable. We shall return to the notion and practice of hierarchy in a later chapter. But at this point it is important to mention that the marginalization and humiliation that the communities like the dhobis suffer at the hands of the upper castes also contribute to the creation of stronger horizontal ties and internal solidarity. For them the *biradari* is not just an identity; it is also a community of support and social security.

The Dhobi *Biradari*

The dhobis call themselves the dhobi jati, and when they say that, they are specifically referring to their occupation, based on birth and inherited from their ancestors. The jati of launderers, or dhobis, are found all over India, even if they no longer follow the traditional occupation in many regions. They are also among the ones mentioned in very ancient texts, indicating that this is one occupation that has existed from early times. In some versions of the Ramayana, when Rama brings Sita back from exile and instates her as his queen on the throne of Ajodhya, he overhears a dhobi telling his wife that the king (Rama) has done something wrong, for he cannot be sure that his queen is still chaste, having spent time at the palace of another man (Ravana). In this version, Rama asks his wife to undergo the fire trial, only because of the words of a dhobi. The lesson meant here is about the dharma (duty) of a king, and reference to the dhobi is only to indicate that a king must heed the opinion of all his subjects, no matter how humble. The fifteenth-century Bengali poet Chandidas is famous for his love poems addressed to the washerwoman Rami. He was a poet of the Bhakti or devotional poetry genre, and his devotional verses describing the love between Radha and Krishna are famous for their erotic as well as spiritual content. The Bhakti movement was directed against the dictates of Brahmanical Hinduism and decried caste and gender hierarchies imposed by them. The love of Radha and Krishna is eulogized by them, as Radha was a woman from the lowly cowherd community and Krishna was a prince, although his foster parents were also cowherds (Yadava). In the same vein, Chandidas, belonging to an upper caste himself, justifies and idealizes his love for the low-caste Rami. The dhobi therefore has played key roles in classical literature and is a ubiquitous community everywhere.

When the dhobis refer to their *biradari*, they are again referring to several levels of association. The widest and the most inclusive is what they call the All India Dhobi Mahasabha, a body that includes all the persons who identify as dhobi, all over the country. This body is just a spontaneous formation that had actually come into operation in 1953, when the movie *Rami Dhoban* was released. This was a time soon after independence when the rhetoric of equality of caste and laws against caste discrimination were becoming well known among the people of

India. The Dhobi Mahasabha at that point was comprised of the heads or *chaudhuries* of the various dhobi *biradari* across India. There were protest movements by the dhobis against the title of the movie, specifically to the use of the term *dhoban*, which was seen as derogatory, as it was a label of being low caste. This was the first movement towards the political mobilization of their caste within the Indian democracy. Democracy and universal franchise had created a potential for competitiveness among the jati groups, who began to crystallize community political identities to push forward a common agenda by pulling together numbers. The jati groups at the bottom of Indian society realized for the first time that organization under umbrella categories that increased their numbers could be used as a political weapon to push forward a self-interested agenda. As pointed out by social scientists such as Kothari (1970) and Brass (1994), caste and religion were seen to be useful as political weapons. But the only stimulus for a larger unity coalesced around reasons that were of a general nature and of significance to all of the dhobi communities. In 1958, the dhobis united under the umbrella organization, to push forward a charter that included a demand for subsidized rates of water supply and removal of taxes on *thela*; the hand-driven carts that were earlier used for carrying bundles of clothes. An important agenda that was being pushed in the seventies was to bring all dhobis under the label of Scheduled Caste, all over India. At that time and even now, the dhobis are included under Scheduled Castes in states like Uttar Pradesh, Bihar, Bengal, and Delhi, but in other states like Punjab and Haryana they are included under OBC (other backward classes). Similarly, the Muslims, not being Hindus, are not included in Scheduled Castes. However, after the implementation of the Mandal Commission giving 27 per cent reservation to the OBC, this agitation lost its steam. The Muslim dhobis have been included in the OBC status after some deliberations by the Supreme Court.

Although the name 'Sheheri' refers to the dhobis who were a part of the city of Shahjahanabad since its foundation, they are not the only community of dhobis who can make such a claim. There are three other communities, or *thops*, as they are called in the local vocabulary; these are the Tijoria, the Campowale, and the Muslims. The Sheheri also use the title of Kanojia, as against the identity of the other three groups. The genesis of these separate communities in Old Delhi can be obtained through the narrative of one dhobi informant given to me in the seventies during the first phase of my fieldwork:

> The earliest community of dhobis who lived in the walled city, from the time of the Mughals were the Tijoria, tracing their origin from the town of Tijarat in Uttar Pradesh. Another group came from Purab (East) at the time of the British, and settled in Delhi. This later group were known as Purbia (also Kanojia). In the early phase of their settlement, the Tijoria and the Purbia considered themselves to be part of the same *biradari*, married among each other, ate and drank together, and shared the same *hookah*.[1] On the day of *jafat* (local name for a communal feast), all the dhobis of the city had gathered on the banks of the river Yamuna. The cook belonged to the Muslim community, but while cooking he dipped his finger twice into the food to taste it. When the Purbia saw this, they refused to partake of the food as they believed it had been rendered impure by the saliva of the cook, who had dipped his finger twice. Had he dipped it only once then it would have been alright, but by dipping twice he had transferred his saliva to the food. From that time onwards, the Tijoria and Purbia formed separate communities for marriage, inter-dining and sharing of the *hookah*. The Purbia later began to refer to themselves as *sheheri*.

This narrative highlights several issues of interest. Firstly, it indicates that the dhobi communities consider locality to be more important than religion, as the Muslim dhobis were part of the communal celebration taking place on the banks of the river Yamuna. Secondly, it indicates the place of the river in the cosmology of the dhobis. Before the banks of the river were alienated from its traditional users in the name of beautification of the city, it was the space par excellence for the dhobis to hold all their important social functions including their monthly panchayat meetings. The reference to pollution by saliva indicates that jati discrimination is practised even by the lower and even untouchable castes such as the dhobis. Dumont (1970) had made this observation that, unlike race, caste is a layered system, where each layer finds its validation in having some above them but also some lower than them. Since most stratification is contested, the lowest point is never determined in absolute terms as even those at the very bottom will assert that someone is even lower.

The third group mentioned are the 'Campowale', those who travelled with the British army, as they needed their own supporting brigade of dhobis, cooks, cleaners, and other service providers and could only be obtained from people of the appropriate jati group. These dhobis were cut off from their brethren, as travelling with the British exposed them to the *mleccha* (Trautmann 1997) lifestyle,[2] and other Hindu dhobis did not wish to marry among them. They form the third category and so the dhobis of Old Delhi are comprised of four sections of *thops*, each endogamous and each having its own head or *chaudhuri*.

The horizontal solidarities of jati, which may cut across religion, region, and even language, are almost always based on common occupations. A dhobi will consider all others following the same hereditary occupation as a *jaat bhai* (brother based on jati). This is the widest circle of the *biradari* that conveys more the feelings of belongingness, identity, and brotherhood than any kind of formal structure. At its most restricted use, it is limited to the circle of endogamy, the extended kin group, within which all marriages take place. The Sheheri (or Purbia) is such an endogamous group, and, since the numbers are not large and they are confined to a limited spatial zone, they form a strongly integrated network of recognition and cooperation. Even today, when there has been some physical dispersal of the *biradari*, although mostly within Delhi, and a fairly extensive shift in occupation, the *biradari* still thrives and there are several mechanisms that hold it together.

One salient aspect of the *biradari* is that all members recognize everyone else. At any point, whenever I mentioned any name of any individual, along with some other marker of their identity, like age, place of residence, or occupation, I was immediately rewarded with instant identification as well as genealogical connections of that person. Secondly, through generations of intermarriage most people can find filial or affinal connections with each other. A large part of most conversations was always about who is related to whom. In the rest of this book, the term *biradari* will be used for this core centre of identity and other levels by their specific qualification.

Beyond this immediate and closely knit group comes the regional identity, namely the Delhi dhobis, and here a careful boundary is drawn between migrant and 'original'. The city-based *biradari* includes representatives of only the four *thops* originally belonging to Delhi; namely the

Sheheri, Campowale, Tijoria, and Muslim. A higher level of identification would be of a common spoken language. At present, a few marriages have taken place with dhobis outside the *biradari*, but who are closer in terms of culture—that is, able to speak in Hindi. The other levels, other regions, are abstractly recognized and part of an abstract social and political identity that has no immediate implications but remains as a shadowy entity with possibilities for mobilization only under duress. The dhobis are not the only community in this region to have a *biradari*. Similar organizations are found among almost all the traditional occupation-based groups of this region, and of Delhi.

Ahmad (2018: 62–3) gives a detailed account of the meaning and scope of the term *biradari* as it is used among the Muslim butchers or Quarashis of Old Delhi, although she recognizes that the name 'Quarash' must have been adopted by them during the 1911 census, when a lot of communities upgraded their status. It is possible that those referred to simply as Kasai (butcher) elevated their position to Quarashi, linking themselves to an Arabic ancestry and delinking from low-caste Hindu Khatiks. She too defines *biradari* as having the attributes of a common traditional occupation, kinship, and a unit 'within which marriage relationships are restricted' (Ahmad 2018:62). This restriction of marriage that defines a *biradari* is often a result of occupational necessity and gender relations related to division and sharing of labour. As Gupta and Channa (1996) have explained with respect to the Muslim Zardoz, a loose aggregate of workers, the Zardoz became an endogamous group because it was always more convenient to have a woman come in from a similar background where she would have skills for the craft and would be an additional help in the household economy. For the butchers too, the women in the household were involved in cleaning and storing leftover meat and, although not involved in the actual process of slaughter, they were helpers in other aspects of the butcher's work. Moreover, marrying within the same occupational group creates a support group for various forms of economic exchange.

A more recent and interesting example of the formation of an occupational category based on caste with respect to a relatively new and not 'traditional' occupation is Kaveri Gill's work on the plastic recycling industry forming an important although informal sector of the urban economy of Delhi. She has shown the 'numerical dominance of a single important SC of north India, the Khatiks among three categories of labour working in the plastic scrap market, that is plastic godown owner, itinerant buyers, and plastic mazdoors' (Gill 2010: 157). Unlike the dhobis, these do not belong originally to Delhi but are migrants from the nearby states of Rajasthan and Uttar Pradesh. But even within about two generations, they have developed an intensive kinship/marriage network that makes them almost similar to an endogamous *biradari* of the dhobi type. As reported by the author, 'From the total random sample of traders, 96 percent had brothers or in-laws engaged in the same work. Intrafamily specialization was also widespread, with each brother undertaking the role of a different kind of trader' (Gill 2010:159). The narratives of her informants also validate the prevalence of endogamous ties that support the business aspect as well as provide moral universe of support. As her data indicates, the Khatiks made the transition from dealing in human hair, leather, and waste collection to dealing with plastic waste. They also transitioned from more 'polluted' work like pig breeding, pig butchery, and the bristle trade to the collection and processing of newer material like scrap and plastic waste.

Gender Relations and *Biradari*

An interjection about the significance of the *biradari* as an endogamous group is important at this point, for it reflects on the gendered power hierarchy as well as the relative significance that horizontal solidarity has for different jati groups. In most of North India, the term *biradari*, or *bhai-bandh*, is used by the upper and dominant landowning castes to designate an exogamous group where the men are conceptualized as brothers and the women as sisters. This *bhai-bandh* is the entity that cooperates and stands up for each other, in ways that has great implications for political and economic goals and manoeuvres. The Jats (Pettigrew 1975), for example, are well known for having powerful *biradari* relationships, where they support each other in standing up to a common enemy, to help in times of need, like the marriage of a daughter, or in more secular activities like pushing a land deal, winning an election, or pursuing a political agenda. The practice of exogamy is a powerful technique of keeping the group together as consanguine relationships are always seen as more trustworthy than affine relationships. Moreover, in North India among the upper castes, the wife-givers are seen as at a lower position than the wife-takers, keeping the relationship between them full of tensions. Most of the upper castes in North and North-west India were often engaged in conflict with continued invasions from the outside as well as with each other. In all such situations it was expedient to have a strong group that identified as a strong male bonding community. The unequal gender relations, the seclusion of women, and the need to protect their honour from men of other groups also led to male domination and greater restrictions on women's mobility. Women were seen as outsiders from birth, as they would transfer to another male lineage and have a different group identity from their brothers. Incoming women, although merged with the lineage ideally were never trusted as much as one doubted their loyalty. Chowdhry (2004) has written in the context of the Jats of Haryana that a household always tried to bring their married daughters to help with the delivery of a baby, as the family did not trust sisters-in-law or the wives of the brothers to be faithful to each other. Since the women married into the same household came from different lineages, they were seen as competitors and childbirth was a key space of contestation. The status and position of women were closely tied to their motherhood, and sisters-in-law would compete to become the mother of male children. The upper-caste *biradari* are therefore groups of male bonding, kept carefully exogamous so that they are not internally divided by relations of marriage. Among upper castes the one single divisive aspect of marriage is the hierarchy between wife-givers and wife-takers; this is also a source of gender inequity and aversion to the birth of female children.

The dhobis have a different sense of relationality and gender conceptualizations. To the dhobis *biradari* is a term that applies equally to men and women, irrespective of their relation through blood or marriage. There is no special significance attached to masculinity in their culture, where both men and women play important roles in the work that takes place in the household space. This in turn negates the dichotomy between public space and domestic space, a division that informs gender inequity in many other situations. Marriage does not dislocate a woman from her natal home, as within the constraints of limited space a woman is often married just a few lanes away from her parental residence.

Married women are frequent and constant visitors to their parental home and are always around to help or be useful. More importantly, there is no hierarchy between bride-givers and bride-takers, as everyone within the *biradari* is treated as equal. The service castes have never played any role in warfare or any kind of masculine aggressive activities. Their role at any time, even of conflict, is to wash clothes and take care of the aspects of purity and pollution to which they have been assigned. In this sense, even when they accompanied troops or were near any zone of conflict, they were never expected to exhibit any qualities of valour or perform any task that would bring them glory. They were always the shadow people, doing their job, wherever they were placed.

This differential cognition about the *biradari* and social status is reflected in the gender relations that show marked difference between the upper and lower castes. The lower castes show significantly less prevalence of patriarchy and son-preference as exhibited by the upper castes of Northern India (Channa 2023b). There is little or no gendered hierarchy among these marginalized communities, as the men have no special status or masculine attributes that set them at a higher level than women (Channa 1985, 2001). Most of the time, when inside a dhobi household, I have seen husband and wife working in tandem, holding the edges of clothes to fold them, or the wife ironing while the husband washes the clothes. The possibility of the reversal of sex roles among a low-caste community has been commented on by Searle-Chatterjee (1981), who has described how men, when required, often do many of the tasks like cooking and household cleaning usually assigned to women. Just as dhobi women help their husbands, the men too are not averse to lending a helping hand. The ego conflict that is seen in middle-class homes is certainly absent among the dhobi couples. What was true in the seventies continues to be true even today, and while a lot of things have changed over the years, the power equation of gender relations has not changed. This can be attributed to the absence of certain key signifiers of gender hierarchy among upper castes, namely that between wife-givers and wife-takers, and the giving and taking of dowry, that I have already mentioned.

At weddings, one cannot tell the groom's side apart from the bride's, as both sides are engaged in drinking and making merry together. Because of endogamy within a small community, most people are connected to everyone else, and it is near impossible to separate bride-givers from bride-takers. About two generations back there was the practice of giving a bride price, but at present it is neither given nor taken. When a few persons of the *biradari* had begun to ask for dowry, following the trend among the upper castes, the panchayat elders strongly reacted, and a collective decision to end this practice was taken. Even today, in spite of substantial changes in the celebration of weddings and imitation of many of the upper caste/class practices, dowry and the hierarchy of bride-givers and bride-takers have not taken root among the dhobis, where two sides to a marriage remain equal as members of the same *biradari*. In the seventies, the only case that I had come across of any kind of marriage payment demand came from the bride's side. In one household, there were only boys who had no sisters. The elderly mother was busy the entire day, ironing clothes in the neighbourhood. They had a desperate need for a young woman to run the house and do the household chores. The eldest son was engaged to a girl whose family was making a demand of 5,000 rupees to finalize the marriage, taking advantage of the void that the young bride was expected to fill in her affinal household and their urgency. The sum asked for was quite large given the economy of those times and the financial status of the household. I remember having conversations with the prospective bridegroom and his father, who expressed helplessness and dejection. I would see them struggling to perform household chores like cooking, even while they had to do work of washing clothes. Those were the days when men had to go to the river for washing, and the work was highly labour-intensive.

Most marriages, however, did not have many financial worries, as they were helped by contributions by all members of the extended family, where the prime objective was to endow the young couple with all that they would need to set up a household. This included an iron for their trade, a few pots and pans, some essential pieces needed for a house, and a couple of sets of clothes. The emphasis in each wedding was on the combined merrymaking and eating and drinking as a community. In the seventies, both men and women were regular drinkers of alcohol and children started early as they were permitted to take sips from their elders. Women told me then, 'we work day and night in water. If we did not take a little alcohol to warm up our bodies, how will we work? It is easy for women of upper castes to condemn us. They do not have to do any work but sit around in comfort and give sermons.'

Alcohol drinking was seen as particularly conducive to maintaining harmonious relationships within the *biradari*. As explained to me by one informant, 'when people wish to vent their anger or frustration on someone, they always take to hurling abuses when they are drunk. The next day, when confronted, they always have the excuse that I was drunk and did not know what I was doing.' The same person had added with a snigger, 'no one is ever so drunk as they do not know what they are doing. They abuse with all their senses intact and because they wish to do it. But next day one can always have the excuse to deny that they ever meant to do it. In this way the *biradari* ties are not affected and people remain united.' Giving up alcohol and especially stopping women's drinking form one of the major changes that have taken place among the dhobis, along with changes in their lifestyle and their efforts at sanitizing their lifestyle to fall in step with the upper castes. This change is reflected clearly in the generational transformation between the older and the younger women. The latter are cast more in the sedate and conservative model of the upper-caste women, although with education and exposure they exhibit more visible characters of the middle-class women. At least unmarried girls and those going to school and college wear Western dress, and some newly married women do too. But none of the younger women, or even those of the middle-aged group—that is, born after the eighties—have the habits of their older generation of taking alcohol or smoking 'bidis'.[3] Therefore, in the 2020s only a few women of the grandmother's generation partake of alcohol. Men too have largely stopped drinking, at least openly. The reason, as explained to me by an elderly dhobi, was that the weddings no longer took place in the dhobi *katras*, near the residences of the dhobis. From the period of 2000 onwards, they have begun to rent community centres to celebrate weddings outside of their residential areas. Here they fear public exposure and the humiliation of being told that they are not behaving in a respectable manner. This avoidance of public shaming is one reason that free consumption of alcohol at weddings, as was the custom earlier, has been stopped. As young men and women have begun to go to schools and colleges, they are getting exposed to the middle-class values and gaining acceptance among their colleagues, as they try to appear as close as possible to them. As of now, it would be difficult to differentiate a dhobi boy or girl from those of the upper castes, and they are only defined by class.

One could make out rich or poor but not by occupation or jati, as was evident in earlier times.

However, such changes are still at the level of aesthetics and outward appearances. It would be wrong to attribute to the younger generation of dhobis the patriarchal values of upper-caste society, especially with respect to the hierarchy between marriage partners. Even among the most highly educated of India's upper castes, this hierarchy still persists, and most families treat their sons-in-law with deference and daughters-in-law with contempt, which addsto the wide scale prevalence of son preference (Channa 2023b).

However, such hierarchical relations between wife-givers and wife-takers are yet to make their appearance and may never come up among the dhobis. Marriage among the dhobis results in deepening of already existing ties as it always takes place between families already well known to each other. There is hardly any difference in etiquette and treatment of daughters and daughters-in-law and sons and sons-in-law. In almost every household I have seen daughters-in-law behave with ease and informality with their parents-in-law and other members of the household. However, in very recent times—that is, after 2000—some daughters-in-law have begun to cover their faces from their father-in-law. There are two reasons for it. One is the imitation of upper-caste values, especially those shown on television and other media, and second is the continuation of the two-generation joint family. Before the eighties, almost no household was joint and a man would set up a new household almost a few years after marriage. Hardly any daughter-in-law would have to live with her father-in-law for a long time. This situation is now changing as more and more dhobi households are becoming joint.

Sons-in-law are still not shown any deference or treated like special guests as is common among the upper castes. In earlier times they were mostly living at close quarters and nowadays, with more dispersal, they may come and go, but are not shown any special deference. The difference between kin and affine, so marked among the upper castes, is ironed out by the close intimacy of *biradari* relationships. Women used to address their husbands by the familiar *tu*, but over the years, with the middle-class values coming in and as they are developing their own schema of respectability, they have changed/turned to the more commonly used (among upper castes/classes) *tum* or even *aap*.[4] As I mentioned, a lot of values are imbibed from television, Facebook, and other media, and the dhobis no longer live a secluded life in their own *katras*. However, like appearance these changes are not at a deeper level in that even if the form of address has changed, the nature of interaction has not.

In sum, one can say that the *biradari* identity is one that levels rather than divides, and unites its members in a synchronized identity of one-ness. The *biradari*, living was like that of an extended family, intensi-fied by the clustered life in the *katra*, a pattern that one still finds both in the original *katras* as well as in the dhobi clusters that have formed at later dates.

Life in the *Katra*: Community, Gender, and Morality

In the seventies, when this ethnography begins its journey, almost all the Sheheri dhobis lived in the walled city of Old Delhi. The city provided them space in the form of *katra*, an enclosed space with houses clustered around a small open space like a courtyard that was sometimes, but not always, rectangular in shape. The living quarters of each household, comprised of one or two small rooms, never more than 10feet by 12feet but often even smaller. It is possible that the rooms very initially larger, but as the families grew, they were partitioned into smaller units. Families were divided into households, called *chulah* (literally, hearth), which meant that it was a separate consumption production unit. Joint families are often projected as a norm for India, but as noted by other scholars (Shah 1998:73), the patriarchal joint family is very much an upper class/ caste phenomenon, rarely found among the marginal groups like lower castes and classes and the indigenous populations. Among the dhobis, a man would set up a separate household within a year of his marriage, in terms of separating the hearth that involves often staying under the same roof but simply cooking separately. The reasons were purely practical, as large units of work groups, comprising many members of the household, were difficult to manage. The dhobis earned little in those times and the workloads were large and labour-intensive. The households barely man-aged to earn enough for two meals a day. I have been in situations where I have sat with a woman in the late afternoon of a hot summer's day, while she waited for her young son to return with a few rupees from a client, and she could then get some supplies to start her cooking. It would have been the only meal they would be able to cook that day; the morning meal was often leftovers from the evening before. In their own words, '*din laye din khaye*' ('eat what you get every day') was the usual norm. Since there were no savings and little to inherit, young sons and daughters-in-law preferred not to share their incomes with the older parents, whose ability to earn declined with age. Older people consumed least of all, and as soon as they were unable to earn, they became burdens on the children, who had to eke out their meagre earnings to support them. Few people grew really old, and during the course of my fieldwork I found that most people I knew died by the time they reached the age of 40 to 60. Most of the people I knew in the seventies are no longer there, especially if they were around 40 years old or more at that time. Hard work and alcohol took its toll on both the men and the women. The few old men and women around would sit in the common area, smoking a hookah or just sitting, where they would look after small children but were mostly ignored. Except for the men with some political status, like the *chaudhuries*, old age was not an enviable position to reach.

Katra life began early in the morning, with people performing loud ablutions at the common tube wells, lighting up the *chullahs*, children crying, mothers yelling, and some people getting into altercations. Men and women get ready for their tasks of the day, putting hot coals into the iron, or bundling up clothes to take them to the ghat. Earlier all dhobis took them on carts and mules. At that time the volume of clothes was large and there was no other mode of transport. In the seventies, while there were still a few carts remaining, the cycle was the most common mode of transport. The mules and donkeys have completely disappeared, because of congestion in the city and the lack of space and fodder. Open spaces where the animals could graze freely were all gone with the growth of the city.

In the *katra*, the space for cooking was mostly outside the house, where women cooked on open *chullahs* or hearths, fed with coal and wood. These brick and mud hearths were made and remade often, getting a coat of shiny mud now and then. Once they were lit, the cooking had to be finished, as relighting was tiresome. Usually women cooked two meals a day, one around the middle part of the morning that sufficed for the day, when both men and women were engaged in work, and the other in the evening once the dhobi work was almost over. In those days the men still washed clothes on the banks of the river, loading carts full of clothes to the taken to the riverside, and women would iron them in the corners of the lanes and bylanes. The latter practice still continues, and the neighbourhood *dhoban* or ironing woman is ubiquitous all over Delhi, even in New Delhi and the relatively new neighbourhoods. Because older women were mostly engaged in the ironing of clothes, household tasks like cooking fell to the younger women, either unmarried girls or young daughters-in-law.

Some *katra* have large washing vessels in the common areas in between the houses where men can be seen busy washing clothes at all times of the day. It is an exhilarating sight, seeing men with shining bodies, thrashing the clothes about while soap suds fly in all directions. In some *katra* there are ghat-like structures consisting of cement troughs with taps providing running water attached. One never sees women washing clothes, as in the traditional division of labour it is always the dhobi man who did the heavy work of washing clothes, needing a lot of strength as their way of washing involves lifting and throwing down the clothes on the hard surface. When clothes were washed on the banks of the river, they used to be thrashed on a stone slab, but in the cemented ghats and vessels they are thrashed on the sides of the vessels.

When the men are washing clothes, women go delivering them, or even visit friends or relatives. Women used to spend most of their time inside the *katra*, cooking in the common area, gossiping with each other, and generally taking collective care of the children. When clothes were washed on the banks of the river, the women used to help their husbands, spreading and drying the clothes, and would visit the ghats regularly. I remember, during the early days of my fieldwork, a heavily pregnant woman came back from the Yamuna bank, after spending half a day helping her husband. She had left early in the morning and returned late in the afternoon, without having eaten anything during the interval. It was her first child, but all other members of the family took no special notice, and she became busy in other household work, without much fuss. When the washing of clothes at the river stopped, the women's time schedule changed considerably. They became more housebound and slowly their participation in the household economy shrunk. I still have some examples of daughters (even married ones) helping their mother with the ironing of clothes, but most young women nowadays refuse to have anything to do with the dhobi work. There is in fact a changeover to middle-class values, with taking care of children being seen as a primary task of the mother, unlike the collective caring that was practised earlier.

In the times when women did only dhobi work, children ran around in the *katra*, where all the houses opened into the same common space, so it was not difficult to keep an eye on them. They could eat in any house, as children were fed the same food as adults, except very young babies who were breastfed. Childcare was not a matter of concern. In the period earlier to that of my fieldwork, in the previous generation, survival of children was not taken for granted. Child mortality rates were high. Even in the seventies, several babies and children passed away even while I was working among them. Survival of children, like their birth, was left to divine will. Many children were born but not many survived. At the time of independence in 1947, the average life of an Indian was only 27 years and child mortality rates were high. By the seventies, things had changed and the greater survival of children made the dhobi families large. On average there were four to five surviving children in almost all households. But after the 1990s, things began to change slowly, and today a modern young dhobi couple aspire to have not more than two children. During the seventies, the numbers of children were more, but the norms of taking care of them had changed little.

The *katra* was built in such a way that there was a narrow passage opening, which opened into the rows of houses, if they could be called as such. There was little chance of people entering or leaving the *katra* without being noticed, so children were quite safe. Children belonged to the *biradari* and were a collective responsibility. Young mothers were always very busy, working hard, to cook, iron clothes, or distribute them in the neighbourhood. Most of the collection and distribution was done by women, as men had to go to the riverbank to wash. Clothes that came to the house were ironed by women in the house itself. Since mothers rarely had time to look after their children, they were left on their own, but someone or other kept an eye open, and no difference was made between my child and her child.

Adolescent girls were chaperoned more strictly. In the seventies, I often came across an older woman reprimanding a young girl for laughing too loud or dressing inappropriately or in any way transgressing norms of modesty. The young boys had mostly begun to attend school in the seventies, and some even went to college. The college-goers had their own social circle and sometimes mingled with their peer group in the neighbourhood, even transcending jati barriers. One of my earliest fieldwork experiences was chatting with a group of college-going boys, on a rooftop in the *katra*, where they were joined by curious siblings including their sisters. They spoke disparagingly about the upper-caste and upper-class young women, whom they met in college, saying that they dressed inappropriately and that their moral shortcomings were covered up by the high economic status of their fathers. These boys tried to appear as 'modern' as they could, and copied the hairstyles of popular film stars of that time.[5] One may here refer to Ahmad, who has said that 'Young Qureshis look up towards Bollywood actors as role models' (Ahmad 2018: 66). The aspirations of young men from marginalized communities like the dhobis and the butchers are fired by fantasies borrowed from their favourite film and, nowadays, media stars. At the same time they were keenly aware of their non-acceptance and their marginalization with respect to the students of more affluent families who attended college in those times. In the present day, although the role models are derived from similar sources, the distance felt is much less between the students from marginal communities and others. The reason is both because a much larger number from earlier marginal groups are attending college and going for higher education and because commodities are more easily available and attainable, with cheap substitutes being sold at various sources including online. The markets have expanded both in scope and depth, flooded with mass-produced, cheaply available goods. There has been a significant gender based transformation as well over the last forty years.

With just one or two exceptions, girls in the seventies did not go to school. They were largely in charge of taking care of the household and looking after younger siblings. Adolescent girls were in charge of running the day-to-day household matters, and they often kept the household money, kept accounts, and sent their male siblings out to shop for household necessities. At present almost all girls go to school, and a fairly large number go to college as well. When they marry, they may not work outside the house, and as of now working women in the formal sector can be counted on the fingers of one hand, but their lifestyle has changed. The wives spend time doing normal household work, taking care of children, and doing a lot of *puja* (rituals) at home. Almost always nowadays I find the daughter-in-law doing rituals, cooking in the kitchen, or simply sitting around watching television.

At the time of the seventies, the young wives were busy ironing clothes, and the older wives visited the households for collection and return of clothes, and some of them ironed clothes in the neighbourhood. The latter was back-breaking work, as the woman would stand near a makeshift table and iron clothes from morning to night, taking only short breaks for food and an occasional cup of tea. They use heavy irons, filled with coal, and in the hot summers it is not only hard work but extremely uncomfortable to be near the hot iron all day. Yet the women rarely complained. They amused themselves by gossiping with all the passers-by and by keeping an eye open for all neighbourhood happenings. The neighbourhood *dhoban* is culturally recognized as the eyes and ears of the area.

The *katra* was above all a moral space—a space not only of belongingness but also of vigilance and social control. *Biradari* life was possible only if some norms were strictly adhered to. The most contingent of these was harmony, not only between various members of the *biradari* but also within families, between husband and wife, and between siblings and parents and children. I have already described how alcohol provides a convenient let-off from hostilities that may otherwise become overt. The *biradari* takes recourse to curtail all forms of conflict via mediation by the panchayat, a representative body of all responsible males of the community. At the level of the endogamous community, it operates to resolve marital disputes and any other transgression that threatens the peaceful existence of the *biradari*. At one time there was a sanction against any husband who dared raise his hand to his wife. He was not only publicly reprimanded but also fined 5rupees. In all my years of association with the dhobi *biradari*, I have never come across any serious breach of the peace. The cooperation and genuine affection between husband and wife had always struck me as something that emanated from relations of equality and mutual support. In their harsh life conditions, the inner solidarity acts as a protection against the outer social environment, where they are often faced with adversity and discrimination.

There is also a strong defensive attitude towards the women, whose honour and respect are seen as key to the *biradari's* collective honour and self-respect. Dhobi women always dress with great modesty, and the women who stand on the roadside or on corners of the neighbourhood ironing clothes in the public spaces, who are vulnerable to the gaze of all passers-by, always keep their heads covered and their faces and eyes cast down. Even when they are gossiping and talking to others, they do it with decorum, not talking too loudly or laughing or making any gestures that may be deemed inappropriate. Since they are very conscious of their vulnerability as a low caste, whose women were traditionally open to sexual exploitation, they take extra precautions when they are working outside their homes. In one of my earliest conversations with some young male students, I was impressed by the way they projected the honour and decorum of their own *biradari* girls as against those from upper castes and classes. 'Our women have honour and they know how to conduct themselves. Even if we do not have money, we have respectability' was voiced by some of them. Again, as one older woman put it, 'Our honour is in our hands. If we behave properly then no one can touch us.' Such values are still strong, and even though young women go to college and study, they no longer go out much as they are not doing the house-to-house running around in the new colonies. Older women still go around for clothes collection, especially to known households, but more and more I find that it is the men who do this work. The men's work has transformed also, and many have taken to ironing clothes in place of their wives, who only help from within the home. The question of honour now has the added criteria of respectability, now defined in middle-class terms.

The intense density of *biradari* life also makes everyone open to scrutiny by everyone else. It is this constant gaze that acts as a deterrent to any kind of deviant action or behaviour. I began my work among them as a young woman and often spent entire days in their *katra*, sometimes even at night staying over for a wedding or ritual function. Never once have I encountered even the slightest deviation from propriety by anyone. On the contrary, once my relations with them had reached the level of fictive kinship, I was always showered with extremely protective gestures. Whenever I expressed a desire to visit some part of the dhobi residential areas that were not considered safe for a young woman, a young man would be sent along with me as a chaperone. This included the visits I made to the Muslim areas.

Within the confines of the *biradari*, a constant moral pressure operates such that in spite of bawdy drinking and revelry that characterizes most dhobi ceremonials, such as marriage, there is no chance of any transgression of social norms. I remember that when I stayed back for weddings, and the women were drinking, they would withdraw to a separate corner of the *katra* and keep away from the men. Women never got drunk and only indulged in singing and playing the *dholki* (a kind of drum). Men, as mentioned, frequently got drunk, and many used to pass out. But again, no norms of propriety were broken. A prime reason was the kinship network that provided everyone with their appropriate etiquettes and norms of interpersonal behaviour with every other member of the *biradari*. Kinship terms of reference and address are used for every member of the *biradari* by everyone else. Every member is located on a genealogical grid to be addressed by an appropriate term. Elders of the *biradari*, including parents, guide their children to use appropriate terms of address that take care of generation, gender, and category of relationship; for example, any member from the mother's natal family belonging to a generation above the ego, will be called '*mama*'—that is, mother's brother. This extended kinship terminology covers every member of the *biradari* and is one of the most important criteria of identifying who is considered as belonging to *biradari* and who is not. In other words, kinship is the cementing principle that keeps the *biradari* members together as well as facilitates the close and tight-knit living pattern of the *katra*. Even at present the night-long festivities see the participation of young and old, but *biradari* norms act as a protective shield and transgressions are unheard of and absolutely unthinkable.

The dhobis are so adapted to this close bonding and lifestyle that they tend to replicate it wherever possible. When some of them were relocated to the new colonies during the slum clearance programme of the seventies undertaken by the Congress government, they tried to bring their *biradari* members to live close to them. The *katra* architecture could not be replicated, so they moved into apartments close together, and even here the free movement between the households exists. Even today when I visit any of these new locations, members of the *biradari* are freely moving into each other's houses. Where there are ghats, these are shared and people cooperate in the washing and drying of clothes. Doors are never locked even in the new localities as all households are still seen as one large kinship group.

In my visits to the *katra* over the past decade or so (in the 2020s), some cosmetic changes are becoming evident. The earlier simple rooms with whitewashed cement walls, mud or cement floors, and no doors are now getting transformed into little apartment-style dwellings where, within the limits of the small space and earlier design, individuals are trying to modernize and upgrade the quality of their residences. Doors and even curtains have been added to almost all houses, floors are paved with mosaic or marble tiles, kitchens have been made inside with whatever space is available, and many houses have added toilets, even if small. The outsides have also been polished up, with paint and tiles, so that one can make out different apartments, unlike the undifferentiated rooms that characterized the earlier *katra*. The modernized houses are in tune with the changing lifestyles. Firstly, a change towards pride in one's place of dwelling, having it done up and looking good. This also means that one distinguishes one's own place from that of one's neighbour. People have painted their houses according to taste and have added kitchens so that women now cook in privacy and not in the public arena. Embellishments have been added in terms of some special design or an additional glass partition or a decoration piece. Every household has its own television and refrigerator. If space allows, sofa sets and beds have made an appearance. Some households have added washing machines as well, quite a serendipitous situation for people whose main occupation is to wash clothes by hand. Women use these washing machines for their household clothes as well as for some of the clothes that have come for washing.

There seems to be a slight move away from community living towards more individualism, as well as a semblance of class, where items of everyday use symbolically assert a slight upward movement; a better piece of furniture, a new coat of paint, or something fancy like a glass door. Another reason is the rise of aspirations that lead the dhobis to imagine that they can also live like the upper castes and the elite. This mental erosion of caste-related class values is a primary stimulant for changing lifestyles.

However, things changed over the years and, as I have already mentioned, many households, especially among the better-off, are having more than one generation living together. This is happening where none of the sons are in the dhobi business so that they are earning independently of their father, whether he is in dhobi work or not. When each has a separate source of income, it is not difficult to live together. Under the new circumstances conditions for work are also changing. A kind of incipient class difference is also emerging among them, especially related to education and work. Also a difference has come in in terms of dispersal of living quarters. Earlier, up to the seventies and early eighties, most were living in close proximity to each other, so that a separation of household often did not mean a physical separation but only an economic one. The family would be living in the same house or in nearby ones. Since there is a lack of physical space in the *katra*, a separate *chullah* would mean that the daughter-in-law was cooking a few feet away from her mother-in-law or sister-in-law, and they would cooperate with each other and interact on a continuous basis. With the dispersal of living space, setting up a new household often means moving away from the original place. At times a dhobi household may find itself separated from most others, as I found that some households were living in isolated houses where none of their *biradari* were in close proximity. In such a case the brothers would not separate and continue to work and live together as a support group. I found, for example, a dhobi household very near to Subhadra Colony where my friend Bishanlal lives. While Bishanlal lives in a cluster of dhobis with their own ghat, this household has made its own makeshift arrangement in the very house they live in, putting in tanks for water supply. I found two women washing clothes inside the house, who were sisters-in-law, married to two brothers. They have a joint household of two brothers living together. They told me they both work and live together, sharing the same hearth.

Bishanlal and his three sons are all engaged in dhobi work. His eldest son lives in Pratap Nagar, one metro station away, the second son lives in an apartment close to theirs, while the younger son and his wife live with them. Bishanlal told me that his youngest son had got work from a hotel but had to give it up as he was not able to cope with the workload. When I asked as to why his brothers did not help, he replied, '*Bhai wai aajkal koi nahi puchte*' ('Brothers no longer care for each other nowadays'). All of them do the dhobi work and use the same ghat that is attached to their homes, yet the older two sons keep their work and hearth separate and only the youngest lives with his father. Even in the seventies and earlier, I was told that primogeniture or the youngest son continuing to live with his parents was the norm. The same continues, especially if all of them are in dhobi work. If they are not, then there can be other arrangements including the formation of a joint family.

In another case, a fairly prosperous dhobi whose one daughter is an assistant professor, and whose sons manage their jointly owned dry-cleaning work, has a joint family with both married sons living with him. They have a house in a lower-middle-class neighbourhood across the Yamuna, but the house, though on a small piece of land (50 square yards), is well made and vertically three storeys high. The father and sons work together and run a joint household where the women do not work at all in the dhobi occupation. They aspire to a respectable middle-class lifestyle and have all the outer resemblance to an upper-caste household. Here too the daughters in law observe *purdah* (veiling) in front of their father-in-law. His daughter, who is an assistant professor in a Delhi University college, and her husband, a software engineer, have bought their own apartment but in a neighbourhood close to that of the man's parents. The decision was made so that even while they live separately, they are not actually separated from the parental family; '*alag nahi huye*' ('we are not separate'), as the young man told me. The separation in this case was because of space and lifestyle considerations. The educated young couple want to live their own way. They have a very middle-class apartment with all modern gadgets including computers and study tables. Such was not possible in the house of the man's parents. But they remain close at hand and frequently go over to their parents' houses. There is no weightage in favour of any one set of parents, and both the man's and the woman's parents are visited at random on an equal basis.

As per my own observations and also when I ask them a direct question about when they think the real changes came about in their lifestyles, most dhobis point to the period from 1992, when the economy was liberalized, and more specifically to the decades after 2000. '*Isi shatabdimain zyada zyada badlav aya*' ('The changes have come in largely this century') was the statement from many of them.

The *biradari* also acts as a kind of bank, as most members indulge in what they call *cometi* (committee). A group gets together and each member contributes a fixed sum every month for a period that equals the number of members. This ensures that each member contributes his share to the common pool. Each month a lottery takes place and the person whose name is drawn gets the entire amount. However, till the cycle is complete, everyone has to keep paying their share. As is obvious, such a system works only in a primary group kind of situation and where there is moral pressure for compliance. Whenever I asked as to whether there were any transgressions—that is, whether someone would not pay up—the answer was always the same, '*Biradari ke samne naak kat jayegi*' ('He will suffer loss of face before the *biradari*'). At the time when most dhobis were illiterate and almost no one had a bank account, these *cometi* were the only way of saving, for them. But the only way these microfinance processes can work is within a community that exerts strong moral pressure.

The Continuity of the *Biradari*

At present there have been some transformations, such as some members of the *biradari* moving away from the traditional occupation, having made good in some other business. In the seventies, a few boys were studying in college. A couple of them got white-collar jobs in banks, under the Scheduled Caste quota. They have also moved up the ladder of promotion to acquire managerial levels. There is one particular family I have been following for the entire period of more than forty years, and they have flourished in alternate occupations—from the grandfather being the head of the panchayat, to the son running a dry-cleaning shop, to the grandsons having shops selling antiques in the specialized tourist market near Jama Masjid. The young men, who are now heading the family after the death of their father, are situated completely away from the jati occupation. Yet they are conscious of the identity and the power that this identity has for them.

Earlier, up to the nineties, the fortnightly panchayat was the main occasion for men of the *biradari* to meet. The meetings took place on new moon nights on the banks of the river Yamuna and were a grand affair, with at least sixty to seventy persons attending at a time. However, once access to the riverbanks was blocked, the attraction of this meeting waned, largely because its location was displaced from the original site.

The riverbank had a special meaning for the dhobis, and as they assembled on the riverbank on a dark new moon night, there was a spirit of belongingness and identity in those meetings. Later, when they were ousted from the river bank and meetings became impossible, they had to choose alternate sites, which were often not acceptable to all the members of the *biradari*. The centralized authority of the single leader that had been unquestioned till the eighties was now put in doubt. More than one person began to stake claim to being the *chaudhury*, or leader, and would call a meeting at different locations. Such processes of internal dissent had begun by the late seventies and continued till the eighties. Even though the *biradari* remained unified, the jurisdiction of the *chaudhury* has been diluted.

At present, the meetings are called in specific *katras*, which are not designated as common territory but are usually seen as belonging to a certain individual. I have heard many people mumbling that they will not go to the meeting if it is held at a certain place. I attended a few panchayat meetings; in the nineties, I attended a couple of them, and then one later in 2015 on 19 April, but they were not the same. Few people turned up and there were more arguments and verbal tussles, with little achieved as a result. There was always a sense of confusion and no one seemed to hold overall authority. In the 2015 panchayat, a sum of 100 rupees was collected as member's contribution. This practice had always existed, but in the seventies the sum of money was only 10 rupees, then it became 15, then 20, and in 2015 it was 100 rupees, but people were still complaining it was too little. On that date in April 2015, forty persons gave 100 rupees each. The panchayat is also not held exactly on the new moon day but on the Sunday that follows it. The norm of holding it on a Sunday has slowly come about after 2000, as many working people do not find time on other days. By 'working' is meant those who are running small businesses and not just doing jobs. Since offices and the Old Delhi markets are closed on Sunday, it has now become the day of the panchayat. The dhobi panchayats are still an all-male affair and women do not participate, although they may make comments and discuss affairs of the *biradari* with their husbands.

As told to me by various informants, the main issues dealt with by the panchayat are regarding the collective celebration of certain events, the main being the Shobha Yatra of Nagarsain baba, their patron deity. Other matters usually concern marital disputes, and this has always been a central issue. Since all marriages take place within the *biradari*, any dispute leads to cracks developing in *biradari* relations. One such dispute was resolved that very same year, when the man and the woman had filed for a formal divorce in court. The dhobi elders approached the magistrate to take the matter off the court proceedings and let them handle it at their own level. The magistrate agreed and the matter was handed over to the panchayat, who managed to resolve the issue and patch up the relationship.

Divorce and separation are rare but do happen among the dhobis. Men often remarry, but women rarely do. In one case a woman had divorced her husband, saying he was impotent, but the same man got married again and had four children, who are now grown up. In another case I met a young woman who was living with her parents in Farashkhana, Old Delhi, who had left her husband because he restricted her too much. She told me she felt suffocated. Divorced and separated, even widowed, women rarely remarry, although among the dhobis there is no formal restriction on remarriage of women. According to this young woman, the panchayat did not do much to help, and she took matters into her own hands and came away to her parents.

At present, there are a few strong individuals in the *biradari*, who engage the *biradari* in collective activities. These are mostly ritual occasions that involve the deities specific to the community. Over the years, the dhobi community has managed to strengthen its identity around sacred symbols, most of which were invented during the period from the eighties onwards as the old symbols began to crumble. Yet, as mentioned earlier, even younger members, college-going boys, men working in white-collar jobs, and some doing business other than that of washing clothes, still prefer to adhere to the dhobi identity and specifically to the Sheheri *biradari*. Efforts are on to affirm the identity and continue it for future generations. In a conversation with me, one of the young men, successfully running an antique shop, said, 'When I was in college, I was not happy with my dhobi identity. Other boys would look down upon me, so I avoided it. But as I am growing more mature, I realize that the *biradari* is our strength, we can count upon the *biradari* any time for support.' He also added that he is making efforts to keep up the *biradari* spirit, by arranging for cricket matches for the young boys once a year as an annual event. By giving prizes that he sponsors from his own funds, he is encouraging the young people to retain their identity.

My interactions with the young generation also indicated that almost none of them wanted to be counted out of the *biradari* ties. Almost every marriage takes place within the *biradari* even now, although in recent times I have recorded a few marriages outside of the *biradari* in Delhi but rarely out of the dhobi jati. There are two reasons for this: the dhobis feel comfortable marrying someone of their own jati, and very few people of upper caste would marry a dhobi. Marrying within one's *biradari* reaffirms and strengthens already existing social ties, and makes a person feel that he or she belongs and is acceptable to everyone. One great advantage is that one is not dealing with strangers after marriage, as happens in marriages where one is married into an unknown family. In the upper classes, marriages are negotiated over longer distance and wider marital circles. As is well known, in India, because of restrictions of jati-based preferences and a culture of negotiated marriages, people often end up marrying total strangers. But in a small and endogamous community like that of the dhobis, this cannot possibly happen as most people know each other by sight as well as by interaction. For women it is a safety net, as cases of bride abuse or torture of married women by their in-laws is almost unheard of. The close-knit community ensures a degree of vigilance and moral policing that prevents domestic violence. At the same time the reasons for which violence usually takes place are also mostly missing. The absence of dowry and the equal relation between bride-givers and bride-takers eases out much of the sources of conflict in upper-caste marriages.

There is little competition between spouses and they have a relationship of constant cooperation when they are doing the traditional work. Even when persons move out into different occupations, the culture of cooperation persists, and husband and wife tend to support each other in whatever they are doing. I know in recent times of a young couple where the wife is a college professor and the husband works in the IT industry. They are highly supportive of each other and the husband ensures that his wife has enough space for her academic work, and she supports him as well. The husband is particularly proud of his wife's achievements as she is the first person, man or woman, in their community to acquire a doctoral degree. I have over the years observed this non-competitive and supportive relationship between husband and wife among numerous couples. At least some of such a relationship can be attributed to a household-based economy where men and women play complementary roles. A part is attributable to strong *biradari* ties, and an important aspect is regarding the dhobi's relation to the society at large and the power dynamics of gender relations, which we shall discuss subsequently.

In summing up one can say that identity, security, belongingness, and mutual support are the major factors behind the collective desire to continue with *biradari* ties and identity. The dhobis are not alone in this respect, as most communities or jatis, high or low, have strong affiliation to community identity. Although the concept of jati is ubiquitous among all communities in India, it is especially important for the marginalized communities, which are away from all other sources of power—political, economic, and social. The collective identity is strength in itself. Let me give another example: I was getting some beads strung in a market in Delhi in the year 2016, and the young man who was stringing them for me told me that he would not be available for the next week. He added that not only he but no other bead stringer would be available, as they, the bead stringers (*piroyi wale*), are a community, a 'jati'. 'There is a wedding in our community and all the members of the community are going to be busy in that, none will be working,' he added, also saying that they were a close-knit group who participated in all activities together. The bead stringers are an even smaller community than the dhobis as this is a specialized task with a limited scope. They string beads and pearls for bigger jewellers and often sit on the pavement outside jewellery shops to serve clients who need to fix a broken string or have a new one made to order. Smaller communities like this are extremely vulnerable to outside market pressures and cling to each other for mutual protection and help. This horizontal solidarity has rarely been commented on in the discourses on caste that tend to emphasize either the mutual interdependence of different castes (functional approach) or the hierarchy and relations of inequality (critical and political approach). Yet it remains an integral aspect of a society based on units of distinct identities that are discrete but not divisive. Each unit has its internal solidarity while forming specialized bonds with others, mostly through occupational specialization (Gupta 1991). Where the system fails itself is in the perpetuation of hierarchies and, even more insidiously, the practices of discrimination and marginalization leading to such inhuman practices as untouchability.

Notes

1. A hookah or hubble-bubble is a smoking implement where the mouth is applied to the end of a pipe attached to a smoking pot. To share a hookah means that one is of the same social and ritual rank. A phrase used for ostracization from one's community or groups was *hookah, paani bandh*, meaning that the person could not share a hookah or receive water from those of the community. It was considered a very severe punishment.
2. *Mleccha* is a term used for non-Hindus. An untouchable may be ostracized but is still considered a Hindu, but *mleccha* denotes impurity of all kinds.
3. Bidis are native cigarettes rolled in leaves, which are cheaper and indicate low social status of the smoker.
4. In Hindi the three forms of address have considerable cultural significance and indicate levels of intimacy, levels of status difference, and are signifiers of kinship and social relationships. *Tu*, the most intimate form, is used for people who are either very close emotionally, a sibling, a mother (never father), a younger relative who is very close such as one's children, and also one who holds a much lower status like a servant or a low-caste person. *Tum* is an intermediate category used for those who are close but must also be treated with respect—friends, spouse, mother (again rarely father), younger colleagues, a student's teacher, and so on. *Aap* is deferential as well as indicating social distance and hierarchy. Fathers or both parents may be addressed as *aap*, and certainly all older relations who are to be respected. A son-in-law is always *aap*, but a daughter-in-law almost never. A wife in an upper-caste patriarchal family usually addresses her husband as *app*, but a husband may address her with *tum* or even *tu* (rare).
5. A Rajesh Khanna hairstyle was particularly popular in the 1970s.

3

Livelihood, Resources, and Strategies for Survival

The dhobi life is full of strategies for survival. Placed at the lower end of a social hierarchy, most of them have to struggle constantly to keep afloat. This is not to say that they were ever out of work. There were two reasons for this: firstly, the ritual one of purity and pollution and secondly, the more pragmatic one of inherited skill. During the period when people were deeply entrenched in the caste ideology—a period I would put to up to the 1960s beginning with the settlement of the city—it was necessary to have the dhobi wash clothes as it was considered a polluting task, especially for the upper castes who lived in Old Delhi. Washing clothes of one's own household is a cultural element that came in with the Punjabis, who arrived in large numbers in Delhi after the Partition. As I learnt from my mother-in-law, who came from Punjab to Delhi after her marriage in the year 1921/2, Punjabi women were not averse to washing the household clothes, and only large pieces of linen were given to the dhobi. The north-west region on the border of peninsular India was always less dominated by Brahmanical Hinduism and rigid caste norms. Needy Punjabi women also washed clothes in other people's households, as I have personally seen in my own childhood. But even in more prosperous households, while women washed their daily clothes or had them washed by a female servant, men's clothes were normally given to the dhobi. There was a gendered reason for it. The men's clothes had to be very well maintained as they were going out to work, to their offices, shops, and other public places. The whiteness and crispness of a man's *kurta*[1] was a matter of pride for him as well an indicator of his family's prestige. Women mostly stayed at home and could wash their 'daily-wear' clothes themselves. The very expensive clothes went to the dry-cleaners, an institution that came to India with the Europeans, and till quite recent times they

Dhobis of Delhi. Subhadra Mitra Channa, Oxford University Press. © Subhadra Mitra Channa 2024.
DOI: 10.1093/9780198926238.003.0004

were seen as specializing in European-style clothes such as dress suits and coats, mostly for men. I will be discussing how the traditional dhobis also became entangled with dry cleaning in later times.

Keeping account of the clothes given to the dhobi, and receiving them back, was on the 'to do' list of tasks of most housewives. The dhobi was one of the service providers, or *kamin*, on the list of the *jajman*, in the traditional rural jajmani system (Wiser 1936, Yagi 1999). In the rural areas, the work of the dhobi was limited as the peasantry had few clothes and not much to get washed. They only catered to the aristocrats of the village. But their work was important in the cities, where large numbers of middle to upper-middle households had plenty to give to the dhobi, including bed linen and curtains. In the city, the dhobi was a necessary person to absorb the pollution of the *jajman's* household (Yagi 1999: 269). In recent times, from about a decade in the 2010 to the 2020s, many of the rural dhobis, who were doing subsistence agriculture in the village, have migrated to the cities and are now working as servants for the more prosperous dhobis. In this way, and as pointed out by Prashad (2000), the city dhobis could have had a work history of a variety of occupations, but there is no data or information available on this. My observations on work transformation account for only the decade from 2010 to 2020s; those belonging to the dhobi *biradaris* of the city have no recollection of any other kind of work that their ancestors may have done in the past.

In the more modern and urbanized period, while the ideologies pertaining to ritual pollution has taken a backseat, their work retains importance because of the concept of skill. Skill and specialization are two words that are associated with very modern enterprises, yet they are equally applicable to the traditional caste-based occupations, because these are skills honed over centuries, and, as many people believe, it is imbibed in the blood, '*uske khoon mein hain*'.[2] As the caste-based rationale for the survival of their occupation is fading, the skill-based rationale is taking over. Slowly, the terminology of *jajman* and *kamin* disappeared from the vocabulary of the urban people, and the dhobi is no longer necessary to absorb the pollution of the *jajman's* household (Yagi 1999: 269). Such values faded out with some old and conservative people in the eighties and nineties. In this century, there are few who will even know the meaning of these terms. Yet, in general society, there is an implicit association of caste with occupation, especially those that are known to be hereditary and part of Indian society from antiquity. Even among the most modern people, when looking for someone to wash or iron clothes, it is the name dhobi that will invariably come up. The presence of neighbourhood laundromats is a phenomenon, too rare and in very restricted areas, to have made any impact on the general public. In another context Gill (162) quotes the words of a Khatik involved with the plastic recycling trade: 'Khatik knowledge of plastic and recycling is unsurpassed – by smelling it, seeing it and burning it, we can tell what sort of plastic it is.... Our *biradari* has maximum knowledge of this work.' It is interesting that caste-based skills are seen as irreplaceable even in a relatively modern occupation. Another work that deals explicitly with this aspect is Kapoor's work on the Chamars, who are engaged in leatherwork. Traditionally the Chamars were responsible for the removal of dead animals and then for skinning them and curing the skin to make it into leather products, an activity that was considered to be 'permanently polluting and inherently dirty' (Kapoor 2018: 120). Kapoor has linked the pollution attributed to the Chamars and their consequent untouchable status to the sensorial aspects of being in 'intimate tactile and sensorial contact with animal bodies, raw hide, chemicals and polluted water' (Kapoor 2018: 121), but she fails to mention the pollution attributed to a 'ritual state' in addition to the physical and bodily aspects of disgust and dirt. The dhobis were traditionally assigned to the washing of menstrual and childbirth clothes of women and those of mourners after a death. In addition to the physical dirt, they also absorbed the ritual pollution attached to these life cycle events (Yagi 1999).

Interestingly, when an occupation climbs into the modern occupational category through technological transformation, as in the case of the flourishing leather industry, the upper castes still do not involve themselves with the primary work of labour but prefer to be managers and higher-level technicians—for example, not dealing with the processing of raw hide but the designing and marketing of the final products made of processed skin. A similar transformation, though on a lesser scale, is found in the laundry sector with the introduction of dry-cleaning. The latter is never used for soiled clothes of the kind given usually to the dhobi but to more expensive, finer materials and 'dress' clothes for special occasions that do not entail the kind of physical or ritual pollution as with blood and dirt. A person of high caste may, and does often, own dry-cleaning shops but at the lower end; when it comes to the actual washing of clothes, it is almost always done by a dhobi. Several dhobis had tried opening dry-cleaning shops but they have never been as successful as the big dry-cleaning establishments run by the upper castes/classes. But almost all dry-cleaning shops will employ a dhobi to do the actual work.

This association of caste with skill, with a particular type of knowledge, is something that has rarely been highlighted in the works on caste, except some recent works like Kapoor (2018). This is also because most works on caste have either focused on the ritual and ideological basis of caste, emphasizing the textual and hierarchical ethos of the system, or have taken a critical, humanistic, rights-based approach. The latter point of view has foregrounded the exploitative and unjust nature of caste inequalities. This perspective situates itself within a political discourse related to identity, inequality, and social justice. It intersects similar discourses on racism, white supremacy, and other such areas of socially imagined and executed discriminations on various bodies (Channa 2017). But caste is also a form of identity that leads to the formation of horizontal social ties, and in the case of occupational specialization bestows monopolistic advantage. Because of the politicized view of caste inequalities, and the very real exploitation and inhuman treatment meted out to those stigmatized as 'untouchables', the focus has shifted to a radical politicized view of caste that has either deliberately or inadvertently blocked the social and cultural aspects of caste. While I solidly empathize with the humanist, rights-based point of view and have elsewhere analysed caste-based discrimination within the universalized theoretical framework of marginalization and apartheid (Channa 2005), my long association with the dhobis has also alerted me to another form of discrimination that may arise if we essentialize such a theoretical framework and ignore some of the ontological aspects of their everyday existence. At least for some of them, if not for others, a jati identity has some positive outcomes. Gill (2010: 183), in her work on the Khatiks, has come to a similar conclusion: 'If ethnicized caste identity, as a flexible but easily identifiable social category is an aid to informal coordination and formal cooperation among a certain group, strengthening its ability to capture some of these elusive economic gains by becoming a viable, if unlikely "business community", it appears that it will be used to best effect.'

The dhobi work is still thriving, and in fact has made economic inroads into the emerging market-based economy of the city. The occupation is viable, has potential for adapting to the capitalist market-based economy, and also for bringing in prosperity and an improved lifestyle without having to leave the original caste-based occupation. It has evolved from a household-based productive system, to a semi-market-dependent one. To analyse this further, let us first take a look at the dhobi method of laundry, as it existed about fifty years back, when I first encountered the community in Old Delhi.

How They Washed Clothes, Then

There is no data on how dhobis washed clothes in antiquity. There is no description of the life of the dhobi. How did they wash clothes? What did they use? There is no clue, but there is one aspect of their work that is present throughout—the riverbank. From antiquity, the dhobi has been associated with the riverbank, unsurprisingly, as the river was the original source of all water for the needs of human settlements, both urban and rural. My elderly informants told me that they used a kind of clay for washing in earlier times, but they also learnt to make their own soap as well as starch. Only in the past few decades, with the full commercialization of their trade, have they begun to rely more on soap and detergents bought from the market. Starch used for cotton clothes is still made at home, and an elderly woman described the techniques of making various types of starch from different materials to be used for different kinds of clothes.

The river Yamuna has played a critical role in the life of the city of Delhi, especially in the life of those whose livelihood depends on its waters. The earliest visual impression of the dhobi and the river is from the film *Pukar*, made in 1939 by the then famed film-maker Sohrab Modi, in which we are shown a dhobi washing clothes on the banks of the river Yamuna and an arrow from the palace near the river coming and hitting him. According to the story, the arrow came from the bow of the Empress Noor-Jahan, the wife of Emperor Jehangir, who inadvertently kills the washerman, predictably known as Ramu Dhobi. Jehangir has a large bell installed at the gate of his palace for anyone to ring and call out for justice (the name Pukar comes from call; in this instance the call for justice). The wife of Ramu Dhobi pulls on the bell, ringing it, and when summoned to the court, makes her plea heard. She accuses the empress of having killed her husband. The emperor gets down from his throne, hands her his bow and arrow, and tells her to shoot him, so that justice is done. Since the empress shot her husband, she should shoot hers. The entire court erupts in protest, saying that the life of the emperor belongs to the country and is not his to throw away. The *dhoban* is persuaded to accept compensation in return for her husband's life and to forgive the emperor, to which she reluctantly agrees.

It is significant that in both stories, the one from the Ramayana and the one of the film *Pukar*, there is one thing in common. The *dhoban* or wife of the dhobi is shown as outspoken, fearless in her criticism of the person highest in power (the monarch in both instances) and ever ready to criticize, irrespective of the status of the person under criticism.

In the film *Pukar*, the husband and wife are shown as happily washing clothes together at the banks of the river, singing a song. In the seventies, when I began my work on the dhobis, a similar situation prevailed, and husband and wife were often seen working together on the banks of the river, where the wife would help the husband dry the clothes. On a windy day, one could see husband and wife hanging onto the drying clothes; at other times she would be helping him with sorting and various other tasks. The husband and wife unit is the core of the dhobi kinship and social organization, quite unlike that of upper castes, where this unit is buried within larger kin relations.

In my earlier work on the dhobis (a modification of my PhD thesis written in 1981 and then published in modified form as a book in 1985) I had focused on the dhobi economy, and my work was supposedly research based on economic anthropology theory. Since then, the field of economic anthropology has been transformed to a political economy approach and now globalization is the key domain of analysis, where focus is on the global market network and how smaller, local systems are absorbed within it. At the level of analysis, the local unit is identified by an artificial boundary introduced only as a research method. In actuality there are myriads of ways this unit is articulated with the wider global economy. However, even while it is impossible to isolate any local economy from its wider setting, it is still possible to demonstrate that the local has characters that set it apart from the wider, read capitalist, economy, in which it is embedded. The local may still retain the morality and ethics of a personalized network of relationships, which gives it a different character than the generalized, impersonal nature of the worldwide market of which it is a part. This conceptual disarticulation of the local unit is the key to the logic or rationality of studying the local. Each time we do an intensive, qualitative analysis at the local level, there remains open the possibility of revealing a system, a way of life, dependent on a local version of the formal economy, also called the informal economy. However, it has been firmly established that the informal economy is not a separate domain but a part of the larger economy, as there is continuous interaction between the two. It is now considered appropriate to say that the larger economy has its informal and formal sectors. The formal sectors fall within the legal-jural norms and laws of the state, such as minimum wages, provident fund provision, retirement benefits, and so on. The informal sector does not have the benefits of formal rules and laws, but is not constrained by it either. Just as the dhobis do not charge their clients according to any formal laws pertaining to minimum wages or pricing rules, they do not pay taxes either. As far as I have seen, there are no written records of their earnings, and their work is not governed by any formal laws. In fact, I doubt if their work is recognized as a productive activity at all, at the formal level of the state.

When I began my thesis, I had doubts about the classification of the dhobi work, especially as it was rooted in a subsistence type of economy and originated in the jajmani system (Wiser 1936). The jajmani system is a defining criterion of the Hindu caste system, and intrinsically associated with an agricultural economy. In its traditional form there was no money changing hands; the *kamins*, or servers, were paid in kind, grain and requirements, just enough to keep body and soul together. The payments and gifts ensured that the status difference between the *jajman* and the *kamin* was maintained, and the latter could exhibit no luxury that would put him on a par with the upper-caste patrons. The *jajman* was always of the landholding caste in the village, not necessarily a Brahmin or even of the higher Varna. Srinivas (1959) has explained the concept of dominant caste in a lucid manner to explain that one or more castes have the control of major resources like land and water in a village, and that the lower castes, ritually on lower rungs of the ladder, are kept in their place, so to say, by also keeping them poor (Channa 2019a).[3] The system reproduces itself by keeping the hierarchy between the *jajman* and the *kamin*, and the latter forever dependent on the former. The relationship therefore does not follow the demand and supply norms of a free market economy, being continued as a social relationship based more or less on the model of negative reciprocity as described by Sahlins (1972), which prevents any fluctuations in payments. In the rural economy it was always kept at the level of bare survival.

The Sheheri dhobis, although placed in a cash economy and in the heart of the city, followed more or less similar norms. In the seventies, when I began my fieldwork, the client, referred to as '*grahak*', was an important person in their day-to-day lives. At that time, there were still enough households that maintained the hereditary, jajmani type of relationship with the dhobi. These were mostly the old inhabitants of the city, the Aggarwals, the Kayasthas, the Brahmins, and the Khandelwals. The *grahak* and the dhobi maintained a fictive kinship kind of relationship, where the elderly dhobi, visiting the household over a generation, would be called '*chacha*' or '*tau*' (father's younger brother and father's older brother) by the children of the household. The *dhoban* had a similar status. Although they were not allowed inside the house, they were treated with decorum, made to sit on a small stool or on the ground, offered tea in a glass (kept separate) and perhaps some snacks.

The relationship with the clients is one of the major resources of the dhobis and is one prime reason for their non-antagonistic attitude towards those of the higher caste. This is also one of the main reasons that dhobis do not explicitly subscribe to the Dalit ideology, which they are either not aware of or, even if aware, attribute to the people of South India. I will come back to this point later, but let me here explain how a dhobi relates to his client. In the seventies, one informant, then 90 years of age, recalled his relation with his client whose clothes he washed and who was in charge of carpentry inside the Red Fort during the British period, when soldiers were lodged there. The contractor allowed him to enter the Fort in a surreptitious manner and collect wood shavings from the carpentry work going on. These were then used by this person to light his *bhatti*. Other dhobis had also related many incidences of a close reciprocity between them and their clients. Another dhobi, young at the time of his interview, had related how his father, who washed the clothes of a bank manager, had been told that if any of his sons could get an education, the bank manager would get him a job in a bank. So when this person was able to get a BCom degree, the client got him a job in a bank, as promised. Another dhobi regretted that he had refused the offer of a job from a British person whose clothes he washed, for he, being the eldest son, could not leave his household occupation of washing clothes. If he had left the traditional occupation, his entire household would have been left without work for the future, as they would lose all their clients.

Closer to recent times, in around 2005, a young man got a job as an assistant professor in one of Delhi University's prestigious colleges (Kirori Mal College) as his mother used to iron clothes inside the college campus. She had very cordial relations with the college personnel and when her son got a good education, the college management rewarded her by getting him a teaching position in the college.

It is relevant to note that, although the dhobis have a close cooperative relationship with all members of their *biradari*, they are quite competitive when it comes to the question of their clients. If a dhobi falls sick or is otherwise not able to work, his clients are quickly taken away by other members of the *biradari*, since they are knowledge who his clients are, and also about his health and other intimate matters. When I had questioned them about this, the reply had been quite pragmatic. Most dhobis had said that the clients were a free resource, and anyone could take them if they wanted to. Since there are many kinds of dhobis, outside of the *biradari* anyone of them could take the client. So they consider nothing wrong in taking away the client of a fellow *biradari* man, as they also feel that in times of need they will be there to help, and also it is better the clients remain within the *biradari* than go to someone outside.

But over the generations a subtle change is coming into the dhobi–*grahak* relationship. For example, a dhobi, who was elderly in the seventies, narrated how he held a fictive kinship position in the household of his Aggarwal client, to the extent that the daughters-in-law of the household observed *purdah* (veiling) from him, just as they did from other male members of their affinal household. A newly married daughter-in-law, not knowing the nature of this relationship, had once scolded him for not washing the clothes properly. Her husband had come upon the scene and reprimanded her, saying that 'dhobiji was now old and could not do as much work as he used to, but that does not mean that she has the right to scold him'. The daughter-in-law had burst into tears and left the scene, and later on never dared to scold him again. But such deference and respect are waning from both sides. The younger generation of dhobis are more cognizant of their rights and do not wish to be servile to anyone. They want to be treated as equals and be just paid for the work that they do. With the shifting of work towards the formal sector of the economy,[4] this personalized relationship is taking a back seat. Even during the earlier period of my fieldwork, not everyone was equally comfortable with or close to their clients. The relationship was always one of tension, as the dhobis struggled to reconcile with the hierarchy and their mental cost–benefit analysis.

On the whole, the relationship between the *grahak* and the dhobi was never just one of a transitory economic relation, even though there was exchange of money for service. In my earlier ethnography I had quoted from Cook (1973: 842):

Those performances are economic, or have economic aspects which entail the production, transfer or utilization, directly or indirectly, of material goods with use or exchange value as well as those performances that involve transfer or utilization of services, remunerated in cash and kind, for the purpose of satisfying wants and/or contributing to subsistence. Systematically applied, this formula enables the analyst to handle within a common analytical framework both materially productive activities (labour) and activities that render services but do not yield material products so long as they elicit remuneration for kind. (Channa 1985: 82).

This definition of productive activity originated from within a more positivist framework than the one we are using right now, but there are points of interest that must be noted. While by this definition one can identify the washing of clothes as a productive activity, there is also the point mentioned that remuneration can be both in cash and in kind. For a long period of time, and maybe to some extent even now, the dhobi's relationship with his *grahak* was such that the expectations went far beyond that of cash being exchanged for labour done, on both sides.

In the earlier jajmani system that was located in the pre-capitalist era, and where it was a caste relationship rather than a market one, the main objective of the dhobi's work was not to produce clean clothes but to absorb pollution ritually from his client's body and from that of the entire household. This ritual absorption of pollution was directly proportional in importance to the level of pollution involved, and it centred on the woman's body more than that of the men. Within the framework of Hindu norms of purity and pollution, women's bodies are more polluted because of the production of menstrual blood and the pollution incurred at childbirth. The dhobi had to wash clothes from both these polluting events as well as of the mourners at death rituals.

In contemporary times, and in the city, at least from the time I began my association with the dhobis, the concept of purity and pollution was getting diluted but not quite gone. With the use of sanitary towels and births taking place in hospitals and not at home, the dhobi's task of absorbing pollution from the female body was reduced. The dhobi was given the clothes that were bigger and heavier to be washed at home, as well as those that needed to be done up really nicely as formal clothes, especially for the men. The traditional Indian attire for men, the cotton *dhoti* and *kurta* as well as the *pyjama* and *kurta*, were very amenable to being washed by the dhobi. Women's clothes, with the exception of the finer ones, were mostly cleaned at home, and the use of synthetic fibres had made the work of washing easier. So the dhobis had continued relationships with the individual households, even by the seventies and to the present day, in many parts of the city, especially Old Delhi. In a visit in 2015 to a dhobi household in Shastri Nagar, I found that the clothes being prepared were mostly from households, and a similar situation was observed in the Old Delhi *katras*.

The dhobis were, and to some extent continue to be, dependent on these household *grahaks*, not so much for money as for various other forms of remuneration and support. To give a very recent example, the dhobi who irons clothes in the Commonwealth Games complex in Delhi was without work during the COVID-19-induced lockdown in March 2020. The residents decided to send money into his bank account to help him tide over the difficult times. He returned happily back in service after the lockdown was lifted. There is enough evidence to show that similar help was given all over Delhi. In the seventies, while collecting 'household budgets', I found that many items of daily consumption were missing. In other words, the dhobis did not have a budget heading for them as they did not spend any money on these items. The first and foremost was clothes. Nearly every household that I had interviewed gave the answer that they wore the clothes of their *grahak*. This seems to be an unwritten rule, not mentioned nor openly acknowledged, but was repeated by every dhobi, man or woman, I talked to. From ancient times there is a proverb, very popular in Northern India, that 'The king's head gear is the dhobi's loin cloth'. Yet it is amusing to note that no person giving clothes to the dhobi will accept that the dhobi wears them, while the dhobis are very open in admitting that they do.

Many dhobis also mentioned that they got a variety of aid from their clients, such as help with children's education, loans at time of distress, old clothes, household goods like cycles, old appliances, and help in a variety of forms—getting a job for a son or daughter for example. What is important to note is that all this help comes in an informal and unmeasured way. It is accepted as a part of the continued family like primary group ties that bind the *jajman* and *kamin* in the traditional system, transferred from the rural to the urban areas. The dhobi always felt free to ask his client for any kind of help. It was never felt that he was overstepping his boundaries as would be the case in a market relationship. But this help came with a price, of accepted hierarchy and inequality. Hindus, especially those entrenched in caste-based values, consider giving *daan* as an act of charity that passes from the high to the low (Raheja 1988, Channa 2005). There are therefore norms of giving and receiving. The giver does not have to make out the objects given as gifts. They are at times practically thrown at the person receiving them. Except when gifts are given ritually on special occasions like Deepawali or at the life cycle ceremonies of family members, things may just be passed on to the service caste persons without any attempt to camouflage the inequality. One may use Sahlin's (1972) concept of negative reciprocity to describe this kind of giving, where in return for material goods a kind of slave-like deference is expected. Yet there is also a sense of rights on the part of the service caste; they feel free to demand and expect to get, especially if there is an occasion where gifts are customarily given, like the birth of a male child in the family. This expectation and its fulfilment legitimize the relationship; for example, a dhobi or any other service-caste person may feel aggrieved enough to leave the work in a household, where he or she feels that their demands are not being met, or that the *jajman* is not fulfilling his or her obligations.

Dhobi work was therefore not exactly productive work; it was not even a commercial exchange, but was more a part of a moral economy than a commercial relation. It was embedded within a larger social network of relationships informed by age-old value systems that were sustained through time, as people's values changed but slowly. One may here refer to Godelier's (1972) work on the inner and outer relations of an institution like kinship, where the same relations that serve as those of kinship serve as economic ones. The dhobi household is definitely a productive unit as well as a consumption unit. Here production is defined in terms of Cook's definition, by which even the sermon given by a priest in a church, if he is paid for it, is a service and an economic act. It has a complex technology and a knowledge system backing it up that needs years to learn to perfection and can be considered a professional achievement. Yet its social value is low.

What Work Does the Dhobi Do?

The traditional work of the dhobi has three main parts. The first was the collection and distribution of clothes. Apart from the physical collection and then distribution back to the clients, this task involves the marking of the clothes, which is a highly specialized task, as it involves evolving a well-developed coding system so that clothes are distributed back to the same houses. While doing fieldwork in the seventies, I remember the words of an elderly woman, who told me, 'You people think, we are illiterate, but that is not true. We also write books, we write on our clothes, we mark them so well, that no piece is ever lost. Can you imagine marking hundreds of clothes and returning them to their owners, never making a mistake? This is how we write our books.' The markings were in earlier times embroidered with needle and thread, but by the seventies they were using a berry known locally as *bilama* that secretes a black juice that is indelible. Once marked, a garment remains the property of a particular dhobi, and this is also a way of marking ownership, not just of the cloth but of the client too. In this respect also a change has come about over time. At present the household clothes are sometimes marked with a marker pen and not with *bilama*, the use of which is almost forgotten except by those of the older generation. The clothes that come from commercial establishments like hotels, restaurants, and hospitals have their own labels or markers on them, and the dhobi does not have to do anything with them. Clothes that are taken for ironing only are wrapped in a cloth by the household, which allows both the dhobi and members of the household to recognize their clothes. At times, as I have seen in Old Delhi, men or women simply sit with the dhobi or *dhoban* and get their clothes ironed. But at the same time, it is quite remarkable that most dhobi women remember the clothes that they get from regular households and can recall from memory which belong to which house. It is memory that is mostly relied upon rather than markings for a dhobi to identify clothes of specific clients. This is also part of the skills that they acquire, something that is imbibed in them.

This coding, which was done secretly, is part of the hidden agenda of protest that is carried on by the oppressed towards the dominant (Scott 1985). It often involves derogatory representations, picking upon some personal aspect of the individual and the household taken as a whole. In describing the marking of clothes as writing, '*likhte hain*', the woman was saying exactly the same thing as Derrida, when he says that writing should not be restricted to alphabetic writing but should be defined in terms of an expanded view, where it takes into account all the creative forms of expression of human beings. Writing is just one form of communication, and there are many ways in which a people 'write'; for example, the folk art of *patachitra*, where narratives are communicated through a serial mode of drawing. Most indigenous people do not paint or draw, just arbitrarily, for creative or aesthetic satisfaction; they do so with a purpose, to communicate (Channa 2021). Since these are cultural forms of coding and expressing, they also serve as ideal modes of expressing resentment, anger, and ridicule. In this sense, by claiming a knowledge status for their work, the dhobis are trying to critique the division between 'knowing' and 'doing' that forms the basis of the caste system according to Kapoor (2018: 128). In fact this division is unacceptable to most untouchables, who take pride in whatever they do and consider themselves knowledgeable. All the dhobis I have interacted with, who engage in the caste-based occupation, consider that they are both knowledgeable and skilled. A conversation with a woman about starching clothes, for example, led to her telling me all about how different kinds of starch are made, what different materials are used, and which kind of clothes require which kind of starch. At the end she told me proudly, 'Yeh sabke baska baat nahi hai. Yeh to sirf hum dhobi logon ko hi pata hai and sirf hum hi kar sakte hain' ('This is not within the capacity of anyone to do. These are known only to us dhobis and only we can do these processes properly'). In the same way I have been instructed on the making and use of soap, bhattis, and so on, which are never described only as 'doing' but very much as 'knowing'.

In earlier times clients did not have the agency to change their dhobi; rather, the dhobi could use his discretion to pass on his clients to his son or brother and sometimes to a biradari member, like the situation after Partition when many Muslim dhobis were practically left without any clients. Here it may be mentioned that most service-caste groups have a trade union-like arrangement where it is considered unethical to take away another person's clients, except under exceptional circumstances such as severe illness, migration, or death. In describing the sweepers or the Balmiki caste group in Delhi, Prashad (2000: 4) says, 'Each mohalla was serviced by a sweeper whose employment was guaranteed by an unwritten agreement with other sweepers rather than by the householders.' While such unwritten codes are very strong among the sweeper castes, they are not so strict among the dhobis. But usually there is a division of neighbourhood among them, and one rarely finds intrusions taking place. While breach of conduct is rare within the same biradari, there are different levels of the biradari and varying thicknesses of relationships exist among them. But by and large the traditional forms of long-term temporal relationships are not broken easily.

The dhobis often ridiculed and looked with contempt upon the very people they paid overt deference to. Today, when the coding is no longer done by the dhobi, they may still evaluate the clients from other kinds of markers, such as the nature of the clothes that come, the number and frequency with which a household gives clothes, the readiness with which payment is made, and commercial establishments come with their ready-made codes that are derived not from personal evaluations but from their position in the market system. The class and caste of a household were and still remain an important marker, and size and economic status mark out commercial establishments. The way a dhobi presents himself or herself to the client is an enactment, in the sense that they will present themselves on the basis of their inner evaluation.

This frontstage acting, or overt display of a deferential attitude, can also be interpreted as an economic act, an act directed towards material gain. Most of the lower castes grow up imbibing through experience and socialization the value of overtly expressing one's inferiority in front of a socially superior person, from whom they have expectations of gain in one way or another. However, this does not imply that they actually hold such people in esteem, unless they have some proven qualities. In other words, inequality by itself does not generate deference, especially within the secular world. But because of the gains that are perceived from those in higher positions, and in the case of caste there are some inevitable hier-archical positions, a respectful front is maintained. One may here also refer to Erving Goffman's theory of frontstage and backstage behaviour, where Goffman (1956) describes all social behaviour as a 'performance'.

When the dhobi women and men interact with their clients on their rounds to pick up and deliver clothes, there is a performance involved, which is both conscious and deeply imbibed into their actions by encul-turation of a culture that has evolved over many generations (Channa 1975, Natarajan 2012). It is not professional as it would be defined in the context of the modern corporate sector, but it is professional in the con-text of the social environment in which they work and have worked for generations.

After collection, they sort the collected clothes and mark them. As men-tioned, the marking is a very different kind of activity than the performa-tive one of collection and distribution. In the privacy of their homes, the dhobi men and women give vent to their inner feelings, putting marks as they wish, sometimes making an implicit criticism of the household or the individual to whom the clothes belong. They are also free to use the clothes as they like. They can wear them, spread them, or put them to any use as long as their safety is largely ensured. As an indicator of the informal setting, the dhobis give no guarantee about the clothes. In this informal transaction, there are no written agreements; nothing is written, and nothing is signed. There are occasions when clothes get spoiled or are lost. The maximum that a client can do is to verbally abuse or make a din. In most cases, the long-term relationships are not broken, and continue with some grumbling on both sides. Most people take it for granted that a few clothes will be damaged or lost in transactions with the dhobi.

Next, and in the second phase, the clothes are washed and ironed. This is the main part of the dhobi activity, and here considerable transformations can be seen. Earlier, the clothes were taken to be washed at the river Yamuna. The river water was free of cost and the slabs of stones on the banks served as washing ghats, where the clothes were thrashed to clean them. There are folk sayings among the dhobis that, although the dhobi stands in water the whole day, he is never harmed by any creature of the water; no water snake, for example, will ever bite the dhobi, nor any poisonous insect or any other pest in the water. The action of the dhobi in raising the clothes high above their head and then bringing them down with a swinging motion to dash them on the stone is a typical gesture attributed only to them. It also symbolizes dhobi masculinity, associating it with physical strength. Dhobi men pride themselves on their strong bodies, and some of them also become *pehlwans* (or bodybuilders). They also take up being masseurs and bonesetters, as a secondary activity. Although the water of the river was free, an additional cost input for washing clothes at the river was their transportation to the riverside. When the city was built in the sixteenth century, it was built right on the banks of the river. By the 1960s, the river had changed its course considerably, making the Old city move away from the riverbank. This necessitated transportation, increasing the input costs in terms of labour and maintenance of transports of various forms. The labour input for washing clothes at the river was further enhanced as someone, mostly the wife or a young son, had to deliver the food at the riverside in the afternoon for lunch. Most of the time, however, the dhobis would eat a meal in the morning and then come back and eat in the evening. If a vehicle like a rickshaw was hired, it added to the expense, which at that time was a great burden. By the turn of this present century, however, most dhobis were using a motorcycle for transport, although a few were still using a bicycle, but in the early seventies even the ownership of a bicycle was a luxury.

In the seventies, the dirty clothes were still being loaded on the *thela* (a kind of wooden cart) and pulled by a bull or a cycle, to the Yamuna ghats or to other ghats in the Old Delhi area. I saw the *thela* in use even up to 2015, at the Minto Road ghats. By the seventies, there were few bulls left with the dhobis, but the *thela* parked near the *katra* was still the marker by which one could identify that dhobis lived there. Like the river, bullocks also had an almost mythical association with the traditional occupation and were treated as family members, given names, and fondly addressed. I often heard a dhobi address his bull as '*beta*', a term that is used for a son. Even when they died, they were not handed over to the butcher for skinning, but buried on the riverbanks. I was often told that they could not treat the dead bull with disrespect, as it was a faithful member of the household and had been a means of their livelihood during its lifetime. I remember on one occasion a man had bought a new bull and wanted me to photograph it, as I used a camera for my fieldwork (in those days smartphones were unknown). He made me photograph it from various angles, but unfortunately the bull took ill after sometime and could not survive. I was then told by another person that because it had been photographed so much, the bull had caught the evil eye (*nazar lag gayee*). In another case, a man had spent about 1,500–2,000 rupees (an astronomical sum in the seventies) on treating a sick bull and did not have money to buy another, when it died. But he did not regret having spent the money, for as he explained, 'it was like for my own son'. The cost of losing a bull was not for them just an economic loss but an emotional loss like losing a member of the family.

Dhobis generally displayed a mixture of pragmatism and emotion towards the activity of clothes washing and associated paraphernalia. The bull and cart, along with cycle and *thela*, were not just technological supports but also associated with masculinity, and only men had privileged access to them. Women would just walk. Women in most cultures have to take the hard and tortuous route, and dhobi women had to walk for any work they did, come rain or shine. Washing clothes in the river, in spite of its increasing cost, continued till the seventies, although the water was increasingly polluted. Women would tell me even then that the water has become so dirty that '*paani itna ganda hai ki nibala bhi gale se nahi utarta*' ('one does not feel like eating one's food after coming from the river').

I remember walking around on the riverbank in the seventies and even eighties, when it was still full of sand and the water, though dirty, still flowed. The riverbank was strewn with large vessels and the *bhatti* (brick ovens) that the dhobis used for steaming the clothes. This again was a special technique used by the dhobi to clean large and heavy clothes like bed sheets, curtains, tents, and other material that was heavily soiled and needed deep cleansing. The *bhatti* is a hearth, about 2feet in diameter, sunk about 6inches below the ground with a raised edge made of brick, stones, or daubs of earth, on which an iron grill is placed for the vessel containing clothes to be heated. The hearth is lit by firewood. Other resources used for washing clothes are soap, soda, bleach, starch, optical whiteners (obtained commercially), and chemicals like acids. The use of these depends on the nature of the clothes and their value. Expensive clothes are treated differently than the cheap ones. Additional factors are the time that is available to deliver them back and, of course, the money that can be charged for them. When clothes are very dirty, small amounts of caustic soda or a large amount of washing soda can be added. If the cloth is of good quality and the client is paying well, washing soda is used, and if the cloth is coarse and the client is paying less, caustic soda is used as it usually reduces the life of the cloth. An alternative way to reduce cost of washing very dirty clothes, like those hired out by the tent-*wallahs* (shops hiring out tents) for weddings, is to use spent lye instead of water. This is a by-product of soap-manufacturing units, comprising a small percentage of caustic soda along with glycerine and other chemicals left over from the manufacture of soap and is very cheaply available. The clothes are arranged in neat piles after being coiled and covered with a sheet on top. This sheet protects the clothes from the spurting liquids from the soap and lye boiling below and also prevents yellowing of cloth from the smoke coming up from the hearth. The entire process is highly technical and cannot be done by a layperson. There is also a series of decisions to be made: what material to use, how much to spend, how much labour to expend all are matters of deliberation that a dhobi has to make, keeping in mind the status of his client, the amount of money the client is ready to pay, and also the nature of the relationship. It is a known fact that a dhobi does not treat the clothes of a casual customer very well, but he has deep commitment for an old client and is much more professional towards a well-paying one.

The very dirty clothes were steamed overnight in these *bhattis*, and the dhobi would sit and watch over them through the night. There were many stories about ghosts and ghouls seen and felt at the river, and for many dhobis the nights spent at the riverbank were something one could talk about, and which were distinctly a part of the dhobi way of life. The romantic association with the river, of dark nights spent waking up on the riverbank, were part of the dhobi's urban legends, but as they moved away from the river, these stories, oral in character, died away, and no one ever mentions them anymore. One evening, however, sitting in the home of an elderly couple, we recounted the days spent on the ghats and they would reminiscence about it as a way of life that is gone but that had its moments worth remembering.

The *bhatti* still remains in use, lit by firewood wherever possible. But it is getting replaced by washing machines that heat the water for better cleaning, enhanced by the use of detergents and commercial stain removers. Since the dhobis need large quantities, these are bought in bulk from wholesale markets. Talking to one Muslim dhobi, Anees, who was washing clothes at Malka Ganj, I was informed that being a resident of Farash Khana, deep inside the Old City, he was washing clothes in the Yamuna river till 2006/7, but then the Delhi government under Chief Minister Sheila Dikshit destroyed most of the ghats on the riverbank, in the name of water pollution. Since then, he has been washing his clothes at this place. It is interesting to note that Malka Ganj is not quite near to Farash Khana, but he had to make use of his personal *biradari* ties to get a ghat to wash his clothes there. Also, while most of the dhobis here were Hindus, they had no objection to a Muslim dhobi washing clothes with them, as he belonged to the larger *biradari* of the Sheheri dhobis, as discussed in Chapter 2. Anees also told me that they are forced to use expensive driers as they are not washing on the banks of the river. When they did, they would leave the wet clothes on the sand for the night and the water would drain away, and in the morning they would shake them and spread them on the sand to dry in the sun. But nowadays they neither have the sand to spread clothes on, nor does the client wait for them to take so much time. 'The clients want their clothes quickly, they will give in the morning and want them back in the evening. No one has time to wait, so we have to dry them in the drier.' But because of using a drier, he has to pay a monthly bill of 5000–6000rupees for electricity. On a visit to his house at Farash Khana, I found his mother and brother washing clothes in a ghat that they had built inside their house. The woman was very reluctant to talk to me, unlike the frank and easy conversation I had with her son at the Malka Ganj ghat. At that place, there was a work environment, several dhobis were present, and he was at ease. But at his home, deep inside the Muslim residential area, his mother was reluctant and suspicious, especially as it was around 2015, a time when Muslims had begun to feel insecure. Previously I had been visiting Muslim dhobi households in Matia Mahal and other places and found them quite at ease and comfortable with talking to me. Although the situation has changed somewhat, the dhobis still have easy relations with their Muslim counterparts, as I have found from my visits to the mixed neighbourhoods.

The dhobis had begun to move away from the river, even by the mid-sixties, when the water in the river began to recede, and the flow got restricted due to pollution as well as the building of several barrages and dams that control much of the water flow in the Yamuna. Most of them found it difficult to wash clothes there anymore. In 1966, the Congress government at the centre built some ghats for the dhobis at Minto Road. In the seventies, an agitation was begun under the leadership of Mr. Arya or Arya ji as he was known, who was residing in Railway Colony near the ITO bridge, and whom I had interviewed during my thesis research for providing greater facilities to the dhobis of Delhi. Because of this agitation and according to the Delhi Urban Shelter Improvement Board, forty-two ghats were built and handed over to the dhobis, including those at Malka Ganj, Gulabi Bagh, Jehangir Puri, and Hailey Road. Just like Mohammed Anees, another dhobi, Ram Chander, had also moved from Bazar Sita Ram, deep inside Old Delhi, to Malka Ganj for the washing of clothes. Several of them had built their own ghats adjacent to their houses, within the *katra* itself. In the seventies, when the first phase of the research was done, the breakdown of the data of the 102 households surveyed for this purpose had revealed that twenty-nine had their own ghat, twenty-four washed at the government ghats, three washed at someone else's, and twenty-seven still washed at the Yamuna river. Seventeen out of the 102 households were not washing clothes at all. Some of these were only ironing clothes, and a few were doing other work (Channa 1985).

Out of the twenty-nine households that had their own ghats, ten were sharing it with their kin, who were not part of their households and formed separate consumption units. The initial effort for making a ghat always came from an undivided unit of father and sons, who pooled in the money to build the ghat, and later, when they separated their consumption units (*chullah alag*), they continued to use the common productive resource. In this way, while they were sharing at the level of work, they separated at the level of consumption. On a day I had visited the household of my friend Bishan, with whom I have a close relation, they had large numbers of clothes all piled up and the youngest son and his wife were working on them. Bishan's wife walked in carrying a large vessel of starch that she had made herself. His son put washed and ironed clothes in neat bundles and was going to deliver them. They were all household clothes, and they told me that they still had clientele with individual households along with purely commercial clients like restaurants and hotels. From the seventies, I had noticed that when it came to the sharing of resources, dhobi families were always ready to cooperate with each other, but it was a different matter when it came to the sharing of clients. There were always two sources of work—the clients that one inherited from one's father and those that one made on one's own. But there was always a limit to the amount of work that one could do, and most cooperating units, mostly consisting of father and sons or male siblings, did not like to share physical labour and distribution of remuneration. Each dhobi, forming a work unit with his wife and unmarried children, wished to keep his household expenses separate and his accounts independent. They felt that their work was very hard, and each person deserved to enjoy the fruits of his own labour and that of his wife and children. If a man found that his work was getting heavy, he would give away a few clients to his sons, so that as a man grew older, he kept giving away his work, till by very old age he would keep just as few as he could manage. Unless absolutely debilitated, neither men nor women would stop doing any kind of work. Most dhobi households could not support non-working members, and only the very debilitated were supported by their sons and daughters-in-law and sometimes by the daughters. The kin bonds, however, remained strong and undivided. Only in one case the ghat was shared with one non-kin on payment of rent, and in another case with a friend out of an emotional bonding. This sharing with non-kin became more extensive later, as more and more dhobis moved away from the Yamuna and their populations increased.

In the seventies, the cost of building a ghat, including the making of the *bhatti* and all the fittings like the taps, was about 1,000rupees, a prohibitive cost at that time when the cost of washing and ironing varied from 25 paise to 1 rupee.[5] A ghat always needed a *bhatti*; the type with an iron tank would cost some money, but one made from bricks alone did not cost anything, as they got sand from the river and bricks from anywhere where a building was being pulled down or newly built. When a *bhatti* is shared, then the cost of the firewood is shared. In the seventies, however, I knew the case of one very poor dhobi, with few clothes to wash, being allowed to put his clothes in a *bhatti* without having to pay anything or share in the cost. This particular individual was suffering from ill health and had small children to feed. As he was not able to wash many clothes, he barely made enough to survive. The *biradari* members helped him as, being one of them, he could not be allowed to be absolutely destitute and starve. Sometimes sharing a *bhatti* becomes necessary, as a *bhatti* needs a minimum of 40 kilograms of coal to be operative. If two or more persons did not have enough clothes to be washed, they would share a *bhatti* and the cost of the coal. If a person had too few clothes, he would just boil the clothes in a vessel on the fire and dispense with the use of the *bhatti*. However, the *bhatti* is to be used only when there are heavy cotton clothes like bed sheets, curtains, and towels. Smaller and more delicate clothes and those made with or mixed with synthetic fibres cannot be steamed and need to be washed by hand. Gradually the use of the *bhatti* became less important as more clothes were being made with synthetic fibres. Earlier the washing of clothes by the dhobi was almost synonymous with treatment by the *bhatti*, which was seen not only as an efficient way to clean very dirty and heavy clothes but also as an icon of a dhobi's skill. No one except a dhobi is known to be able to use a *bhatti*, although anyone can wash clothes.

The large vessels used for washing large clothes, called *hauda*, are also shared if the *bhatti* is being shared. When clothes were washed on the riverbank, one could use the vessels that were lying scattered on the sand, left by people who were washing clothes a long time back. They were a kind of *biradari* legacy, and treated as common goods. But once washing on the banks of the river stopped, there was no more access to these vessels, which were probably destroyed or thrown away when the riverbanks were 'beautified'. Another hallmark of dhobi technology is the use of the heavy iron, made of solid iron and heated with coals. At the time of marriage at least one iron was traditionally given to a girl as part of the gifts she brings with her, but the practice has been discontinued as women rarely iron clothes anymore. I remember a dhobi telling me with pride,

'Among us, even a small girl of ten years can pick up this heavy iron and press clothes'. When a girl went to her affinal household after marriage as a newlywed bride, the first task she was asked to do was to pick up an iron and press a few clothes. It used to be the initiation of the bride into her new household. Compare it with that of an upper-caste household, where the bride is usually asked to prepare a sweet dish like milk pudding to serve to the family. However, this practice increasingly went into disuse as girls began to get educated and their roles began to deviate from the earlier ones. When I mention this to the young girls now, they laugh and think I am joking. It is no longer expected that a girl will iron clothes when she goes to her affinal home.

However, even now the dhobi technique of ironing and folding clothes is very specialized and valued. This is the reason why people want to get their clothes pressed by the dhobi rather than doing it at home. Even when most households have stopped giving clothes to the dhobi for washing, the clothes are still preferably given to the dhobi to be ironed. The use of an electric iron is restricted among them, as most of the time they work where there is no electricity connection, such as at a street corner or under a tree. Those that work inside apartment complexes may use heavy electric irons. Apartment living is becoming more common, with gated communities coming up during the last decades of the twentieth century, and the dhobi manner of working is largely changing within these complexes. But in the Old Delhi area, one still sees the dhobi with the heavy iron standing under a tree or at the corner of a lane. It is almost always the dhobi woman who is so found as she continues to iron, as she has been doing for a long time in the past, with the sari still drawn over her head as she works, come rain or shine. Irons usually need replacement after ten years, and they can be mended. In the seventies, when electric irons were being first introduced among the households of the dhobis, there was a great deal of fear, especially from the women, about their use. Many told me that they feared their blood would dry up because of the 'heat' from the electric current. If it was used at all, it was by the men and never by the women.

The dhobi's identity revolved around these resources, the hallmark of their trade and their traditional skills. The *bhatti*, ghat, and iron remain the markers of the dhobi occupation, and some of the previous ones, like the bullock and cart and the donkey before that, have vanished. Slowly, with the use of washing machines and driers, even these are disappearing, though they are not altogether gone. Even in the resettlement colonies, with their relatively recently built ghats, the *bhatti* remains. But what has continued and seems to be continuing into the future is the heavy iron they use to press the clothes, although its gendered use is changing and it is getting transferred from female hands to those of males.

The persistence of the dhobis in remaining in their hereditary occupation can be seen in their willingness to shift to wherever their ghats have been built by the government. This process has been happening in several phases, beginning in the 1960s. All the ghats are provided with water by the Municipal Corporation, at subsidized rates. But electricity rates, earlier supplied at cheap rates by the Delhi Electric Supply, run by the state, have increased considerably since electricity was privatized and put in the hands of corporate companies like Tata and Ambani. The Aam Aadmi Party chief minister, Arvind Kejriwal, had reduced charges and also made electricity free for up to a small level of consumption. This level of 400 units was set keeping in mind the consumption level of a poor household. The dhobis, however, use electricity for commercial purposes, running their washing machines and driers, and hence run up huge bills. At times, they may in desperation resort to the theft of electricity, as reported in a newspaper item on 23 July 2008 about a dhobi located at the dhobi ghats at Minto Road, who was fined by the Special Electricity Court for stealing electricity and using it for commercial purposes. Later, however, most of the eighteen ghats at Minto Road were demolished, although again there was a news item with a photograph of the then minister for state for urban affairs, Hardeep Singh Puri, talking to the dhobis at Minto Road and telling them that their *jhuggis* (temporary housing) would be replaced by proper houses. But this news coverage did not include the information that these houses were planned in Dwarka, a place far away from the dhobi means of work and client resources. The dhobis are still more interested in their livelihood than in their housing. The relocation of the dhobis is a typical example of what Baviskar (2002, cf. Gill 2010: 191) has referred to as 'bourgeois environmentalism', in which 'middle and upper classes push their concern with visual beauty, entertainment, cleanliness, and safety in an organized way to shape a metropolitan space in their own vision'. Needless to say, the poor and marginalized have no say in this decision-making process. The dhobis are still grateful to the previous Congress regime, for it at least listened to some of their grievances and Indira Gandhi had ensured that they can continue with their livelihood in the resettlement colonies by building ghats there with regular water supply. Present regimes, especially after the liberalization of the economy and the overtly corporate leanings of the state, turn a deaf ear to their issues and whatever solutions are offered are with least regard for their needs.

Doing Other Things

None of the negative factors affecting their occupation have deterred the dhobis from carrying out their work, which is becoming more and more lucrative as the city is getting commercialized and is also expanding greatly in scale. The expanding city is seeing the expansion of the dhobi work to the extent that, by the early twenty-first century—that is, nearly forty years after I began my association with them—I found that they are also developing an incipient class structure. The affluent layer is still a thin one and comprises just a few households, most of whom belong to the earlier few families of entrepreneurs who had made it good in the seventies. At the Minto Road ghat, I had come across an individual, the son-in-law of one of the most prosperous dhobi families of the earlier generation, who now acts as a middleman, hiring the services of fellow *biradari* men to work for the big hotels and establishments located in the New Delhi area, near Minto Road. He takes the contract from them and uses his *biradari* contacts to hire dhobis for work. I saw him walking around the area with a cell phone in his hand, looking important.

While most dhobis continue with their work, some of them have begun to either break away completely or take up some supporting occupation or a hobby like wrestling, which some have managed to make into a career. In the seventies, there was one entrepreneur who had a tyre shop in Old Delhi. There were many rumours about his prosperity, the most prevalent being that he had once found a large amount of money in the pocket of a garment that had come for laundry. Instead of returning it to the owner, he had used it to build his shop. Some said he won the lottery. But there was no praise or admiration for his prosperity among the fellow *biradari* people. No one told me that he had made good by his hard work or acumen. It was always a story about a piece of luck. But he remained a part of the *biradari*, and his sons and daughters were all married within it. One daughter was among the few girls at that time who went to college and wore Western dresses. I attended his son's wedding, to a girl from the *biradari*, whose father was a dhobi, doing traditional work, and not very prosperous. At the wedding, the bridegroom, who was somewhat educated, had asked his wife to shake hands with me. When she was feeling shy, he urged her on, saying, 'Go on, she is a madam, who is educated. Learn how to behave with educated persons.' The middleman, whom I met nearly forty years after this wedding, was the son-in-law of the same family, who seem to have retained their somewhat superior financial status, although the tyre shop had been closed and the proprietor had died, most probably of alcoholism at a fairly young age of around 50years. But the *biradari* ties had not been broken and all marriages of that family had taken place within the *biradari*.

Another upwardly mobile family was that of Chaudhari Bulakhi Ram, who had welcomed me into his household, encouraged me to do research on his community, and provided me with the first entry point into the tight-knit boundaries of the *biradari*. His only son, Suraj, was the first to open a dry-cleaning shop. Later his two grandsons built up their own lucrative business selling antiques and metal items in the busy Jama Masjid market. This is one family that seems to have moved partially away from the *biradari*, but not entirely. They continue to live very near to the *katra* at Farash Khana, their original home, although they have now moved to an apartment. The older women of the household still frequently socialize in the *katra*. It was clear that, in spite of their class elevation, their social circle was still largely confined to the *biradari* and the *katras* in the Old Delhi area. The younger men of the household seemed to have their own circle of friends, but the elder one told me that, while in college, he was embarrassed about being a dhobi; as he is maturing, he has begun to realize the importance of the *biradari*. He is now getting actively involved in the affairs of the *biradari*. They were not the only dhobis who remained part of the *biradari*, even if they were not working as dhobis; most other *biradari* members continue to remain so irrespective of changes in occupation and lifestyle.

In the first phase of research done between 1974 and 1977 (Channa 1985), I had collected data about occupations from 375 individuals divided into three age groups: above 45 years of age, 86 persons; between 30 and 45 years,105 persons; and below 30, 184 persons; all males. It must be mentioned here that at that time women were not doing any other work except assisting in the household economy in ways already described. At that time, in the first age group, there were only two individuals who were not in dhobi work, and I have already mentioned them—one was the owner of a tyre shop and another the proprietor of a dry-cleaning shop. In the second age group, there were thirteen persons not in a traditional occupation, and they included peons, milk vendors, lower-division clerks, persons doing bookbinding and file cutting, and salesmen in the local cloth shops. In the last age group, there were seventy-two persons not doing dhobi work, and the maximum number were engaged in paper cutting and bookbinding, a large number were motor mechanics and salesmen in nearby cloth shops, and the rest were engaged in various petty occupations. During the course of the next forty years, I did not find much change in this type of occupational breakdown. As of now, a significant number of them are still engaged in the dhobi occupation; a large number of the younger boys are engaged in bookbinding, file making, and paper cutting, and there are still hardly any who are working at higher levels. Several of the younger persons, who were working in alternate occupations like paper cutting, reverted to traditional occupations once they became older. There are only a few who have managed to gain entry into what may be called skilled white-collar jobs such as software engineers or teachers. In fact, at present there is only one young couple, in their twenties, where the wife is an assistant professor in a woman's college in Delhi and her husband is a computer professional. There are still hardly any office-goers. In 2023 one young man got an assistant professorship in another Delhi University college, and some more are in office jobs. One young man is a doctor at AIIMS (the All India Institute of Medical Sciences) in Delhi. But the trend is still slow and reflects the general trend of the job market and the larger policies of the government to keep people in contractual and temporary employment and encourage more young people to create their own jobs, or in other words to keep to the informal sector or become an entrepreneur. A majority of the dhobis not doing dhobi work are in the informal sector doing private jobs and petty commodity transactions; for example, one elderly dhobi sells children's garments on the pavement in a big market area. In the Old Delhi area housing the poorer section of the dhobis, women are engaged sorting spices, shelling peas, or even working as household helps by the local people.

In the seventies, there was a young boy named Hemch and, working in the ministry of defence; later he got married and had four daughters, whom he educated very well. The eldest—was married to the son of another good friend and informant, Omi Pehlwan. The young man to whom she was married is a well known body builder. The girl in question had done a double Master's and a BEd but was yet without a job. In an interview undertaken in 2015 her father was very critical of the political situation in India and especially of the treatment meted out to the Scheduled Castes (SCs). In fact, as he pointed out, the reservation for the SCs had hardly benefited anyone in their community. His daughter was sitting without a job, having worked on an ad hoc basis in a reputed private school for seven years, from where she had finally been thrown out. He himself had held a government post till his retirement, but was bitter and resentful at the way he had been treated all the years of his employment. His son-in-law, Shiv Kumar, the body builder, on the other hand, was a successful and happy man. Shiv Kumar had two sons with an age gap of more than ten years. When I asked his wife as to why such a gap, she said that her husband was always travelling because of his professional commitments and that he had even gone abroad as a wrestler and bodybuilder. I was told that every gym owner in Delhi knows about Shiv Kumar, which seemed to be a tall claim, but within the *biradari* people are very proud of him and many carry video clips of him showing off his body professionally in athletic meets. Shiv Kumar did not live in a *katra* but in an apartment complex in a separate apartment, which was furnished like any other modern house, with sofa set and dining table. When I visited his house, his first son was just born and was lying in a crib, and his wife was looking after him. I was reminded of his mother returning from the Yamuna river, when she was carrying him, walking all the way and coming home tired, but with no one to care for her. I saw this family at very close quarters and saw how they changed over the years. By 2020, Shiv Kumar had been promoted as an officer in the railways because of his excellent performance as a wrestler and the recognition that he was getting. His father, Omi Pehlwan, was a wrestler in addition to being a dhobi and also had a shop where he treated patients. He was also a bonesetter and gave indigenous medicines for sprains, minor injuries, and bone-related issues. In around 2015, when I visited their shop after Omi's death, his wife was sitting there wearing makeup and nail polish, and disbursing medicines. She was helped by one of her sons and a person from another caste group, who told me he was trained in a *gurukul* (traditional school) for indigenous medicines. More recently, after her death, a son is taking care of the shop, which is situated in a prime location, although very small. Omi's son Shiv Kumar is a star in the *biradari*, but at the same time he is deeply entrenched within it. He has a highly educated wife but she is not employed. His father-in-law had a coveted government job and he educated his daughters, and at least two of them have decent employment.

In the seventies, there were several young boys going to college, but not all of them did make it to being successfully employed. One young man, who used to sport a fashionable hairstyle, became a bank manager and rose to a fairly high position. But others, like my good friend and long-time associate Bishanlal could not manage to pass college, and while he could clear the first year, he failed the second and third years. In the seventies, Bishanlal was a teenage college-going boy living in Kucha Pati Ram, and I remember attending his wedding. He wore a Western-style suit for his wedding, as recognition of his college-going status. He shifted to his present residence in 1984, and he, along with other family members, have eight apartments in this complex that also has a ghat for washing clothes and a running-water connection. The dhobis cluster together, not only because of kinship and *biradari* ties but also because they need to share the resources like ghats, *bhattis*, and space for drying clothes and running water. Bishan's sons are all into dhobi work, and he could not persuade any one of them to get an education. They are, however, literate, use smartphones, have Facebook accounts, and watch National Geographic on television. All the sons are married, and only the eldest lives away from his father, about one station away by metro at a place called Chuna Bhatti dhobi ghat at Padam Nagar. All have two sons each. Bishan's daughter is the youngest and was studying in class VIII in

2015. At that time Bishan told me very happily that she wanted to be a photographer, and he was hoping she would be able to join the media in a professional capacity. Later, however, after she had finished her graduation, I walked into their house one day and found the girl and the family very dejected. I asked her about her photography and she told me all her life is now ruined. It seems that there was a slight mistake in the spelling of her father's name in her tenth board certificate and because of that she is unable to collect her graduation certificate as the names do not match. She told me that for two years she has been going from pillar to post, meeting authorities and putting petitions, but nothing has worked. This again is an example of how the system treats the marginal, although she has certain rights as an SC student and the government machinery is overtly geared to help everyone in a democratic set-up. At ground-level reality the situation is very different.

Rationality and Irrationality

Traditional workers and indigenous economies have usually been understood as not being rational in the modern economic sense. From the detailed description of dhobi work given here, it becomes clear that there is always a fine balance between emotions and pragmatism. Even while maintaining primary group relationships with their clients, the dhobis always try to tip the advantage in their own favour. They manipulate the clients into giving them extra advantage, at the same time making stringent calculations in investing their own resources on them. Within the *biradari* too, they take pains to keep up relationships but are quick to take economic advantages, even overriding *biradari* and family ties when they have to. The *biradari* ties are themselves seen as a resource that comes to their rescue at dire times. The dhobis can be seen as pragmatic and rational and yet humane, believing that human relationships encompass those animals and non-humans they consider to be part of their social universe. One agrees with Appadurai (1986) that any kind of 'othering' or creation of anthropological subjects is a figment of theoretical imagination. In this work at every step the dhobis have been understood as 'no different' in any respect from the anthropological self.

Notes

1. A kurta is a long garment worn in the upper part of the body. The lower part is accompanied by a pair of pyjamas.
2. Kapoor (2018) has made similar observations with respect to the tanners or Chamars of Uttar Pradesh.
3. However, there might be exceptions, as in some parts of the country, especially in the North-West, the Brahmins are highest in ritual hierarchy but rank low in economic and social status, with the agricultural castes like the Jats and Ahirs being dominant. The Brahmin is still attached to them as his *jajman*, and receives gifts and sustenance from them, while remaining poor. Here class and caste are not equivalent.
4. Dhobis wash clothes for the formal institutions such as hospitals, hotels, and offices, where their payment and relations are bound by formal rules of that particular institution.
5. A rupee is 100 paise, so that 25 paise are one quarter of a rupee.

4

Living Life as a Dhobi
(Man and Woman)

A dhobi, in India, is an ascribed identity, and one has to be born into a dhobi jati to be a dhobi. The term dhobi can be used for an amorphous mass, as described by De Certeau (1984), 'a flexible and continuous mass, woven tight like a fabric with neither rips not darned patches, a multitude of quantified heroes who lose names and faces as they become the ciphered river of the streets, a mobile language of computations and rationalities that belong to no one'; or it can be deconstructed into individual actors, who have lived or who still live, in flesh and blood. They are and will remain unsung heroes, with no names, no recognition, and, in the city of Delhi, anonymous to the extent that some people may deny having seen or known about them. This chapter attempts to describe the dhobi individuals whom I have met and many of whom I still meet, who have names and who exist as real persons.

Then there is the abstracted category of the 'dhobi'. One that does not exist, is constructed, and through which an attempt has been made to give a brief understanding or rather a feel of what it means to live life like a dhobi, man or woman, on an everyday basis. Here the 'everyday' is taken in the sense given to it by Guha (2009: 420) in that it stands for a collective experience transcending actual time: 'It enables every lived instant, every "now" to escape the discipline of linear succession occasionally to hark back and look ahead.' Also I have followed Sax (2009: 94) to analytically assign agency to the collective in order to be able to use the collective noun to describe thoughts and practices.

A dhobi by birth remains a dhobi by jati, irrespective of their actual occupation. There are some essential nuances to the identity. Some dhobis, who have struck out independently, becoming shop owners, or entrepreneurs, or working in private jobs, may not openly use the dhobi identity

Dhobis of Delhi. Subhadra Mitra Channa, Oxford University Press. © Subhadra Mitra Channa 2024.
DOI: 10.1093/9780198926238.003.0005

that also makes them synonymous with being untouchables. However, if they are in a government job where they are taking the benefit of reservation, they have no other option but to declare their caste status.[1] I recall here the narrative of one person, who retired in 2005 from a government job, where he was an upper-division clerk in the Ministry of Defence. He told me that he had a very good friend in office, whom he used to help a lot in his work, and they shared lunch together. But one day the friend asked him his caste, and when he told him that he was a dhobi, he began to avoid him completely: *'Pehle to hasta bolta tha, har cheez mein mere se madat mangta tha, par jaise hi suna ki main dhobi hoon to muh mor liya'* ('He used to laugh and talk to me and ask for my help in everything but turned his face away as soon as he came to know that I was a dhobi'). In the seventies most young dhobis talked to me about facing discrimination in schools and colleges, but such open aversions are no longer felt by the present generation of dhobi young men and women. In the seventies a woman told me, *'Mere bacche school jate hain to master kehta hai, tum kyon padne aa gaye ho. Ghar baitho, yeh padai likhai tumhara kaam nahi hain'* ('When my children go to school the master tells them why have you come to study, go back home, this studying is not your job'). However, at present no one would be able to make such a statement without fearing some kind of reprisal, although plenty of people may harbour such sentiments in private.

In fact, a young woman, now serving as an assistant professor in a college affiliated to Delhi University told me that her supervisor and mentor regarded her with great affection and always encouraged her: 'They love me and always encourage me to do better.' But at the same time, at the time of writing of this book, the very same young woman, who has been teaching in the university college for ten years, has not got a permanent tenured position. There is some ambiguity in admitting the identity of a dhobi. The father of the same woman, who owns a dry-cleaning shop but at the same time has a religious group for devotional practices for Balaji (the Hindu deity Hanuman), told me with pride in his voice that the people around him now refer to him as *'woh Balaji wale'* ('that person who is associated with Balaji'), meaning that they no longer see him only as a dhobi but assign him an identity transcending his caste identity.

A dhobi places emphasis on the jati-based identity when he or she is identifying as a member of their *biradari,* and as part of an endogamous marriage group. There are also dhobis who are dhobi by jati but not a member of the particular *biradari* to which a dhobi may belong. Such dhobis are also treated as fellow dhobis, and this extends beyond the religious boundary, and Muslim dhobis are also treated as brethren. A person who is not a dhobi by jati, even if doing dhobi work like having a laundry shop, will not be considered a dhobi and never as part of the social universe to which only those who are dhobi by birth belong. There are, however, subtle hierarchies, like distinguishing those who are part of one's own *biradari* from those who are not, and those who were born in the city from those who are migrants.

At present (from around a decade earlier than the writing of this book), some very poor migrant boys with no means of subsistence had a preference to get attached to a dhobi as a servant and learn the trade. They are the most marginalized even among the dhobis, who look down on them, not including them in their social universe. Those migrating from the villages do so under extreme circumstances, where they are left with little option but to leave their native places. However, they are considered migrants only for the first generation. There are many who now claim to be city dhobis but say they migrated from rural areas several generations back. In the absence of any system of record-keeping, as they were mostly illiterate till recently, it is not possible to trace the genealogies of these dhobis, but I will write about what I observed with respect to the newly migrated dhobis.

I met a young man named Ram Chander, about 25 or 26 years of age in 2015, at the Malka Ganj ghat. His story was that he belongs to a dhobi caste but was born in a village named Hardoi, where the dhobi work hardly attracts any clients, as the villagers have only a few clothes that they wash themselves. He was living with his young wife named Seema, who sat in the bitter cold January day with a small baby wrapped in a shawl. She told me that there are twenty to twenty-five households of dhobis in Hardoi, but none of them have any work washing clothes. They all do subsistence farming, growing a little for home consumption, and also work in the sugar cane fields, a major cash crop in the region. Her marriage was arranged by her mother, and she came to live in the city with her husband. They had a miserable little shack, built on top of a storage room provided with the ghat for storing clothes that came to be washed. The shack had a tin roof and its height was such that a full-grown person could not stand up in it. She was even cooking inside it and living with her 1-year-old child there. Ram Chander was employed as a servant by a Sheheri dhobi belonging to Old Delhi. His employer was at that time quite elderly and lived in Sita Ram Bazar and had a dry-cleaning shop in Old Delhi. He began working with his employer when he was only about 8 or 9 years old. He had come to see the city with the sons of his father's elder brother, and stayed on. He preferred the city life to that in the village and, having found employment, did not go back. Before marriage, he was staying at the ghat with a couple of other boys. These boys stay for free, use public conveniences, and eat at the local cheap eateries, called *dhabas*. The employer pays for their food directly to the eatery and deducts the cost from their salary.

Ram Chander told me proudly that after getting married he no longer has to eat at the *dhaba*, since his wife cooks for him: '*Ab meri shaadi ho gayi hai, mujhe dhabe mein nahi khana padta aur paise bhi bach jate hain*' ('I no longer have to eat at the dhaba and save money at the same time'). Unlike other dhobi women, brought up in the city, his wife does not know any dhobi work, and cannot help him, but she keeps house, cooks, and looks after their baby, and that is enough for him. He then gets his full pay without any deduction, as the employer is not paying for his food. We see this boy's tactics in inching his way towards a better life; first he came to the city with his brothers, then the glamour of the city enticed him to stay on. A factor other than the glitz of the city lures these marginal persons—the impersonality and the space in which they can live an anonymous life, not always recognized and stigmatized for their lowly status, both caste- and class-wise. It gives a sense of freedom to be lost in the crowd, to be able to eat at a *dhaba*, without being asked about one's caste, and to travel across the city without overt disgust being shown for their presence. Ram Chander's marriage improved his position, in terms of both personal comfort and a small gain in position, as he was no longer treated as an immature boy but as an adult. In addition, his finances improved, ever so slightly, with his wife's cooking. His aspirations may be much bigger, but at least he was a satisfied person, as he could assess his life as having improved and not gone from bad to worse. At the edge of subsistence living, this is a lot to achieve.

There are now several migrant dhobis at various ghats, a phenomenon that was quite rare in the seventies. The perceived inferior status of the migrant dhobi creates an additional layer of hierarchy. There are several reasons for this. Firstly, they are not part of the Sheheri dhobi *biradari*, and therefore not integral to the close-knit social network of which all these dhobis are part. Secondly, they work as servants for other dhobis, as they do not have the direct rights to the ghats, which belong by an unwritten ethic to the dhobis who claim have been living in the city from much earlier times. Thirdly, they come to the city with no clients of their own. The Sheheri dhobis, with their legitimate access to local ghats as well as a well-established clientele, find themselves in a superior position to the migrant dhobis. At the Minto Road ghat, during my conversation with a few elderly women, I was told that only migrant dhobis act as servants; *'we don't'. 'Woh hamare naukar ka kaam karte hain, hamari biradari wale kisi ki naukri nahi karte'* (They [migrants]work as our servants, *we* of the biradari do not work under anyone). The *'we'* are the city dhobis, with a functional *biradari* and long-standing relationship with clients.

An important factor to be considered when we are trying to understand the values carried by the majority of dhobis is their emphasis on independent earning. One often repeated refrain was *'hum kisike gulam nahin hain'* ('we are not anyone's slave'). To a dhobi, the free life on the riverbank, the luxury of taking one's time over a particular task and working according to a self-created schedule, is an important aspect of self-identity. It is this sense of independence that is their way of coping with the ascribed stigma of being untouchables, of never being accepted into higher social strata irrespective of economic status, and forever living on the margins of society. The small sense of superiority at being able to employ someone as a servant goes a long way to bolster self-esteem, but then this status is also achieved by only a few. But for the others, like the women sitting under the shade of a tree with whom I had a conversation, there is a vicarious sense of superiority, to know that there is a category of 'migrant' (*bahar se aye huye*) that is even inferior to them.

Their daily life in the city has always been fraught with the realization of their ritual and social marginality. In the initial period of my fieldwork, I was once told by a dhobi couple that they had tried to open a tea stall near their house in Kashmiri Gate but were unsuccessful, as the people around them started talking about *'dhobi ki chai'* ('the tea of a dhobi') that directly referred to their untouchable status. It was also the first time I was exposed to the direct implication of caste-based discrimination, a phenomenon that I had no understanding of, at least not at first hand. Spending time in the *katra* made a fundamental difference in me, as I understood not only what it meant to be poor and marginalized but also how people maintain their humanity under such adverse conditions. The little tactics, the manoeuvring of space, the taking advantage of the precise moment, when one could, keep them going, not just as marginal beings but as human beings with consciousness, agency, and a sense of control over their lives.

The Life Cycle

Birth and Childhood

Birth in a dhobi household means that the infant is welcomed irrespective of gender. Unlike the upper castes, the dhobis do not discriminate between the male and female child, a fundamental reason being that the performance of the dhobi occupation is nearly equally divided between men and women. The burden of patriarchy sits lightly on the shoulders of the dhobi household members. In my long years of experiencing the dhobi family relationships and household power structures, I have been impressed by the lack of unequal power relations between men and women as well all forms of gendered discrimination.

Abu-Lughod (1991) has warned against the essentializing of culture, as it is both a way of 'othering' and of creating a hierarchy. Yet there are regularities in values, in norms and a sense of ethics, which come out very clearly over a long period of association with any community. With respect to the Sheheri dhobis, this is also made possible by the relatively fixed boundary that is put around this identity, to enclose a few hundred people, a small enough group for everyone to know everyone else. The density of social relationships at the core is identifiable enough to make the Sheheri dhobi an analytically sustainable category. In this sense it is also valid and legitimate to assign some characters to their collective experiences, their lives together, their ways of understanding the world, their core values, and their norms of behaviour.

Dhobi infants are born and raised in crowded environments. Seeing a dhobi child sleeping soundly under conditions of loud noise and commotion, one is bound to compare them with children in affluent families who need quiet rooms and sound machines to sleep. As children grow up, they also get used to multiple handlers and being ignored when crying or hungry. A mother's primary duty is seen in breastfeeding a baby, and with perhaps few exceptions all babies are breastfed till at least one year of age, and often till the next one comes along. I never found any dhobi mother in a hurry to wean her child, and they are allowed to wean as they please. The babies are also fed on demand and often fed almost every half an hour, since a crying baby is seen as a distraction and also distressful to the adults around. A mother is always busy in household matters, including the work put into the processing of clothes, and it is easy and convenient to pick up the child and breastfeed it while continuing with what she was doing. Giving bottled feeds would require far greater time and other resources, and most women never felt the need for it. A baby was directly weaned from the breast onto adult foods like bananas and *khichri* (a mix of rice and lentils). There is no effort at conscious weaning and a child begins to eat by getting bits and pieces of food from older siblings and adults. The youngest child was often breastfed till the age of two and a half or till such time as it began to eat and get used to adult food. Till a couple of decades back, I have never seen children being given milk other than breast milk. Most dhobis could not afford it. Only recently on a visit to a household, I saw the young mother bathe her baby, put on a nappy, and leave it with a bottle of milk, to be cared for by the grandfather while she got busy with other work around the house. Nappies and bottle-feeding came to them with the education of girls, the expansion of the market (dated to around the turn of the century), and improved economic positions, and is still a mark of a better-off household.

Once weaned, children are mostly left alone. An adult will take care of them only when that person has the time to do so. Small children are hardly disciplined in any way and they cling around their mother's saree as they work. When a child is hungry and demands food, the mother will place some rice and lentils in front of it, or hand a piece of biscuit or other available snack. The same is done by other adults. The children have no fixed food timings and munch their way through the day. Only when they are much older do they begin to eat regular meals.

In the seventies, the young women, who were daughters-in-law then, complained furtively to me about their mothers-in-law, saying that they were prevented from taking care of their children by the senior woman in the household, who believed that children grow up anyhow but that work that brings in the money and needs to be done first. From one point of view the dhobi women had more agency, especially with respect to their husbands, than upper-caste women or women from better-off families, but on the other hand, as long as they were in the household occupation, it was also a hard life. At the time when there were lesser amenities and most women were engaged throughout the day in the work of ironing clothes and doing household chores, there was little time left over for full-time childcare. Looking after children of all ages was also a collective responsibility in the *katra* way of life that I have already described. Maybe this was similar to the joint family living of upper-caste/class households, but there the women had the luxury of household help and servants, who often took on most of the work, even of looking after children.

But the seventies were a time of transition. This was the period of mass access to education, of rising aspirations of living a life outside that of being a dhobi. The then young people had begun to dream of becoming middle-class. They wished to bring their children up like the upper-caste families in their neighbourhood. The city was changing around them and they also wished to be part of that change. The most frequent lament that I heard from young women in the seventies was that they wanted to take care of their children but were not able to do so: '*Hum apne bacchon ko nahi dekh pate hain, hum chahate hain ki hum unki achhi tarha se parvarish kare par majboor hain. Saas kehti hai ki ghar ka kaam karo, bacche to apne aap pal jayenge*' ('I cannot look after my children I want to bring the up well but my mother-in-law tells me to concentrate on the household work, the children will grow up on their own').It was not as if they were always being controlled by older women in this respect, but the burden of work did not allow them to take personal care of their children. In the nuclear households, where they could do as they pleased, the burden of work and limitations of resources also prevented them from taking care of their children as they aspired to. It is perhaps for this reason, when this generation of women became mothers-in-law after a couple of more decades, that they no longer insisted on their daughters-in-law doing dhobi work. There was a shift towards encouraging them to take care of their children. This shift was informed by the middle-class values to which they were more exposed and also came about because they carried the sense of frustration that they had when they were trying to raise their own children. As I mentioned in the last chapter, few young women in the 2020s are expected to do dhobi work as a full-time job. At the most, if the household is still engaged in traditional work, they help around.

The 1970swere a transitional phase in city life, as industries, markets, and education were becoming more prevalent among all classes of society. This was a time when the first generation of young dhobi boys had graduated to attending college. Even a few girls had begun to attend school, and there was exposure to some media, although television had not yet become popular. By the eighties, television had also entered many houses and even some of the dhobi households. By the nineties, with the liberalization of the economy, a variety of goods entered the market, and individual earnings also went up. The variety of goods in the market was tempting and much of dhobi way of living underwent a change from this time onwards. Most dhobis I talked to pointed to the 2020s as the threshold at which real changes could be observed in their society.

But during the seventies times were hard, earnings were less, and many households barely eked out a living. A young couple lost their firstborn child, a boy, when he was barely 6months old. They had taken him to a wedding and during the celebrations the child was neglected and died of dehydration, as the weather was hot. The mother had been busy with the wedding revelries and did not pay much attention to the small baby. Later the couple were very depressed, but as the young mother told me, she was expected to be at the beck and call of everyone during the wedding celebrations. She could not pay attention to her child, as that would have been considered inappropriate behaviour: '*Mujhe sab yeh karo woh karo kehte rahe. Main apne bacche ki taraf dekh bhi nahi payi, woh garmi mein rota raha. Baad mein doctor ne kaha dehydration ho gaya tha*' ('Everyone told me to do this, do that, I could not even look at my child. He kept crying in the heat and later the doctor told me that he was dehydrated'). The children were seen as taken care of by divine powers. If a baby died, it was very sad, but it was the will of divinity. Most people did not blame any person, neither the parents for negligence nor the elders who had prevented the mother from taking care. Even in the *katra*, I found that babies would be crawling around by themselves, while someone would just pick them up and put them on the side, to keep them out of harm's way. Somewhat older children would be running around and eating wherever they could. At that time, not much attention was paid to children's education. No special adjustments were made to enable the children to study in the crowded environment of the *katra*, where there was the constant noise of clothes being washed, children playing, women gossiping, and men shouting at each other.

The houses were congested, with little room left for anyone to sit and study. Nor were the parents aware of any manner in which children could study, or had any kind of familiarity with formal education. This was the first generation of dhobi children going to school. Little girls were mostly entrusted with the care of younger siblings, and helped the older women with household work, as soon as they were able to walk and talk. A girl would pick up an iron as soon as she was able, mostly around the age of 8 or so. Girls would be professionally ironing clothes by the time they were 10 or 12. Boys too rarely went to school beyond the first few years. As mentioned, the parents had no knowledge of formal education, nor did most of them consider it as anything useful. Young boys dropping out of school would be sent for some gainful employment. The Old Delhi area is heavily commercialized and home to a variety of informal sector occupations that provide livelihood to large numbers of unskilled or semi-skilled persons—men, women, and children. The dhobi *katras* are close to some of the major centres of commercial activities. In fact, more trade takes place in Old Delhi than anywhere else in the city. The Sadar Bazar area is famous for its paper trade; likewise, there are particular areas known for trade in cloth and traditional attires, for gold and silver ornaments, for household goods, for cycles, for motor parts, for various kinds of food, and so on. During the seventies I had seen that a large number of dhobi boys, as young as 10, were employed in the paper cutting, binding, and file making small industry that thrives in this area. Even in very recent times, some households are still engaged in the paper business, but now they are engaged in it as trade and not simply as cheap labour. Several of the boys, who learnt the trade when they were young, continued with it as adults, and are now making a fairly good livelihood out of it. Most of the big publishing houses, including Oxford University Press, Macmillan, and other such major national and international publishers, have their offices here, and there are many smaller publishers and large numbers of printers and suppliers of paper.

Similarly, several young boys were employed as salesmen in the local cloth shops, for which this area is also well known. Childhood was mostly about work, earning a few rupees for the boys and for the girls, to help with raising their siblings and helping out with household work. As I was told by the elderly dhobis, things were much worse in the colonial period and earlier, as the rate of child mortality was very high, just as it was in all parts of India. Children were primarily regarded as assets for the household, for providing additional labour and help; only later, by the seventies, not earlier, was there some cognition that children could go to school to study and to get some qualifications that were other than that of doing dhobi work.

From the nineties onwards, attitudes towards child-rearing had changed to some extent, in that most children went to school, although still there were many more dropouts than ones that actually passed out. The optimism and changing aspirations that I had witnessed in the seventies have now been replaced by more pessimism and sense of defeat with the entry of the Indian economy into the neoliberal period of the 2020s. 'Hamare jati ke logon ko koi phayda nahi hua' ('Our jati did not get any benefits') was a common refrain repeated by many people in the twenty-first century. In the 1970s and 1980s, there was a new generation getting educated, and they had hopes for a better life. But by the year 2000 or so, most of them did not achieve the dream of leading middle-class lives, as many found that they had actually made very little progress in social and economic terms. Only a handful of men, who had got an education then, made it good. One became a bank manager and shifted to a neighbourhood in a middle-class locality. Another man, who held a government job, is still living in his old house in the katra, and while he educated all his four daughters, only two of them were able to get jobs to their satisfaction. The situation was more frustrating as the economy was liberalized in 1992 and the aspirations of people had risen much higher than before. Earlier the people were satisfied with what they had, as they expected this was what was ordained for them according to the status of their jati. But by the turn of the century, with much more exposure and a rise of consciousness of equality and democracy, most people aspired to at least some of the good they saw around but which was difficult for them to attain as the formal sector did not yield many jobs even for the educated.

This situation is better understood in the context of the larger economy, as summarized by Gill (2010: 173), who points out that very few net jobs were created in the 1990s and most of regular jobs were at the high end of the service sector, accessible only to the upper classes as they had the resources, such as education and sophistication, to apply for them. Data indicates that 60 per cent of regular employment in the 2020s was held by upper-caste Hindus. In addition, of the net jobs created in this period, most were concentrated at the lower end of the service sector filled by lower-end casual labour, often migrant labour, and simultaneously even the better category of self-employment showed a decline. As indicated by Mohanty (2006), most SCs are likely to be employed in the insecure and unregulated sector as compared to upper-caste Hindus. Further quoting from Mohanty (2006), Gill identifies the shrinking of the public sector and transference of most institutions to the private sector in the post-liberalization period as another blow to the SCs as to their chances of getting a job. Previously they could get jobs under quota in the public sectors, which stand considerably diminished with increasing privatization.

In the post-liberal era the feelings of equality have increased considerably, and aspirations override all jati identities, increasing the gap between the available and the attainable. Goods flood the market and advertisements entice people to buy them, but the means to do so are severely limited by that same market economy.

The dhobis followed the prevailing trends. Children were pampered and given toys and good clothes, a significant change from forty years back, when they all went around semi-naked in the summer and dressed in shabby woollens in winter, often wearing cast-off clothes given by clients. Toys and books were unknown, and children played with whatever they could lay their hands on. Most children did not play but were engaged in adult work, helping parents and others—little boys learning to wash clothes, or distributing them, taking food to their fathers, or working in various petty jobs. The little girls duplicated the work done by adult women. A child would accompany an adult to the riverbank to help in drying and spreading clothes, and once there could play in the sand in his or her spare time, while they watched over the clothes. Small boys over the age of 7 or 8 were often sent to nearby markets to fetch small items. Girls at this age began to do household work like washing vessels, picking up younger siblings, helping their mothers fill the irons with coal, and so on. At later dates most children±—girls and boys—were sent to school, but not all of them completed their education, dropping out if unable to cope with studies. Few made it to higher studies. To inform those who criticize the system of reservation in government jobs for being unfair, for promoting mediocrity, I have always wondered how any child brought up under the conditions of the dhobi *katra* could ever make it to college, and yet some even graduated and got jobs. This is an issue that continues to raise debates and is seen as contentious.

Marriage and Household over the Years

The transition from childhood to adulthood, as understood many years ago by Margaret Mead (1949), is smooth, with a child becoming an adult almost unknowingly. Marriage is a landmark transition to adulthood, as almost every couple sets up their own household soon after marriage. It is only in recent times, as young people are diversifying their occupations, that they are finding it more convenient to continue to live in an undivided household, but the impetus to separate is always there. For example, a young woman who is teaching in a college and whose husband works in an office were living with their in-laws, but as soon as they were able, they set up their own house near to that of the in-laws. Those who are following the traditional occupation always set up a new hearth (*chullah*) almost immediately after marriage. The father and maybe other members of the kin network give them a few clients to enable them to run their kitchen, and then leave them to fend for themselves. But there was rarely too much of a physical separation, as most of the time the newlyweds would move into an extension of the original house, or into a room nearby. When a man got married, while doing the traditional occupation, his newly wedded wife was expected to be able to help him not only in setting up a new kitchen but also in the household occupation. This again, as I understood it, was a strategy to maximize the work and earnings of the household.

Since the dhobi household has little hierarchy and there is no one in overall control of the household work organization, increasing members of the household does not increase efficiency but, rather, decreases the work output. Household members begin to depend on each other for work, and it may happen that no one works to their full capacity. Once separated, each husband-and-wife unit has to devote more time and energy to their work. But in real life, people do not think in these terms. The pressures of sharing work lead to quarrels between members, especially the daughters-in-law. Each person may feel they are putting in more work than the other, and since the common hearth implies equal consumption levels, this might lead to feelings of being cheated, and negative emotions erupt. While men attributed the break-up of household units to quarrels between women, the women pointed to ego clashes between father and sons and between brothers. It is likely that multiple factors were at play, but the overall outcome was nearly all the households breaking up into nuclear units. Most men would blame the women: '*ghar ki bahu ek saath nahi rehe sakti hain, aapas main takkar to hoti hi hai*' ('women in the house cannot live together, they will always clash'). A common saying is '*Bartan ek saath rahe to khadkenge hi*' ('Vessels kept together will make a noise'). Women's perspectives can be summarized in this statement: '*Baap aur beta to aapas mein ladte hain, har koi apni baat manvana chahata hain. Ek doosre se aapas nahi karte*' ('Father and son will fight with each other. Each wants to have the upper hand, they do not want to compromise on anything').

At a more abstracted level, looking from the point of view of common sense and rationality, the resource-starved dhobi household has no incentive to stay together. There are no common assets like property and business to hold them together. Sometimes father and sons may hold clients together, but there is an inevitable separation after the death of the father. Shah (1998) warns against making a direct link between joint households and wealth, but mentions two important economic factors as affecting household composition: firstly, that joint households have a tendency to create assets and wealth, and continuity of the joint organizational structure then becomes necessary for the preservation of wealth; secondly, 'low assets tended to hasten dissolution of joint households' (Shah 1998: 73). In the situation of the dhobis, the lack of hierarchy and absence of authority of the elders, considered essential for the management of the joint household, appear to be a key reason why it cannot be held together. In almost all joint households that I know of personally, including in my own kinship circle, the household functions under the supervision of a patriarch or a matriarch or both. The dhobis, as I have already described, are averse to any kind of authority within the household, including those based on age and gender. All members contribute to the household economy and functioning and have decision-making power, but as soon as they lose this capacity for work, they rapidly lose their influence. The deference shown to elders among the upper castes is totally absent among them. As pointed out by Shah (1998), this may be related to the lack of asset creation by the elders. The only fraternal joint household I have seen is that of the wives and sons of Suraj, which will be described presently, but in that household assets in the form of shops had been created by the male elder.

At the time of my early work with the dhobis I had collected narratives from women regarding their marriage and early lives. A woman who was then about 80years old told me that she was married when she was only 9years old. She was married from Chitli Qabar to Sita Ram Bazar (where I met her), a distance of about 2 kilometres. Sitting on a cot, bent with age, she recalled how she would stay at her in-laws' place for a few days and then run off to her parents' house and not want to come back. She stayed there most of the time, but occasionally her parents sent her back. As she was only a child, the mother-in-law would give her small tasks around the house, and if she did not do them, would give her a few whacks; later, as she recalled, the mother-in-law used to pet her. She had two younger sisters-in-law, who were her playmates, and after her marriage her mother-in-law, still a young woman herself, gave birth to four sons, of whom two survived. In those days children were seen as gifts of God, and expected to grow up on their own. No particular human agency was recognized either in the matter of birth or the survival of children. As my data indicated, there was a high degree of infant mortality till the 1960s, and after that things began to improve, with better availability of medical facilities, yet infant mortality was an accepted state of affairs even till the later part of the twentieth century. But dhobi family sizes increased considerably by the 1970s, with better medical care and lack of planning. That was the time of very large families, sometimes comprising ten or more children per couple. After the last part of the twentieth century, with better understanding of planned parenthood and more exposure to media as well as the impact of a market economy, family sizes have reduced somewhat. Earlier, around the seventies and eighties, I recall even young people making fun of the government's programme of family planning, saying that for the dhobis two children were the beginning of the family and not its end.[2]

The elderly woman whose life I am recalling had narrated that since she was not able to do any household work, her father-in-law told her one day, 'Come, I will take you to the ghat with me. You can help me there as you cannot help your mother-in-law.' So she went to the ghat, but once there, she and her young sister-in-law became very naughty, away from the supervision of the mother. As she recalled, 'We pulled away all the tags that had been attached to the expensive clothes, to mark them, and then picked up slime from near the river bed and smeared them all over the clean clothes.' The furious father-in-law came back home and threw both son and daughter-in-law out of his house. They were put in a small shack near their original home and left to fend for themselves. She said, '*Hum bhukhe rahe teen din tak. Ghar mein kuch khana nahi tha, phir mera shauhar bahar jaakar do rupai lekar aaya aur hamne aaloo aur atta kharida bahut mushkil se tab roti banaya khane ke liye*' ('We were hungry for three days, we had no food in the house, then my husband went out and got two rupees and we bought some wheat and potatoes and with great difficulty made some *rotis* to eat'). '*Mujhe roti banana nahi ata tha par ek buddhe ko taras aa gaya aur usne mujhe roti banana sikhaya. Par who bhi mujhe bahut marta tha agar main jaldi nahi sikhiti to*' ('I did not know how to make *rotis* and a kindly old man near our shack helped me with my cooking. But he too would beat me if I did not learn quickly enough'). However, even if they were hungry, she never felt any fear, for 'there were always so many people near us. We were within the *biradari*, and very close to our home. There was nothing to fear, and people helped us occasionally as and when they could.' Finally, she learnt all the household work as well as dhobi work, by the time she was 10 or 12, and set up a home with her husband, who was grown up, being about seven years older than her.

This was referring to a time of famine (it appears she was referring to the Great Famine of 1899–1900), for she told me that when she was separated by her in-laws, things were very expensive because of the famine. Nothing was available and they had extra hardship for that reason. While at other times she had bought 40 seers' worth of wheat (approximately 35 kilograms) for a rupee, at that time they could get only 2 seers for 1 rupee. She talked about the *biradari* closeness and how as a child she was able to survive with the help from the *biradari* members.

Another narrative, from a woman who was then about 22 years of age, also gives a clear account of what it was like to grow up as a girl child among the dhobis in the seventies. She recalls that she was born in Sitaram Bazar to a full family of parents, brothers, and sisters. She had practically no childhood and she could not remember a time when she was not working:'*Jab se hosh samvala hain bas kaam hi kaam kar rahi hoon. Kabhi aur kuch nahi kiya*' ('Since I have gained consciousness I am only working. Do not remember doing anything else'). At first she was sent to the market to purchase small items, and then she began to help cooking meals and would sometimes go to the ghats on the river to help her father with the washing of clothes, when she would help in their spreading and drying. At home she would do the cooking and also iron clothes. As she recalls, this was her routine from morning till night and day after day. There was hardly any change or any days that were different from the others. Initially she was sharing this work with her elder sister, but after she got married, the entire burden fell on her shoulders. As she said,

My mother was always busy with working outside the house, like bringing clothes from the houses, ironing them, folding them, returning them to the clients. She had no time for any household work. It was all left to me. I was barely 14 or 15 when the entire burden of household work was on me. I took care of the household money as well. Then a brother got married and I was expected to carry out the entire burden of arrangements of the wedding by myself.

Things changed a little for her when the sister-in-law came to the house and she had some free time on her hands. She also had the responsibility of teaching her sister-in law some of the ways of the household. Then another brother got married and, with another female member, things became easier: 'Now I could go out and do a bit of gossip with my friends in the neighbourhood.' But when the sisters-in-law began to have children, she left all the household work to them and took care of them. This meant she was no longer confined entirely to the house. She could pick up the baby and roam in the neighbourhood of the *katra*, or, in other words, her life became somewhat easier. She described a situation that I found recurring in many households:

> The household expenditures were all in my hands, right after the time of marriage of my elder sister. I would go to the ration shop, give them the ration book, collect the sugar in a bag and let my brother follow me with the wheat and rice on his cycle. I would clean the grain and ask him to get it ground at the *chakki* [wheel], and bring it home.

This went on till she got married at the age of 18, when naturally enough her sister-in-law or the daughter-in-law of the house took over. Here it is interesting to note that the unmarried girl in the house had greater authority than the sister-in-law who comes into the house, and this authority remains with her till she gets married. However, if a girl is married into a house with no unmarried girl, then she would be handed authority almost immediately. Here also we see that the mother-in-law does very little household work, for as she gets old enough to have her son married, a woman can safely work outside of the house and is mostly found at the corner of a lane, ironing clothes.

The young unmarried girl is most vulnerable and needs to preserve her virtue, so she stays at home and takes responsibility for the household. The daughters-in-law succeed her when she gets married and the cycle begins again. The underlying logic of this practice is, however, to be found not just within the dhobi household and *katra* but outside of it, in the inter-caste relationships and the vulnerability of jati groups located at the bottom of a ladder of inequality (Channa 2001, Chakrabarty 2003). From traditions handed down from the past, probably originating in early medieval times, the upper castes had the privilege of access to the bodies of lower-caste women. The dhobi women were particularly vulnerable, as they had to go to the client's house to pick up and deliver clothes. In fact, this practice was particularly resented by many younger dhobis, especially women, even during the early period of my work. As one woman put it,

> They will not even come down and give you the clothes. Even if one is not well, is tired or having a back ache, or if my feet are hurting and I ask

the mistress to come down with the clothes, she will just stay up and ask me to come up and collect them, and same with the delivery. People expect that you will bring the clothes and drop them in their lap. I have to keep climbing up and down stairs apart from walking to and fro with the clothes. It is very tiring and frustrating.

Add to this the possibility of sexual harassment. Given the social conditions of Old Delhi, this is an unlikely but not altogether impossible event.

The dhobis are therefore very careful about their young women, who were earlier hardly allowed to go out, except within the *katra*. It made sense to them to allow the young women to run the household and let the older women manage the outside work. In all my conversations and all my interactions, the honour of women is something that is implicitly emphasized, often comparing it with the loose morality of the urban upper classes. A moral superiority is something that is claimed by most persons belonging to the lower castes, a morality that is often denied to them by the upper castes but which forms a strong core of their identity. One may here refer to Bama's (2005) work *Sangati: Events*, which is so near the truth even in its fictionality. The elderly grandmother, widowed at an early age, boasts that no man can touch her because she has the power of being a one man's woman, one who has remained loyal to her dead husband, all her life.

In the *katra*, older women considered it their right to reprimand any young woman they thought was behaving inappropriately, telling them to walk and talk with decorum. Even elderly women, while standing for long hours in public spaces, take care to keep their body language very proper and subdued. No man is allowed to look at or behave inappropriately with them. At the same time dhobi women are very fond of gossip and fun but keep it among themselves.

In the early period of my interaction with the dhobis, I sometimes had conversations regarding marriage with some young men, and they would tell me laughingly, 'We have to marry a girl from the *biradari*, for as soon as she enters the household, she will be asked to iron clothes. After a few days she will be asked to go to the ghat to help wash clothes. How can a girl from another jati do this?' The dhobi unit of work comprises at least one man and one woman, and the conjugal unit is seen as ideally fulfilling the condition of being such a unit. Furthermore, the manner of living of the dhobis would not allow any girl from outside the cultural coding to be able to adjust to the environment, where there is a constant occupation with washing and drying clothes. It is true that in the present time some dhobis have moved out to residential units outside of the dhobi *katra* or clusters. Some of them live independently in mixed neighbourhoods where there are no clothes being washed or other dhobis living nearby. But even up to the 2020s, and at the time of writing this book, such households are very few. There is one family living in the East Delhi area, in a non-dhobi neighbourhood, and all their children are educated and employed in various jobs, while the man who heads this household owns a shop in the Old Delhi area. His wife, who was born in the dhobi *katra* and is quite used to doing dhobi work, is now a full-time housewife, and her daughter-in-law is a pampered young woman, who gets up from sleep late in the morning and wears Western clothes. While seeing her coming down from her bedroom at eleven in the morning, I was reminded of the young married women of her age living in the *katra*, who would be up at dawn, lighting their coal-fed *chullahs* and their irons, and getting ready for a long day ahead. But these young women have also become docile and conservative and spend much time in looking after their appearance and dressing up. The women who were into full-time productive work, helping their husbands, had value of their own. They never bothered about appearance and had a great deal of agency in doing work and also controlling household affairs. The young daughters-in-law in the better-off families live with their parents-in-law and to some extent follow the middle-class family norms of decorum.

In a household where the family still does dhobi work but the youngest son and daughter-in-law live with the parents, I found the daughter-in-law to be very well dressed but to cover her head in front of her father-in-law, but otherwise not to be constrained in any manner. Strict rules of *purdah* and strict rules of avoidance are disappearing from almost all middle-class families and are getting diluted in even very conventional households in Delhi, so it is not surprising that such norms do not make their appearance in a dhobi household. But what is to be noted is that in the earlier households the married women did not observe any *purdah* from anyone and lived quite independent lives. It is notable that, in the households moving away from the traditional occupation, the women are assuming more conventional roles and losing the freedom they enjoyed earlier, even though the equality of relationship between the husband and wife, a norm that has been handed down over generations, still exists. If the husband is not doing dhobi work and the wife is only doing household work, she spends a lot of time dressing up, applying nail polish, and so on. Husbands always help in household work and also in looking after children, though this task has become important only in the past few decades. The women also spend more time on ritual activities, to which we shall turn in the next chapter.

There was never any particular mealtime in the dhobi household, and the practice of eating together at a dining table is unknown among them, irrespective of their economic status. Meals are cooked about twice a day and kept for people to eat whenever they like. There is hardly any practice of serving a meal, and in earlier times the women would take the midday meal to the men, who would have left early to go to the riverbank. But nowadays the men are mostly at work at ghats near their homes, and can come and eat whenever they are hungry. A wife may or may not serve her husband, depending on the situation. Mostly people serve themselves and eat singly. A family meal is an unknown concept. A man may call upon his wife or daughter-in-law to serve him food as he is going out to work, or a woman may serve herself or be served by a daughter or daughter-in-law, but there are no fixed patterns. The dhobis have adjusted their daily routine to their work pattern, and as there is no fixity in the work pattern, there is no regularity as such in the eating of meals. There is also no sequencing as to who eats first and who next, a matter of great importance in upper-caste households, where there is always a strict patriarchal order of serving and eating meals or, as in modern-day households, everyone sits and eats at a dining table. Among the upper classes, servants often serve meals so that all family members can eat together.

As I have noted in various places, there is no overt patriarchy in the everyday life of the dhobis, as many norms such as the sequence of eating and serving food are not possible to follow. A woman may have left in a hurry with a bundle of clothes to be delivered to the clients, and her husband then has to serve himself if he is hungry. Men and women, adults and youngsters, have no pattern to follow; the only criterion is to take immediate and situational decisions depending upon the work at hand and the task to be completed. While in an upper-caste household a woman's refusal to serve her husband may become a major issue, it is of no consequence in a dhobi household. In one household, for instance, the elderly husband and wife had a fairly heated exchange, as the wife was in a hurry to leave for some ritual at a relative's place and the husband wanted to have his food first. She left in a huff, with some other women from the *katra*, leaving him to eat on his own. In a similar situation in a middle-class and upper-caste household, the wife would have had to serve her husband first before she could leave, if she could leave at all without him. This incident was observed in 2015 and not something that happened a very long time ago. In another recent incident, I was in a well-off dhobi household when the young husband came in with a shirt in his hand and asked his wife to iron it for him, as he had to go out in a hurry to deliver some clothes. The wife, while doing some other work, showed no interest in ironing his shirt, instead reprimanding him for not asking her earlier and making a din at the last moment. His mother, instead of saying anything to her daughter-in-law, also asked him to wear another shirt instead. He said that none were dry and he had to wear this one. His wife then very leisurely ironed his shirt, taking her time and paying no heed to his pleas that he was getting late.

In the 1970s and 1980s, and even in present times, the women would set up a separate household quite soon after marriage and take charge of their own households. In this situation they have a lot of control over household affairs, especially in the spending and use of money. Most men leave the running of the household to the women, a practice that is continuing over the generations. If a household was practising washing and ironing of clothes, the women were primarily engaged in the distribution of clothes to the houses and collecting the money, although it was not an essential norm. This was a task that anyone could do, including fairly small children upwards of the age of 8or so. The person who actually ran the household budget was the young girl, yet to be married but grown up, such as a teenager. Such a girl was generally neither sent to the ghat nor to iron clothes outside the house. Before the 1990s, there were few girls going to school or college, although now it has become much more prevalent. A young, ready-to-be-married girl was mostly kept at home, but being at home she took charge of the household affairs, sending her brothers off to get grocery items from the market, cleaning and taking care of household items, cooking, and so on. She would keep the household money, as it was safe with her. She also took daily decisions about what to get from the market, what to cook, and how to manage the household expenditure, while her parents were busy washing, ironing, and doing the other tasks involved in the dhobi trade, and the brothers were helping in tasks outside the house, sometimes going to school and college or doing some work in the informal sectors of the neighbourhood economy. A girl was therefore seen as indispensable to the working of the household. When she got married, her tasks were taken up by the newly married daughter-in-law, if there was any. Women began to venture outside the safety of the *katra* only after they had a few children and were seen as past the age of sexual attraction.

Demography did not always support the ideal situation of daughters being replaced by daughters-in-law. I have known households where there has been desperation at not having a daughter. One young couple were planning to go to the shrine of Vaishno Devi in the Himalayas, to pray for a daughter. In another household, comprising grown-up sons only, the father was getting desperate to get his daughter-in-law home, but her family, assessing the situation, were then demanding 5,000 rupees (an astronomical sum in the seventies) to send their daughter to her affinal home. The middle-aged mother was busy the entire day, ironing clothes. The father was busy washing clothes, and the sons were helping the father. On a visit, I found the men struggling with the cooking, trying to make a meal on their own. They seemed quite used to kitchen work, as there never had been a girl to help them, but yet they missed having a woman in the house. The father was lamenting that the parents of his daughter-in-law were adamant on the payment of cash before they would send their daughter. 'They are taking advantage of our situation,' he sighed.

At this point it is relevant to bring up the issue of marriage prestations, as Goody (1973) refers to them. Since the dhobis were at the bottom of the economic and social ladder, marriages were not a matter of exchange of wealth or gift-giving, except at the community level. Although a certain amount of bride price could be demanded, as in the case cited, it was not what always happened, although norms of the community supported bride price and not dowry. Dowry, which is widely prevalent in India among the upper castes, has been referred to as anticipated inheritance by Goody (1973), and is seen by some persons as giving share of the family wealth to daughters, who do not otherwise inherit. It is also more of an acknowledgement of the superior social status of the bride-receivers. As explained by Mayer (1960), in North India the bride-givers are seen as inferior in status to the bride-receivers, and dowry helps to compensate for the status difference, an analysis that is supported by the fact that the higher the economic and social status of the bridegroom, the higher the dowry. Many parents in North India did not wish to educate their daughters too high, as it would lead them to look for very high-status bridegrooms and consequently entail payment of a higher dowry. It is my personal knowledge that many highly educated women in the 1970sgeneration were unable to get married for such reasons. But among the lower castes this aspect is missing, as the bride-receivers belong to the same low social strata and cannot make much claim to high status. A dhobi or a scavenger or a barber, belonging to the lowest economic, social, and ritual status, can hardly make a claim to dowry, nor is there any wealth to be distributed to the offspring in such families. At the same time, a woman is an invaluable asset to the household, both as an active worker and as a reproducer of workers for the family. Keeping her value in mind, it is not considered amiss if her parents ask for some compensation for her transfer to another household. However, among the dhobis, who always lived on the edge of subsistence, such demands were rare, as most families knew the inability of the parents on either side to pay anything or give anything.

In the seventies and eighties, the marriages that I attended were more like community affairs, with the expense being shared by the larger kin group, each giving according to their ability. The aim was to provide enough to the newly married couple to be able to set up an independent household. Unlike the practice in upper-caste/class households, where the bulk of the dowry goes to the kin of the bridegroom, nothing is given to the kin here. The usual and essential gift to a bride is of an iron, some vessels for cooking (a minimum of five in number), a few pieces of jewellery, and one or two sets of clothes. But the number of gifts and expenditure had already begun to climb up by the late seventies, when the aspirations of the dhobis had begun to change.

In all Indian marriages, the gifts given by the parents and close kin are usually in the form of a generalized exchange (Sahlins 1972). People give as much as they can, and also according to the emotional or sentimental ties that they may have to the person getting married±—a favourite niece or a much-loved cousin. There is another category of gift-giving called *nyota* that comes from the guests to the wedding. This is in the form of a balanced reciprocity, and all families keep a systematic account of such gifts received. A responsible person is delegated to keep account of such gifts, a practice followed among the dhobis also. But for the dhobis, such accounting was done only for those beyond the immediate *biradari*, the location of all kinship relations. All *biradari* members are invited to all weddings, and there is again no equivalence working here, as no matter what, each will have to be invited. But there are persons coming from outside this immediate *biradari*, the ones that are dhobis but not Sheheri, others that are Sheheri but not part of the endogamous group, like the Muslim dhobis, and then there are friends, neighbours, and sometimes even clients. Although earlier such persons were negligible in number, given the low ritual and social status of the dhobis, over a period of time their numbers are increasing. Many dhobis are now in jobs and even going to college or otherwise engaged in practices that give them more exposure to people outside of the *biradari*, extending the social network of the dhobis.

A major transformation has taken place in the celebration of weddings as, following middle-class practices, the dhobis who have attained some respectable status according to their own evaluation no longer have the wedding at home. Even today the homes of the dhobis are located in crowded areas and are usually small and situated within narrow lanes and clusters of houses that are, more importantly, designated as low-caste/class areas. The weddings that I attended in the seventies and eighties took place inside these cramped quarters with no visible decorations or lights or overt signs of celebration. The only way one could tell a wedding was in progress was by the presence of a large number of people, the singing by the women, and the free flow of alcohol. There was a lot of hustle and bustle but nothing else. At best there would a small *shamiana* (awning), as permitted by the limited space available. However, from around 2000 onwards, the dhobis have begun to hire community halls in the manner of middle-class people for their weddings. These halls are lit and decorated and also located in respectable areas where people would not be reluctant to come. The rituals that are followed are copied from upper-caste marriages, such as the exchange of garlands (*mala badalna*), and also the pandit (Brahmin priest) now officiates at these weddings, possibly as they are no longer taking place inside the dhobi *katra*. The bride now goes to the parlour to get her make-up done and wears designer *lehngas* (a North Indian wedding outfit) and costume jewellery to match. The days are gone when she would be wrapped in a white sheet from head to toe and sat huddled up. Nowadays the young brides, grooms, and their friends and relatives want to capture the event on video, and the entire process is geared to being photographed, videoed, and then put on Facebook for everyone to see and share.

The weddings have now reached the public domain and they compete with the middle classes for glamour. However, the basic rituals such a *pair-pujna* (feet worship) of the bride and bridegroom are still done. In this, the bride and the groom sit next to each other, all covered in white sheets touched with yellow turmeric, and all the relatives and guests, including the parents, come and touch their feet and offer gifts. This was the main ritual done in earlier times and one by one other rituals were added as they were being copied from other castes in the neighbourhood. Even in the seventies and eighties, the rituals of garland exchange and that of going round the fire were added on. At that time, since no one knew how to do them and since there was no pandit to guide them, the situation was sometimes quite hilarious. I remember that two elders were trying to light a fire for the couple to go around and they had no idea of the *havan kund* that are used in a upper caste marriage.[3] They had got some newspapers and bits of wood and were trying to light them with matches, which kept going out, and the two elders were very drunk and unable to get the fire going. The couple finally took some kind of rounds around a fire that was hardly burning but without the chanting of mantras and the actual rituals that accompany the Hindu marriage. At present the process has been sanctified and done by the priest, who follows some though not all of the upper-caste norms of marriage. The marriages also keep the norms of respectability in mind and no alcohol or non-vegetarian food is served, both of which were a must for a dhobi marriage. The ritual of offering goats at the shrine of Nizamuddin is still followed, but quietly by the parents of the bride and the groom. Their core beliefs have not yet shifted and will be discussed later. An addition that has been made is the matching of horoscopes. The father of the girl who teaches at a Delhi college told me that he had got his daughter's horoscope matched, not once but several times: '*Aajkal janampatri milana bahut zaroori samjha jata hai. Humne to ek baar nahi kai baar milaya, alag alag pandit se'* ('Nowadays it is considered an imperative to match the horoscope of the boy and girl. I had it done for my daughter not once but several times from different pundits'). The emphasis on vegetarian food and not serving alcohol has also been done keeping in mind that people from different castes will also attend the wedding. If the boy and girl are educated, their friends from college are expected to come, and if they are working, colleagues from the workplace would also come. As the circle of relations is widening, the norms of acceptability are being consciously imbibed, and this acceptability is in terms of the norms set by the upper castes.

With respect to the extension of social networks, it is significant that the untouchable and low status of the dhobi has not yet changed completely. I have, for example, almost never seen a person not of a dhobi *biradari* visiting a dhobi in their house, but I have seen a few persons visiting dhobi friends at the ghats, at public spaces, as at a wedding, or at a public ritual. There is a qualitative difference in visiting someone at their home, where one is expected to partake of refreshments and drink water and tea, if not to have a meal. Such intimacy is rarely indulged in by people of upper castes. But at a wedding or a ritual, which takes place in a public space, and where food is cooked on a large scale by a professional caterer, people outside of the *biradari* may take part, although these are few in number even to the present day. When I began my fieldwork, there was a lot of surprise about my not only coming and sitting inside their houses but also accepting food and water, to the extent that I was often asked about my jati, and sometimes also asked if I was a Christian, as I did not exhibit any caste-based restrictions. It is also pertinent that the dhobis themselves believe in jati restrictions, and while they have very cordial relations with the Muslim dhobis, they do not eat or drink at their houses or even at their weddings. They would also not wash the clothes of those they consider lower than their jati, for example the scavenger-caste groups. Over the years a significant change has been the withdrawal of social interactions with the Muslim dhobis, although it has not disappeared altogether.

Marriages were always negotiated within the *biradari*. Since the *biradari* is not a very large unit, generations of marriages within a small circle have linked practically all members of the *biradari* in multiple ties to other members. Most persons in the *biradari* know each other, or, one might put it, *everyone* in the *biradari* is aware of the others. So potential matches for their wards are known to most people, but the issue is of arranging the marriage. There are designated relatives, who are known as *bicholia* (mediators), which category includes the father's sister's husband and the sister's husband. The choice of an affine as a *bicholia*, instead of a kin, is that if a person who is already married into a family gives a good opinion about them, then it is more likely to be genuine than that of a blood kin, who will try to hide the flaws.

Since all marriages had to take place within the *biradari*, there was always a limited choice. The dhobis and other lower castes never had child marriages like upper castes, and most girls were married earlier in the immediate postcolonial period, on which I have data, from the age of 9to 16, and boys from the age of 15to 20. In present times the age at marriage has changed in the natural course following general norms. There is also the additional factor of education, since most girls and boys are going to school and some are going to college. Yet all dhobis expect that all marriages will take place within the *biradari*. At the same time unheard of practices like the consultation of horoscopes is entering their community. There was a time when I could not get people to answer a question as to what was their age. But nowadays, with the practice of everyone mandated to have a birth certificate and the compulsory entry of date of birth for school admissions, they are aware of their age and date of birth and are even celebrating birthdays.

In the early 2020s, doing fieldwork, I found that several households of dhobis, even doing traditional work, have taken giant leaps towards a middle-class lifestyle, now living in a way that was not seen at all during the 1970sor 1980s. The household of Rajeev, who caters to a hotel client in Paharganj, is one such example. Their clothes are washed at Malka Ganj and he employs dhobi boys who are migrants. His house was a joint household consisting of his ageing parents and his wife, and also other brothers and their wives. It was a large apartment on the first floor of a building, and had a spacious living room with all modern amenities like a large refrigerator, television, sofa sets, and other furniture. The women were housewives here, and while Rajeev did go to the ghat, the women were staying at home and not ironing clothes. On the day when I visited their house at around noon, Rajeev was just going out on his motorcycle and had a bundle of clothes with him to be delivered. He told me he would go to the Malka Ganj ghat for about two or three hours and then leave for Paharganj. His work consisted mainly of collecting, distributing, and negotiating deals. The actual washing was done by the servants hired by him. Here we see an emerging internal hierarchy, that of the ghat owners and original residential dhobis of Delhi and the poor migrant worker dhobis who are mostly exploited as servants.

I have also been to Rajeev's father's brother's house across the street. This family had moved here from Kucha Pati Ram, after it was demolished, the only dhobi *katra* to have suffered that fate. This apartment was equally spacious with a wide veranda where a middle-aged woman was ironing clothes and a young married woman in a T-shirt and trousers was sitting in a chair nearby. The older woman told me that this was her married daughter who had come to visit her but was now relaxing in her casual clothes. This was again among the few times that I had seen a married woman wearing Western clothes, but now it was in her mother's house, who told me indulgently, 'if she cannot be comfortable in her own mother's house, where else she can be? At her in-laws' place she must wear a *saree* and cover her head.' Kamla, the woman ironing clothes, told me she has six daughters and a son. The son, being eldest, is married and lives separately. The daughter told me that she had studied till class twelve when her father got her married, but her sisters are studying in college. I enquired from the woman as to why she was allowing her two daughters to study in college but did not allow this one to do so. She told me that the two younger ones had protested that they did not wish to marry before they finished their studies; they said, '*kuch karke dikhana hai*' ('we wish to do something worth showing').

Out of her six daughters, the first three are married; the one sitting there was the third daughter. The three younger ones were studying. Her only son was also studying, and the parents did not want him to do the dhobi work. So, then I asked her as to why not. Was the dhobi work not paying enough? She told me that it was not about money but about the hard work involved. When I asked the daughter as to whether she could also iron clothes like her mother, she said yes, she could. In turn I asked the mother if she was going to let her daughter help her, so she said no, she has come to her mother's house to rest, so she was not going to make her work. All her three sons-in-law do not do dhobi work: the husband of the girl present was working as a shop assistant in Chawri Bazar and another son-in-law worked in a medicine shop in Chandni Chowk, all within the vicinity of Old Delhi. In this household, the parents, Kamla, and her husband were still doing the dhobi work on a full-time basis. They had a washing area on the terrace and water storage tanks, which they filled with the help of a pump. They also hired migrant workers to help them. Those helpers were not dhobi by caste, but they taught them from a young age, so they learnt. She was continuously ironing clothes as she talked to me and these were ready-made clothes to be delivered to a shop in Chandni Chowk.

Kamla had experienced *katra* life and agreed that the *biradari* ties were very strong in the *katra*, where women looked after each other's children and helped each other in many ways. According to her, 'In the earlier days, mothers had no anxiety in leaving even babies behind and going to the *ghats*.' With a show of resentment, she added, 'But now most of the *ghats* have been demolished by the "Sarkar"[government], who broke them to no purpose; they are just lying idle now, of no use to anyone.' Her resentment at the breaking of ghats is echoed by many other dhobis who are critical of the *sarkar* (state), and it also indicates the awareness that collectives at the bottom like the dhobis have about their lack of voice in decision-making.

As mentioned earlier, most households among the dhobis are of the nuclear type. There are a few exceptional households like that of the sons of Suraj, who was the owner of a dry-cleaning shop, and he had married two wives, as the first wife did not have any children. This too was an exception among the dhobis, where no such incidence of bigamy was known, before or after this case. Suraj was the only son of Bulakhi Ram, who was the panchayat head when I began my research work. When his first wife did not have any children, he married again and the second wife had four children, two boys and two girls. I used to note with a degree of surprise how the two wives lived in great harmony with each other. When Suraj passed away leaving quite young children, his elder wife, the one without children, began to sit in the shop, and the younger wife, who was the biological mother, stayed at home to keep house and look after the children. In 2015 I visited their new home in Chippibara, which is close to the *katra* where they had lived originally. This household comprised two older women (co-wives), and their two married sons with their wives and grandchildren. Everyone appeared organized under the authority of the oldest woman. The apartment that they now occupied was on the second floor of an apartment building occupied by people of various kinds, not a dhobi cluster. It was like a middle-class home, with sofa set, television, and refrigerator, items that I now found in practically every dhobi household, quite a far cry from the earlier homes with no doors, a cooking area outside, and mud floors. The older mother was sitting on the sofa wearing a gown (the only time I have seen a dhobi woman wearing a gown), and she had well-plucked eyebrows and painted nails that looked like they had been manicured in a salon.

This family had always been upwardly mobile; in the seventies, the eldest daughter of Suraj used to attend St Anthony's school in Paharganj, a Christian school catering to the lower classes. But now his two grand-daughters attend Presentation Convent, an upper-class convent school for girls for well-to-do families. Suraj's elder daughter had done her Master's and was now married to a businessman who makes wedding cards—a very lucrative business. The younger daughter was good at her studies, did an MBA, became an entrepreneur, and now runs her own business. She is married outside of the *biradari* to a brahmin boy who is a chef in Bombay (I was informed by another dhobi that he is a Bengali). She lives in a middle-class locality, drives her own car, and lives a life completely away from the *biradari*. However, she has close relations with her own family, her mothers, and siblings. The eldest woman's brother's son gained admission into AIIMS and is now a medical doctor. He is the highest qualified person in the *biradari*. This particular household can be taken as an example of the maximum social mobility that has taken place among the dhobis. Yet even here the members retain their ties to the *biradari*. The younger mother's brother lives in a nearby *katra* in Farash Khana and is a dhobi who stands by the roadside ironing clothes. His son was married to the daughter of another dhobi, my earliest contact in the biradari, Omi Pehlwan. It is also true that while the younger generation have broken away from dhobi work, most of their closest relatives are still working as dhobis.

One primary reason for all marriages to be confined to the biradari is that no upper-caste family will give their daughter into a family where most members are into the washing and ironing of clothes. A dhobi girl, on the other hand, can be accommodated into another caste group if she moves away and does not keep up too close relations with her extended family. There is also the unwritten rule of hypergamy that works in all Indian marriages. In more traditional times, it was known as the rule of *anuloma* (in the direction of the hair), a form approved by the ancient texts. According to the rules prescribed in Manusmriti, a man from a higher caste could legitimately marry a woman from a lower caste, but the opposite, *pratiloma* (against the hair), was not prescribed. Women from upper castes could not marry below themselves. In later times, when marriages became confined to one's own jati, this rule was reinterpreted in terms of the status of the bride's house and the groom's house. By the rules of hypergamy a dhobi girl could marry into a upper caste but a dhobi man could not hope to do the same. As of now I have found no exception to this rule in the marriages that have taken place in the dhobi *biradari*.

Another upwardly mobile household was that of a person who owned a tyre shop, as I mentioned earlier. I had attended his son Kishan's wedding in the seventies, and his wife was the sister of a woman who is at present the highest qualified girl in the *biradari*. While Kishan continued the family business, his younger brother became a director in the Sports Authority of India (SAI), and the youngest brother, Kanhaiya, was also doing business. Although this family was fairly wealthy, they have all married into the *biradari*. Several families now have educated children, and educated boys are able to get educated wives.

However, in all the upwardly mobile households, the women do all the household work, which is quite contrary to upper-caste and middle-class households in India, where having servants is the norm. Sheetal (the assistant professor), who has to leave for her college in the morning, comes home and makes the evening meal. Before leaving for her college, she cleans the house as well as the vessels and kneads dough for the morning meal. Her mother-in-law washes the clothes. This is the daily routine, although there can be minor changes on certain days. At the level of their jati, it was probably inconceivable that the household work be done by servants, although several of them have started to employ migrant labour as servants for washing clothes. Here the gender difference becomes apparent. While the men's work can be delegated, the woman's work is not seen like that. Women continue to do whatever they were doing earlier, even if they are educated and are even working outside the home, like Sheetal.

Changing Identities

It must be understood that in the decades following independence of the country, when democratic values were being permeated throughout society, the dhobis had an idea that there were things they could do other than dhobi work, but they still could not imagine that they could do what the upper castes/classes were doing. Till the seventies, they were participating in the thriving commercial urban space in which they were located, but only in fringe and low-grade occupations that did not require many skills or professional training. They also had an aversion to working in a formal set-up, in an 'office' as they put it. The only alternative occupations conceivable for them were to become minor sales assistants in neighbourhood shops, to be in the paper cutting and bookbinding business, or to become an apprentice to a motor mechanic—and at best to get a petty job in any informal-sector occupation.

They looked up at their clients, the *babus* and *sahibs*, and rarely thought that they could be like them. Not only was there no aspiration, there was actually no desire. Most dhobis did not even think that they could do anything else; they were destined to be dhobis and they had to do the best in that situation. But in the years after independence, when there was a gradual spread of education among all sections of the population, a slow awareness about a possible change was coming about. But it has taken more than five decades at least for a significant change in mindset and attitudes.

In the seventies, when I talked to the older generations, they were sceptical about any major change in occupation. There was the realization about limited resources, the daily struggles to survive, the little time they could spare from the work that they had in hand, and also doubts as to what else they could do. Most dhobis, both then and today, are not happy to be working for someone else. The idea of doing a job under anyone's authority does not appeal to them. The most common narrative was, 'We do not like to slave for others. We like to live independent lives. Even a frugal meal, *do roti* (literally two wheat cakes) are enough for us, if we can have them in peace.' As already mentioned, the dhobi worldview places them in a very different cognitive dimension than what their clients think. A dhobi considers himself to be in control of his work and of the clothes that he gets for washing and ironing, till such time as they are delivered. There is a sense of ownership that is lacking in working for others. Rather than getting educated and taking up a white-collar job, most dhobis aspired to a dry-cleaning shop of their own, or even to have some independent enterprise.

In the dhobi household, there is little hierarchy, and very little control is exerted on the children, who are mostly left to do as they please. An adult will shout at them if they are seen to be destructive or get in the way of their elders' work, but there are no instructions on decorum or on controlling their activities. All the while I spent sitting around in the dhobi *katra*, there was little attempt to socialize the children in any particular way. They grew up watching each other and the adults. Most parents had little time to spend with their children, who were left to raise themselves. Yet community living made most of them well behaved, and the young adults are polite and well spoken. The dhobi work requires constant interaction with others, presumably of higher status, and from whom the dhobi expects to earn a living. For this reason, most dhobi adults, men or women, are non-aggressive and follow norms of appropriate behaviour. This was a major factor in making my research easy, as few would turn me away or behave rudely. Although on a few occasions I have met hostility, these have been very rare. Most persons are ready to talk and give information, and many took me into their houses, offering me food, water, and refreshments, giving me a place to rest on a hot day and treating me with affection and care.

The dhobi–client relationship and adjustment form a key aspect of the dhobi way of life and play an important role in deciding what kind of a person a dhobi man or woman is, and even their political ideology. The dhobis have never found themselves outside of the society that surrounds them, yet they have always felt discriminated against. Their mode of adjustment, as I have been describing throughout, is to present a face, appear to be compliant, but in the end do what they want to do.

They have always been made to feel that they are low down the social scale and that they will not be accepted, even if they get educated or do a good job. For example, parents of schoolgoing children, in the 1970sand surprisingly even much later, almost to present times, reported that their children are discriminated against in schools and colleges, treated as outsiders to the mainstream and looked down upon. The teachers in class mostly ignore them or treat them too harshly. There are many stereotypes about the dhobi that prevent their easy movement in society outside of their *katras*. Some dhobi parents of schoolgoing children complained to me that the teachers would tell their wards that 'they did not look like dhobis'. 'What does looking like a dhobi mean?' 'Does every lower caste have to look like Babu Jagjivan Ram?'[4]

Here comes a very important dimension of dhobi identity, and that of all lower castes, originating from misinformation concocted and popularized during the colonial period by what has since come to be known as 'race science' (Trautmann 1997, Channa 2011). Such was the power of the colonial hierarchy that not only upper-caste Indians but to a large extent even the lower castes accepted this formulation, giving rise to the stereotype of the dark, broad-nosed lower-caste person. At the same time the dhobis are quite aware of both the process of stereotyping and the fact that negative physical appearance is fictional and not substantiated by reality, seen in the actual looks of the members of the *biradari*. Here it is also pertinent to mention that the dhobis who were more exposed to the dominant culture, such as those who had gone to school and college, were more likely to know about and even to accept the stereotypes. For those not so exposed, matters of physical appearance were largely unimportant, as physical looks rarely played a role in the traditional jati-based values that guided caste and *biradari* interactions. A dhobi who had gone to college was among those who often mentioned physical appearance, for example; while referring to a young man, employed as a computer software engineer in a private company, he mentioned that the tall and smart-looking young person 'did not look like he was from the dhobi community'. However, I have rarely heard any person, who is not educated or doing the caste-based occupation, mention any such appearance-based stereotype, and most people had no particular cognition about the aesthetics of appearance, something that seems to have seeped into the indigenous cultures more with market-based values and only after the 1990s with the liberalization of the economy (Channa 2011).

Within the jati-based society, norms of jati have always been more important than what one looks like. As one of my close dhobi friends told me, 'They spend 30,000 to 40,000 rupees on what they call "bridal make-up"; what is the use of it? As soon as the girl washes her face, all the make-up is washed away, and all the money too is gone. It is better the parents put that money in a fixed deposit for the girl to use later.' A person grew up more conscious of where he or she belonged in society in terms of caste and class than any other criteria. It is only in the last few decades that personal appearance and other acquired characteristics like education and economic status are gaining priority in the formation of a person's identity, yet jati still plays a critical role. Even for people in public places the first criterion of identity that is pointed out is the jati—that is, the caste and the region to which the person belongs in conjunction with their religious identity. In everyday conversations, in terms of constant evocation, jati remains at the forefront of cognition with respect to identity, even though in many contexts it may have ceased to be a criterion for interaction or practical aspects of action. For example, while travelling on public transport or eating out in a restaurant, many persons may not care who is travelling along with them or who has cooked the food they are eating, but in more intimate contexts it has not ceased to matter. Even in schools and colleges, in hostels and barracks, jati discrimination remains alive to a large extent. Since there is still prevalence of a more or less coeval occurrence of caste and class, there is little likelihood of untouchables entering into the social circle of upper castes, except when it comes to government jobs that carry reservation.

As I have described elsewhere (Channa 2005), caste discrimination is pervasive at a symbolic level, and is particularly resented at the levels of more coveted jobs and high-status positions, as in the medical profession. There have been many cases of panchayat heads being killed for being untouchables, as the upper castes find it almost intolerable to accept a person of lower caste in a superior status. People in offices are highly resentful, although perhaps not openly, of a low-caste boss, especially if the person happens to be a scheduled caste. The present generation of dhobis, many of whom have done well in life, are holding different kinds of jobs, are sometimes earning well, and have found out that they will remain dhobi, no matter what they do. As told to me by Rishi, the young man with a flourishing business in antiques, 'it is the *biradari* that matters in the long run'. It is the dhobi identity that dominates their way of life, their aspirations, and their future as they see it. What they are today aspiring to is not to break away from their identity but to be accepted as dhobis, but with dignity. As Roy (2022: 6) says aptly, 'Today the poor, the marginalized and the minorities have begun to imagine themselves through their own eyes. Dignity issues have acquired a new salience'.

Notes

1. The untouchable and marginalized caste groups are entered into a government schedule for the purpose of positive discrimination and are therefore commonly referred to as Scheduled Castes (SCs). For most official purposes the term SC is affixed to the name of a person who belongs in this category. The reservation policy is applied for admission to institutions of higher education and also for government jobs.
2. The family planning slogan very popular at that time was 'Hum Do, Hamare Do', meaning that husband and wife are two so they should have two children; two for two.
3. A *havan kund* is a copper vessel shaped in a specific way used for lighting a sacred fire in various rituals.
4. Babu Jagjivan Ram was the first person of an untouchable caste group to rise to the rank of a cabinet minister in the first ever cabinet of independent India. A highly qualified lawyer, he was very dark in complexion and had thick set features with a bulbous nose.

5

Negotiating Power in the Realm of the Sacred

Scholars like Scott (1985) and De Certeau (1984) have analysed the ways in which the ordinary person, the anti-hero, the one not glorified, deals with the problems of everyday life, the oppressions and marginalization through negotiating, manoeuvring, dodging, and confronting. For the powerless, there is the power of contra-culture, of subversive movements, of situational wins, withdrawals, and silences. In De Certeau's terms, 'Many everyday practices are tactical in nature.'(1984: xvii); and so are, more generally, the many ways of operating the little ingenuities of everyday life that make possible the victories of the weak over the strong. Weak and strong are definable in many ways in many situations. The weak can be those who are left voiceless or without material resources. The strong entity can be the people who have a voice; it can be the dominant and imposed order, the enforced rules, the coercive mechanisms of forcing compliance, or all of them. The weak often use the power of strategy and manipulation in lieu of overt power and the use of force. The dhobis have been using several such practices and tactics with the world outside, with the hierarchies of the jati system, with the external political order, the '*sarkar*' (Mathur 2016: 22–3) with all its polysemic connotations, the market with its dictates and coercions, and the clients with whom they have an overtly dependent yet subversively controlling relationship. But then there are also the intimate relations within the family and the kin group, the *biradari*, and the social networks of which they are a part. Finally, there is the sacred, the powers beyond the human realm, beyond the material world and the instrumental relations of jati, family, and occupation. Each is dealt with and negotiated in its own way and in its own context. 'Religion of the oppressed is a means to articulate their dreams for freedom. God is the congealed will of the people who cannot

Dhobis of Delhi. Subhadra Mitra Channa, Oxford University Press. © Subhadra Mitra Channa 2024.
DOI: 10.1093/9780198926238.003.0006

afford to exert their own sovereignty against those who monopolize the forces of repression' Prashad (2000: 64).

The two major external sources of power are, firstly, the superhuman, the gods and deities of the dhobis, and, secondly, of course the political, the order to which they are subjected as members of the state and of local political bodies. The first of these will be taken up in this chapter.

The Ala and the Sufi Influence

During my initial contact with the dhobis I was somewhat mystified by the presence of a small alcove in every home where, in the evening, a small earthen lamp was lit. Any senior member of the household would light the lamp and fold his or her hands in prayer. I had met an elderly woman, from Sita Ram Bazar, the grandmother of a young man now working as a web designer who was happy to recall the old days with me, and when I mentioned the Ala, she said that yes, they would fold their hands before it early in the morning before getting down to work. Her daughter-in-law, however, did not acknowledge any such activity and said that they hardly had time for performing that small ritual at the Ala. The elderly woman told me that the Ala was their only sacred place before, and that they never heard of so many *devi*, *devta*, and *puja* as are happening now: 'Now people are worshipping Ganesh, even dhobis are bringing in Ganesh idols to worship at home.' In the seventies, apart from the Ala, I did not find any shrine, temple, or place for prayer in the crowded homes of the dhobis, where even an inch of space was a luxury. The walls were always plastered with pictures, mostly cut out from old calendars or bought during Deepavali, of various Hindu gods and goddesses.

From the beginning of my work, I observed that the dhobis were visiting Hindu shrines like Vaishno Devi, having Devi *jagarans*, and so on. But being untouchables and lower-caste, they did not have access to the ritual paraphernalia of the upper castes and, most importantly, to the services of the Brahmins. In the Hindu jati and Varna hierarchy (Channa 2018a), only the twice-born jatis belonging to the first three Varna are entitled to the services of the Brahmins for their life cycle rituals such as birth, marriage, and death. The last is very important, as Hindus place considerable weight on the right performance of death rituals considered essential for the soul to go on its right path, including getting a proper rebirth. By denying the services of the Brahmins to the lower castes, the upper castes believe that they retain their dominance to a point even after death, but the lower castes almost never subscribe to this hegemonic ideology and engage in active protest by seeking out alternate divinities that they identify as their protectors. Mohan Sanal and Joel Lee (2022) have pointed out that, rather than subscribe to any particular religion, the marginal or Dalit groups selectively engage with *all* available traditions in South Asia, what they refer to as 'restlessly critical and heterodox', where they choose some elements, reject others, and modify the chosen ones according to their own needs and worldview. As an example, Channa (2005b) has described how a pastoral nomadic community reinterprets and absorbs particular elements of the Hindu epic Mahabharata and also their eclectic mix of rural Hindu, Buddhist, and Bon beliefs (Channa 2013d). In a classic work Spiro had described the cosmology of the rural Burmese (Spiro 1967) and very pointedly described it as the 'explanation and reduction of suffering'. For most marginal groups with little resources, religion comes as a possible succour, a cathartic experience to overcome some of the sufferings that they are always subject to.

The dhobis have been attracted to those sects or worldviews that have been critical of established hierarchical religions such as Sufism, the dangerous as well as protective deities of Hinduism such as Bhairava, and their own divinities, who help them in projecting an independent identity, such as Baba Nagar Sain. Till about the 1990s, the most pervasive influence observed among them was that of Sufism. The lower castes of North India, like the dhobis and the sweepers, had cultural elements that appear Islamic at least by their use of language and symbols.[1] They are also largely followers of Sufi saints and cults, possibly as a result of rejection by upper-caste Hindus and the absence of Brahmin functionaries. Prashad (2000: 104) has written: 'Earlier the Churhas offered lamps in small alcoves to the Pir Bala Shah but in the 1920s, the shrine was changed to a Valmiki temple.' It is relevant to point to a difference between the Churhas and the dhobis, with the former always oriented towards a public space and collective actions and the latter towards individual actions, although they also share workspace. Instead of having one Sufi shrine for the entire community, the dhobis had and still have alcoves in each house individually.

The Sufi consolidated in India around the twelfth and thirteenth centuries (Dehlvi 2010: 158), at about the same period as the Bhakti movement. While Brahmanical Hinduism privileged the upper castes, and by default the upper classes, the heterodox sects of both Hindus and Muslims gave space to the marginalized to express their religious sentiments and aspirations. The Sufi movement was based on the notion of devotion and surrender to the divinity and did not involve any elaborate rituals or dictates from the clergy. It also rejected all forms of organized religion and their hierarchical institutions. As already shown in earlier chapters, the dhobis tend to be individualistic because of the nature of their work. Up to the 1990stheir core beliefs and rituals centred on the shrine of Nizamuddin Aulia (Dehlvi 2010: 184), a Sufi saint revered equally by Hindus and Muslims. It sealed the bonds between them and their Muslim counterparts, who, like the Hindu dhobis, were placed at the bottom of the caste hierarchy among the Muslims. Being equally marginalized, both Hindu and Muslim dhobis found solace in a common place of worship, a platform which facilitated cooperation and solidarity. The marginalized had no need to visit any temple or mosque; they only needed to light a lamp in an alcove and express the devotion in their hearts. As Prashad (2000: 66) articulates, 'Both Sufism (in the idea of *Fana* or nothingness) and the Bhakti tradition (personal devotion) offer two powerful devices which were well developed in the collective love of the Dalits.'

Over the years the practice of offering a lamp at the Ala has become covert rather than been given up by the Hindu dhobis. Even in 2023, a senior dhobi informed me that they still offer worship at the Ala. As he said with folded hands and in a serious tone, '*Miya ko chadava nahi dene se, nahi manne se bahut nuksan ho ja sakta hai. Sab kuch barbad ho jayega*' ('If one ignores Miyan, then there can be a disaster, the person can be ruined'). The person who told me this is overtly a devout Hindu who has an organization devoted to Balaji (Hanuman) and goes regularly to visit the Balaji shrine in Rajasthan. He has a big and ornate temple conspicuously situated in his house but has the Ala, kept inside, carefully out of sight but deeply revered. Gradually, while talking to others, I found out that worship at the Ala has not been given up but only made less overt. The dhobis still believe strongly in the power of the Ala or the spirits it represents, the Miyan. There are two of them; one is older, married, and known as

Badsha Miyan, and the other is younger, unmarried, and known as Nanhe Miyan. When I asked the Muslim dhobis, they too told me that only went to the mosque and not to the shrine of Nizamuddin. Again, I could not verify if this was true or that they had just made it covert like the Ala of the Hindus. On the face of it, the Hindu and Muslim dhobis have begun to drift apart overtly towards more organized religious activities, although at the ghats they still share a cordial relationship. While I know that the Hindus still cherish the earlier Sufi deities, although more surreptitiously, I could not find out about the Muslim dhobi situation in actuality. In the last few decades, religious performances have been affected by the increasing drift between religious communities at a much higher level than the *biradari*—at the pan-Indian level. These changes can be traced to both the consolidation of a Hindutva ideology at the centre (Narayan 2021) and increasing economic prosperity accompanied by a need for status elevation in wider society. Although the dhobis do not overtly subscribe to a Hindutva ideology, they have realized that to gain respectability they must assert a Hindu identity rather than one merged with that of the Muslims. The gradual shift towards Hindu ritualistic behaviour is stimulated more by a desire for social recognition than a change in religious sentiments.

As I have described, considerable renovations were done in the houses and *katras* of the dhobis as a consequence of the economic boom in 1992 triggered by the liberal policies of the Manmohan Singh-led Congress government. With prosperity came exposure to various market goods and also to media such as television, and now computers, which colonized most homes. At present it will be nearly impossible to find a house without television, whereas in the 1970s there were practically none. Watching goods flooding the market and being exposed to many kinds of ideas from television, people began to make changes in their homes. With new ideas about good living, the walls were plastered and painted, and in many houses the Ala was either filled up and a wall almirah built over it, or it was converted to a Hindu temple and images of deities put inside it, or it was simply filled in and painted over. The practice of lighting a lamp in the Ala has been replaced by the performance of a daily *puja* in the manner of upper-caste Hindus. The elaborate and ornate shrines that one finds now in almost every home are most likely copied from television and the internet. But although the Ala has disappeared from public view, it is still retained in many houses in another form, mostly as a wooden alcove that is placed near the door or in some other inconspicuous place. It is made its annual offerings at harvest time, during the month of March. The offerings are in the form of fresh grains, fruits, and sweets made at home, known as *gulgule* and *bajra* (millet) *rotis*. At their core the dhobis continue with their strong beliefs in the sacred beings they have inherited from their forefathers. If you ask them, they say, '*yeh to pehle se chala aa raha hai*' ('it is continuing from earlier times') or '*hamesha se hota hai*' ('this was always done'). But what is important is the strength of their belief and their conviction that things can go terribly wrong if the Miyan are not kept appeased. Such sentiments are not attached to any Hindu deity, no matter how much they profess to revere them.

As described by Kapadia (1995), the lower castes and untouchables, being denied the ritualistic performances of upper castes, resort to what may be called devotional religious practices, which involve a degree of abandonment. To the untouchable Pallars studied by Kapadia, the devotion or *bakti* (*bhakti*) was a superior form of getting closer to the divinity than the mechanically performed rituals of the Brahmins, illustrating another form of subaltern critique. The Pallars were of the opinion that Brahmins do things elaborately and logically, whereas the lower castes are spontaneous and do things from the heart. The dhobis were living in a city dominated by Muslims and Muslim clients, and therefore a Sufi shrine was a natural place for them, more so as they were not barred from it by being Hindus (Srivastava 2009: 218); rather, they were denied entry into Hindu temples. The dhobis still follow the practice of the offering of a goat, one in the name of the bride and another in the name of the groom, at the Nizamuddin shrine on the occasion of a wedding. At times they make such offerings on other occasions also, such as the birth of a child or the fulfilment of a *mannat* (vow).

Eclectic Rituals and Gods of Justice

The Ala and Hazrat Nizamuddin did not draw boundaries around the ritual activities of the dhobis or their strategies to manipulate and reach out to the superhuman powers. There was always a greatly felt need to seek help from divine sources, as the earthly sources were both limited as well as restricted for them. In this sense they were making eclectic use of various sources of divinity, as pointed out by Mohan and Lee (2022). Devi *jagarans*, all-night vigils in praise of the mother goddess, have always been popular, especially in North India. From the seventies I knew of small bands of men among the dhobis, known locally as *mandali*, who were specialized in these performances, which require a few instrumentalists, such as a *dhol* (drum) beater, a harmonium player, a vocalist, and some other accompanist like a flute or cymbal player. In one band that I knew, the harmonium player was a Muslim, but this is a common occurrence, and many instrumentalists that accompany religious singing in India are Muslims. Again, not everyone in the band was a dhobi, but as I have mentioned (Channa 1985: 93) they were usually of the low and even untouchable castes; for example, there was a Khatik, a dhobi, and a Muslim in one band, but the presence of a person of a higher caste was most unlikely. Ritual activities like a *jagaran* (all-night vigil) are part of the folk or 'little' traditions (Redfield 1955) of Hinduism or even popular culture, situated far away from Brahmanical Hinduism. With the emphasis on *bhakti* and on the casting away of restraints, they also mock the rigour and solemnity of Brahmanical rituals. Earlier, such performances never involved any Brahmin priests, but in more recent times some upper-caste households may include a priestly ritual in a *jagaran*, usually as part of a larger celebration like a wedding.

The *jagaran* is part entertainment and part a religious affair. The devotional songs are mostly parodies of popular Bollywood tunes and are more conducive to foot-tapping than to transcendence. For the participants, however, these are all very authentic, and high emotions may be triggered during these performances, in the manner of the 'setting of moods' described by Geertz (1973). The performance always begins in a slow rhythm, with soft and lilting music at the beginning, and gradually gains tempo as the night goes on and people need to be kept awake. The *jagaran* is always a public performance, located in an open area. All over Delhi, it is a common sight to see roads blocked, awnings put up, chairs neatly arranged in rows, and a stage with an image of the goddess put up to mark the performance of a *jagaran*. The bright lights, the popular music, the theatrical performances that accompany the singing, and also the chance to let go, to let one's restrictions down, are an attractive proposition for the housebound women, the lower castes, the poor, and the lower middleclass. Quite often the *jagaran* is accompanied by some *prasad*, and even dinner. There is always a horde of ragged children and local pariah dogs thronging the venues, who stay up all night to get some titbits to eat.

Within the walled city, the dhobi *jagarans* usually took place inside a *katra*, and there was little likelihood of people from other jatis joining in, though some immediate neighbours might. Otherwise, they took place in a public park or, as already mentioned, by cordoning off a street. The *jagaran*, as its description suggests, cannot be an exclusively *biradari* affair, and public participation is never discouraged or prohibited; yet in the local neighbourhoods the identity of the person or persons sponsoring the *jagaran* is always known, and most upper castes would not attend a *jagaran* sponsored by a dhobi. In fact, although dhobis act as members of the *jagaran mandalis*, it is not very often that a dhobi household actually sponsors a *jagaran*. In the seventies and eighties, the matter was not just one of money but also of the social sanction for organizing a public ritual event. Around this time, most dhobis were living at the edge of penury; the overall pattern was to get some money on a daily basis and spend it on food and absolute bare necessities. There was hardly anything left for ceremonial expenditures, and all necessary life cycle rituals were celebrated in a low-key way and with participation and contribution from the extended kin network that overlapped to a very large extent with the *biradari*. At that time no dhobi would think of sponsoring a *jagaran* individually. However, by around 2010, some dhobis had begun to sponsor their own *jagarans*, and I attended the first of these sponsored entirely by a dhobi family in 2016, but in a place outside of Old Delhi. In 2023, my informant, who is a college teacher, mentioned that her husband's grandmother (Mother's Mother) had set up a *jagaran* for Kali Mata (the dark goddess) in Old Delhi, and that she was attending it. The fact that dhobis were sponsoring *jagarans* within the heart of Old Delhi also speaks to a significant social transformation; another is the choice of Kali, a predominantly East Indian deity.

The identity of the deity being worshipped is both a matter of dissemination of information and an assessment about their own needs. Earlier, the dhobis had little exposure to any form of deities except those that were talked about by their neighbours and those that existed in their vicinity. The fact that they rarely consider those in their immediate neighbourhood as their patron deities also says something about their exclusion. The deity closest to their Old Delhi *katras* was that of the Lakshmi Narayan temple in Chandni Chowk, a place that has never been mentioned as one where they go regularly or at all. Nor is this upper-caste/class deity ever mentioned by them, indicating that in the past they were not allowed to enter this temple and now they have probably taken it off their itinerary. They are more likely to pick on something that does not belong to their earlier landscape and certainly not to their upper-caste local *grahaks* (clients). The Ala and the *jagarans* were the most predominant form of ritual performed for the divine during the seventies and continuing more or less into the eighties. The nineties, with economic liberalization, marked a turning point. This was also the time of demographic movements. People came to Delhi from rural areas and other states that were relatively backward in economic terms for the booming job market and greater opportunities in the informal sector, including the work of the dhobis. They also brought their rituals and deities with them. Growing up in Delhi, I had never seen a Ganesh Puja being celebrated or Chhath Puja performed on the banks of the river Yamuna. But in present times, with the large influx of people from other parts of India, local rituals from their regions are becoming popular even among the people of Delhi. In the decades leading up to the twenties, I have seen several persons from among the dhobis celebrating Ganesh Puja.[2] The dhobis have taken to it because, again like a *jagaran*, it can be celebrated by anyone and in any space. One need not go to a temple or holy place, nor take the help of a Brahmin to do it. The agency to have one's own celebration and the fact that no one can either socially or legally stop anyone from such celebration are encouraging more and more marginal communities like the dhobis to carry on such ceremonial statements, which provide a language that means that 'we can also do it'.

There are, however, specific local deities that they feel are closer to them, especially those that are not popular with the upper castes. One of them is the shrine of Bhairon at the Old Fort;[3] there are two Bhairon images at this shrine, the second being of Kilkari Bhairon, to whom liquor is offered. Legend has it that the Bhairon temple was built by the Pandavas, especially linking it to the second of the brothers, Bhima, known for his exceptional strength and his marriage to the demoness Hidimba.[4] I was told that many dhobis go regularly to the shrine of the Kilkari Bhairon, especially on a Sunday when the liquor that is offered to the deity is also distributed as a *prasad*. It is the alcohol angle that prevents many upper castes from visiting this otherwise venerated shrine. But for the dhobi, the alcohol-drinking Bhairon appears to be a close kin and they enjoy both the worship and the *prasad*. This is also one niche within the city that accepts them, and they do not face the approbation they face in entering the upper-caste temples. In fact, I do not remember seeing or hearing about any dhobi going inside the temples that abound in the Old Delhi area.

The shrine definitely has an ancient origin, and the numbers of its devotees are increasing by the day. There are two reasons for this. Firstly, of course, the increasing population of the city, especially what is known as the 'floating population'—the migrant workers who come and go in a steady stream. These workers come from the lowest strata of society, both in terms of caste and class, and suffer from great stress. They are likely to visit those places of worship that are specific to the need of getting rid of evil forces. The second reason is that there is a seamless continuity in the Hindu belief of linking medical health problems with divine displeasure or intervention. People have had this faith from times long gone by—that all bodily disorders have a cosmic causation, including that of one's karma. Bad deeds consciously or unconsciously committed affect one's health and well-being. Since the karmic cycle follows its own logical principles, only divine intervention can alleviate such sufferings. In the Hindu pantheon, the higher-order gods are concerned only with esoteric goals like salvation; the lesser concerns such as physical health are taken care of by lesser-order beings like the Bhairon. Moreover, there is a homology between evil forces that cause ill health and misfortune and lower-order deities like the Bhairon, who are supposed to be in shades of grey and control the negative forces of the universe. Sax recounts how, for the low-caste people in the hills, 'Bhairon appears as saviour, who intervenes to rescue weak people when they are exploited and abused by the powerful' (Sax 2009: 32).

The hierarchy of gods in the Hindu pantheon follows the hierarchy of jati in the social world. Usually, the upper castes engage with the higher-order gods like Shiva, Ganesha, Parvati, and Vishnu (along with his incarnations), and the lower order engage with those in the lower echelons of the hierarchy, like Sitala Mata (the goddess of smallpox), the deities controlling snakebite and other misfortunes who, like the Bhairon, are metaphorically dark deities. In a village in Garhwal, an elderly woman told me that gods follow the same hierarchy as humans, and, in her work on a South Indian village, Mines (2002: 236) repeats the same statement—'the pantheon of ranked gods "symbolizes" ranks among human'—and she also refers to other scholars such as Fuller (1987: 33) and Dumont (1986: 460) as being of the same opinion. It does not mean that those of the upper castes do not propitiate these deities; they too go to them for their instrumental needs like specific goal-oriented tasks— getting married, solving monetary issues, getting rid of disease, and so on. In the villages, snakebite is a frequent cause of visiting such deities, to make offerings to their priests who are usually of the lower castes. Mines (2002: 246) mentions a dhobi in the village she studied who is powerful because he controls a fierce deity in the village. This dhobi has a link to the deity that is explained through a myth, giving his family the right to propitiate this particular fierce deity: 'when devotees make their rounds, visiting the gods at the shrine, they pay homage first to Cutalaimatan and his Dhobi god dancer and only second to Muppanar's lineage god and god-dancer' (Mines 2002: 248). Similar situations arise in many other contexts, and control over some part of the supernatural universe is allowed to even the lowest caste in the Hindu universe.

One reason for the popularity of these deities could be that their shrines were usually manned by the lower castes, which also had access to them, unlike the temples of the higher gods to which their entry was banned. They are also viewed as protectors of the marginal. Sax (2009), in his study of rural society in Chamoli in Uttarakhand, mentions that 'Harijans worship Bhairav, the deity to whom the Harijans turn when they are abused or exploited, or when they are the victims of injustice' (Sax 2009: 27). The local mythology of Bhairava links him to Virbhadra, who led the motley crowd of petty demons, followers of Shiva, when he took revenge on Daksha.[5] Sax has cited other myths about the Bhairava among the lower castes in the Himalayas that emphasize how he is the god of justice, one who cannot tolerate exploitation of the weak.

Very similar myths accompany a deity whom the dhobis consider as one of their chief patron deities—Sham Khatu. Like the Bhairav, Sham Khatu is also a deity who takes the side of the oppressed. As narrated to me by my friend Bishanlal, he was the son of Ghatotkach, who was the son of Bhima (the second Pandava) and his demoness wife Hidimba, and named Barbarik. He was a devotee of the goddess Parvati or Shera Wali Mata (the goddess who rides a tiger) and did great penance to please her. The goddess was pleased and granted him a boon in the form of great power by giving him very powerful weapons. The young Barbarik was very happy and was going home at great speed when he was spotted by Krishna (the divine god), who stopped him. Krishna was curious to know why the young boy was so happy, and Barbarik told him that he had been blessed by the goddess and was now very powerful. So Krishna asked him what he would do with his power, and he said that he would take the side of the defeated, the underdog, the marginalized, and all those who were suffering. This disturbed Krishna very much, as he considered this to be going against the doctrine of karma. Krishna knew that at the end of the Mahabharata War the Kauravas were going to be defeated, and if Barbarik took their side, then the Pandavas would also be destroyed and the only person left alive would be Barbarik. Krishna tried to preach to Barbarik that, in the Kaliyuga, the people who were defeated or those who were suffering were the people who were in the wrong—they were suffering the results of their karma[6]—but Barbarik did not relent. He insisted that he would take the side of the weak, the defeated. Krishna wanted to tested him for his power and told him to pierce all the leaves on a tree. Krishna then hid one leaf under his feet. Barbarik's arrow pierced all the leaves of the tree and then hovered around Krishna's feet. He told Krishna, 'Prabhu (Lord) please remove your feet, otherwise my arrow will pierce it and I would not like that to happen'. Krishna realized that Barbarik was truly powerful, so he asked him for a gift—that of his head. Barbarik readily offered his head, and Krishna was very pleased and put the head on top of the Khatu mountain (in Rajasthan). He also told him that he was so pleased with him that he would give him his own name, Shyam. From then on he was known as Sham Khatu.[7]

Bishanlal told me emphatically that the dhobis worship him because he took the side of the weak and the defeated. If we examine this myth, it is a strong critic of the Brahmanical doctrine of karma that justifies the caste system. Sham Khatu did not agree with Krishna that those who were defeated or who suffered were necessarily bad people and that they were suffering for their own doings. He considered it injustice and, like the Bhairon described by Sax, he too is a god of justice. This myth also supports what Mohan and Lee (2022) have to say about the Dalit making a critical appraisal of the religions of the dominant groups. Although Sham Khatu is derived from Hindu mythology, he is not a supporter of Brahmanical doctrines and challenges even Krishna. He is the grandson of Bhima but through his wife Hidimba, who is also a woman outside of the Hindu caste system, a forest-dweller, a demoness (or casteless woman). Through Sham Khatu, the dhobis are making a powerful statement that they are not defeated or marginalized because of their own wrongdoings. It is injustice that is making them suffer and not their own karma.

Sai Baba is an emerging deity of popularity among the dhobis, and there are a number of *mandali* (groups of devotees) associated with Sai Baba, which both arrange for *kirtans*[8] in his honour and also trips to Shirdi, where his main shrine is located. Sai Baba is a deity with universal appeal, as he was a Muslim Fakir but, as is usual in India, is venerated and worshipped by both Hindus and Muslims for his miraculous powers. As pointed out by Srivastava (2009), Hindus, who have a pantheon of numerous deities, are open to accepting others as well. In fact, Hinduism is an ancient form of belief that existed prior to the emergence of bounded, doctrinal religions that are exclusionary. Slowly, Sai Baba has been converted to a Hindu icon, the Muslims having shunned him largely, as he has been enshrined into Hindu temples and is worshipped according to Hindu ritualistic forms, such as having *aarti*[9] performed and offerings made. But he still does not have the upper-caste Brahmanical practices associated with him and is mostly worshipped by the singing of songs, as at Sufi shrines. The devotional songs of Sai Baba also emphasize the unity of all sacred beings and of Hindus and Muslims. The emergence of Sai Baba as a patron deity of the dhobis began sometime in the 1980s, and he had become very popular by the turn of the millennium. Sai Baba, like Sham Khatu, has an association with the poor and the marginal, as he was a *fakir* (Muslim mendicant). The dhobis never mention or even acknowledge the other Sai Baba, the southern one, who is far more of a Hindu icon (being born one) and had followers mostly from the upper classes and foreigners. He was in a way an elite version of the original Sai Baba. Another popular deity is Balaji (Hanuman, the monkey god), and the specific Balaji temple that the dhobis visit is the one that is believed to relieve the sufferings of the marginal. This temple is famous for treatment of the mentally ill. But not all dhobis are devotees of Sai Baba, just as all may not be of Sham Khatu as well. Almost every dhobi man or woman I have talked to about their faith emphasizes that their deities, whether Sham Khatu, Sai Baba, or Balaji, are the ones that take the side of the oppressed and mete out justice.

Religion and Social Mobility

None of these deities are specific to the dhobis or define their identity. To have a religious foundation for their identity was not something that the dhobi community ever thought about before the 1980s or 1990s. This is something that emerged with the changing economic scenario after the nineties, when some degree of prosperity as well as a rise in their educational and social level was achieved by a sufficient number of dhobis to think about elevating their ritual status by having a patron deity, specific to the community.

Ritual and religious behaviours have been viewed by eminent scholars of religion like Otto (1923) and Eliade (1959) to have an emotional and other-worldly content. My initial contact with the dhobis had not revealed any such emotional attitude towards the sacred. Unlike the untouchable Paliyans described by Kapadia (1995) and the Theyyam analysed by Pallath (1995),[10] the dhobis never participated in any kind of shamanistic or ecstatic ritual activities. I was rather impressed by their largely pragmatic attitude to life, relating almost every activity to their occupation or to their *biradari* identity. At that time, however, the most frequent *biradari* participation was at life cycle rituals, especially marriage and death, both events resulting in total participation. They did not have any major group rituals involving the sacred. The only noticeable ritual activity was the daily lighting of the lamp in the Ala at home, but that too was by an individual, there being no collective family gathering for any daily prayers or family rituals, as is more customary among the Hindu joint families. Earlier, it was almost always a man that I saw lighting the lamp, but now I find that mostly women do the *puja*, the daughter-in-law being the most likely candidate for it. The older women rarely perform any *puja,* not being used to doing it. It is the younger generation, those that were between 20 and 30 years old in the years between2015 and 2023, whom I frequently saw doing regular *puja* at home. The rituals being followed—ringing a bell, lighting a lamp, burning incense sticks, and doing *aarti*—are all copied from upper-caste households or from television, movies, and the internet.

Since 2014 India has been ruled by an overtly Hindu regime that has been projecting an essentialized version of Hinduism that is Brahmanical and puritanical. It professes that real Hindus are vegetarian and teetotal, and beef-eating has been criminalized in many parts of the country, especially in the Hindi belt of the North and North-West of India. The dhobis have always known their place to be on the margins of Hindu society, and for a long time they stayed away from any allegiance to ritualistic Hinduism. But under the overarching influence of an overtly Hindu national identity (Thapar 1992: 33) most dhobi households are turning to ritualistic Hinduism as well as turning vegetarian. For many of them it is a symbol of their middle-class social and economic status rather than of an allegiance to a Hindu right-wing party. The dhobis are divided in their support of the right-wing regime, as many of them are enraged at the demolition of many remaining dhobi ghats in the prestigious New Delhi area.[11] So the religiosity of the dhobis and their bent towards the mainstream Hindu religion are not exactly driven by their allegiance to the state, but a mixture of several factors. The present generation of dhobis have climbed a few notches up the social ladder, and there is relative prosperity to be seen in their houses and their lifestyle. Moreover, a much larger number of dhobi young men and women are either educated up to the college level or are now going to school and college. They are imbibing more cosmopolitan values and also a sense of greater equality with the middle classes, a process helped on by the visible and overt dilution of caste-based practices, especially untouchability.

Caste, one may say, now lurks in the nooks and corners, refusing to go away but averse to coming out into the open. With participation in the election process and dissemination of information via the media and internet, a sense of citizenship has now obfuscated caste discriminations to a large extent, especially in the metropolis. The contemporary dhobis have entered a phase of conviction that they are not inferior to anyone, that they have equal rights in a democracy. Some of them are now aware of their constitutional rights, recognize a wrong when they see it, and are in a turnover phase in their self-construction of identity. At this time they are assuming a more cosmopolitan vision of the self, and are trying to imbibe some practices that will eliminate or at least reduce the visual and observable differences between them and the upper-caste, middle-class Hindus, with whom they now wish to identify. These changes may be cast in the language of aesthetics more than of ritual and religion. Here the term 'middle class' has been used loosely; the more apt term would be one used by the dhobis, '*un logo ke jaise*' (like those people) where '*un log*' (they) refers to the neighbours, the general observable members of the city's population that are not ostracized or marginalized in the way the dhobis perceive themselves to have been. The difference between a rural caste/class structure that is tied to landownership and therefore difficult to change and an urban caste/class structure that is far more mobile, as it is tied to a cash economy of great elasticity, is that those living in urban areas, even if poor and marginalized, have the audacity to dream, to imagine themselves as one among the others.

Towards this end, the dhobis of the twenty-first century have marble shrines inside their homes, with idols and pictures of Hindu gods and goddesses, where they do ostensible *puja*. Many have given up eating meat and drinking alcohol as well. Ram Chander, a dhobi who is devoted to Balaji, said, '*Jab se hum logo ne Balaji ki puja karni shuru kari hain hum log meat khane ko galat samajte hain*'. *Hum sharab bhi nahi chute hain*' ('Since we have taken on the worship of Balaji we think that eating meat is wrong. We do not touch alcohol either'). According to him and my own observations in talking to various dhobis since the 1980s, the practice of eating meat and drinking alcohol is waning.[12] At present, as Ram Chander assessed, only about 50percent of dhobis eat meat, and of those who do, about half of them do so only on Wednesday and Sunday, as all other days are devoted to one or other deity. Most among the younger generation who have been to college and school are vegetarian. Yet, as Ram Chander himself pointed out to me, '*Hum log yeh sab chod rahe hain par unchi jaat wale pakad rahe hain. Ab to unke shadi mein sharab hona zaroori hai par hamare mein nahi*' ('Even as we are leaving these habits, the upper castes are taking them on. Nowadays at their weddings it is compulsory to have alcohol but not so among us'). To some extent here too the dhobis are adhering to their moral superiority, an attitude that I had observed in my very initial contact with them, when they were criticizing the upper-class/caste women as compared to their own. Even now, while admitting to taking on a more sanitized lifestyle, they were pointing to the more degraded (in their opinion) lifestyle of the upper castes. In this sense, one may not agree with Srinivas (1966) that the lower level tend to imitate the upper layer because they think they are superior. Here it appears that the dhobis at least, ever since I have known them, have always asserted their *own superiority*, no matter in what way. So even from an outsider's perception, they are imitating the middle-class lifestyle and values; from their perspective, they are actually doing better, outdoing the upper castes.

Another factor contributing to greater overt religiosity at present is the comparatively greater availability of leisure time to the women. Earlier, the work done by women was very hard, such as ironing clothes the whole day with hardly any time even to eat. Nowadays, when visiting dhobi households I find women spending a lot of time doing daily rituals. The coal-fired *chullah* that required considerable effort to light and to maintain has been replaced by a gas oven that lights up at the touch of a lighter. The women no longer have to walk long distances to the Yamuna ghat and spend entire days there helping their husbands. They no longer have to take food to the ghat or even to wash their own clothes; most dhobi households now have a refrigerator and a washing machine. Some older women, and a few younger ones, do iron clothes, but there is always someone at home who can spend half an hour to an hour doing *puja*, in the manner of upper castes. As one elderly woman informed me, she used to give *apheem* (a plant-based intoxicant) to all her five children to get them to sleep while she worked. If women had to give intoxicants to babies, they had no time for daily rituals. Even community rituals were not as elaborate as they are now. The *mandir* in the house has now also become a sign of prosperity and upward mobility. It signifies, or gives out the message, that this particular household has transcended its deprived status, that it can now not only afford to spend money to build a splendid shrine (often made of marble and decorated with expensive pieces like fairy lights and stone jewels) but also spare someone with enough leisure during the busy morning times to do *puja*. Earlier in my memory, the mornings were a time of hectic activity, with a woman lighting the coal-fired hearth, someone ironing the clothes, another person trying to fix the morning meal, and the men preparing to go to the ghat, with the women preparing to go to their ironing spot outside the house and the *katra*, and so on. In present times one can see a woman cooking leisurely in a well-appointed kitchen with modern gadgets, men either washing clothes in the ghat attached to their houses (as in Shashtri Nagar) or in the big *hauda* in their own *katra*, and some putting clothes onto a cycle to take to the nearest ghat to wash. Narayan (2021: 41) explains that 'desire for religious space is not a new phenomenon; it has been there since marginalized groups became conscious of the problem of untouchability. Their desire for freedom from untouchability has been closely associated with the desire for food and water and also for equality within Hinduism.'

Religious pilgrimage was always there and, as I have mentioned already, dhobis visited shrines like that of Mata Vaishno Devi and undertook the Chardham Yatra, but mostly as a once-in-a-lifetime project. Most dhobis were too poor to undertake even this. Nowadays, some families are making annual pilgrimages, and also arranging for group excursions to pilgrim spots like Gar Mukteshwar and Shirdi. Ram Chander organizes regular trips to the Balaji shrine in Rajasthan. He told me that the Balaji they worship is the one that is patronized by the poor and the needy, and he is the one that gets rid of the *bhoot and pret* (ghosts and evil spirits): '*bhoot pret ko bhagaya jaata hai*' (Kakar 1991).[13] There is another Balaji in Rajasthan in visited by the rich Marwaris who never come to visit this shrine. Ram Chander explicitly told me that the rich pray for wealth while the poor go to the deity to get rid of their sufferings (Sax 2009). For this he has formed a formal organization, a committee as he called it, of sixteen people, who form the core group that organizes public rituals (*kirtans*). Each of them contributes 600 rupees a month, and when the annual event of the big *jagaran* takes place, they contribute 5,100 rupees each. For the big event they also collect donations door-to-door and from their circle of friends and relatives. In January 2023, they had a huge event in which Ram Chander estimated that 3,000 people attended. His daughter, who is working, contributed 20,000 rupees for the *jagaran* in January, and she is one of the sixteen members. When I asked him if all the members were from the *biradari*, he said that three were from outside the *samaj* (*biradari*). When I further pressed him to tell me from which community they were, he said they were Punjabis from his neighbourhood. Here again one has to note that communities in traditional patron–client relationships with the dhobis, especially those from the Old Delhi area, will not engage in equal social interactions with them even now.

Punjabis, as I have already mentioned, were not part of the traditional jajmani-type relations prevailing in Old Delhi, where the dhobis were on the wrong end of the pollution schema. If today they have a few persons joining them, one would expect those of similar class and those outside of the traditional caste-based relations.

The acceptance and practice of upper-caste rituals by the dhobis, although superficially similar to what Srinivas (1966) referred to as Sanskritization, is not at core really the same. I have already pointed to the notion of moral superiority that they always maintain. Their goal is not to rise in the scale of caste hierarchy but to rise in class hierarchy. And here one needs to contextualize this religious transformation towards mainstream Hindu practices (as conceptualized by them) in the overall changes taking place in Indian society.

Indian democracy was established on the grounds of liberty, equality, and secularism, following a largely Western model (Brass 1994: 12). But, as Walsh mentions (2011: 243), Indira Gandhi, in the 1980s, was the first to turn towards communalism as a stepping stone in Indian politics. Since then, religion has played a successively important role, both in Indian society and in Indian politics, as the two are interdependent. It is at this point that Hindu fundamentalist parties like the Jan Sangh, the Rashtriya Swayamsevak Sangh (RSS), and the Vishwa Hindu Parishad began to strengthen their hold, to counter Congress policies. The present-day BJP (Bharatiya Janata Party), an amalgamation of various non-Congress opposition parties in India, was not a communal party or a Hindu fundamentalist party to begin with, but when its leadership was taken up by L.K. Advani, who came in from the radical RSS, it assumed and continues to play its role as one. The present Prime Minister (since 2014), Narendra Modi, also has his political roots in the RSS, and is a strong believer in an essentialist view of Hinduism that demonizes non-Hindus. The anti-Muslim sentiments openly projected by the BJP have now filtered down deep into the psyche of most Indians and have affected deeply the life of Indian cities.

The transition of the dhobis from the *ala* to the *mandir* can be explained only against this background. The dhobis rely a lot on their clients, not only economically but also socially, so as to always have a cordial relationship of mutual support. The clients, for the dhobis, are patrons in the classical sense of the term and are expected to take care of their overall needs. The client relationship also sets the moral universe for the dhobis, as they seem to set the norms. In its very first stage, the city was dominated by the rich Muslim clientele, and, from the religious practices of the dhobis as observed in the 1970s, it was apparent that there had been considerable Islamic influence on them. They followed a Sufi path, common to Hindus and Muslims but closer to Islam (Dehlvi 2010). When the Muslim clientele was largely replaced by the upper-caste Hindus, there began a slow shift in their practices. With more and more religious fundamentalism sinking in, the rift between the Muslim and Hindu dhobis also deepened. In the seventies, I was told that dhobis have Muslim friends and visit each other's houses but do not eat or drink tea with each other. But by the 2020s, such interaction was very limited except for the sharing of the ghats, for economic purposes. The rift is deepening by not only the Hinduization of the Hindu dhobis but also the Islamization of the Muslim dhobis. When I recently asked several young Muslim dhobis whether they go to the *dargah*, they very emphatically said that they did not. They only go to the mosque and not to any *dargah*.

As Bhatty (2016: 33) has described, the Indian Muslims are divided into layered castes just like their Hindu counterparts on the subcontinent, although of course without the entire baggage of purity and pollution rules. The lowest at the bottom are the Kameens, believed to be converts from the local Hindu untouchable castes like the dhobis, who continue with their traditional occupations and are known to have adopted a few Islamic practices like *nikaah* but otherwise were living in the ways prescribed by their caste panchayats. The older Sheheri dhobi panchayat had, as already mentioned, included the Muslim dhobis as one of their divisions (*thoks*). In my earlier visits to the dhobi *katra* at Matia Mahal, there was little to show them as distinct from the Hindu dhobis in terms of appearance, both personal and of the *katra*. The Muslim dhobi women never ironed clothes in public like their Hindu counterparts, but they helped the men wash clothes at home and also ironed, but away from the public gaze. The lines as usual were drawn around the bodies of women; while men washed clothes together at the ghats, and still do, the Muslim women did not appear in public. While overt appearances have not changed much, there is a definite trend towards more puritanical forms of religious practices among the younger generation of Muslim dhobis, just as among the Hindus.

As India became more and more Hinduized and politically saffronized (saffron is the colour of the BJP), the dhobis are shifting more and more towards essentialized Hinduism, which involves having Hindu gods and goddesses installed at home in elaborate shrines to do *puja* (a practice that was unknown up to the 1990s). However, they gravitate naturally towards divinities like Sai Baba, who is at present most popular among them out of the generally popular Indian deities.[14] I often found posters announcing Sai Bhajan at various locations exclusive to the dhobis; for example, on 17 April 2017, I found a poster inside the *katra* at Farash Khana inviting people for a *bhajan* (collective devotional singing) in honour of Sai Baba to be held at Ghat no. 7, Minto Road. These ghats were about to be demolished at that time, and some had already been removed. The dhobi holding a community *bhajan* at the ghat sent out two important messages: one, it was a caste-based affair as the *bhajan* was being held at a spot frequented only by the dhobi; secondly, they were laying a claim to a space they considered their own—the dhobi ghat was a *biradari* space, a space exclusive to the dhobi, and others were making illegitimate claims on it. The dhobis had always located their *biradari* practices and performances at their ghats, which they have always considered and still consider to be their own space, a space exclusive to their identity as a jati.

While asserting a greater Hindu identity, it is difficult for dhobis to follow highly ritualized practices, although the young people have begun to keep fasts and avoid eating meat. A casual interview with a dhobi in a lane known as Samosewali Gali (a lane for *samosas*)[15] near Farash Khana, yielded the kind of subtle changes that are coming about in their religious practices. This person is a full-time practitioner of the traditional occupation and is linked by multiple ties of kinship to several of the Sheheri dhobis well known to me. He has a joint household with four married sons, a phenomenon only seen among those who are not in the traditional occupation. In this household, except for the father, no other son was in the dhobi occupation. The eldest was working in a nearby shop, the second son in a bank in Gurgaon (far away from Old Delhi), the third in a company at Scindia House in Connaught Place, and the fourth was still studying. The father said that he, along with his entire family, had gone to his son's friend's place in Bombay. They had visited the famous Ganesh temple (Siddhi Vinayak) and then had gone to the mother-goddess temple near the Muslim *dargah* at Mahalakshmi. From Bombay they had gone to Shirdi to the shrine of the Sai Baba. He told me that the Sai Baba is greatly venerated by all the dhobis, '*bahut manyata hai*' (greatly venerated). When I asked him if he went to the Sai Bhajan that was held at Ghatno. 7, Minto Road, he replied, how could he go as he was never invited? But he agreed that they all go regularly to the Bhairon temple at the Old Fort (Purana Qila). But when I asked him if they still go to the *dargah* at Nizamuddin, he replied, '*Aajkal time kiske paas hai?*'('Who has time to go nowadays?').

From this brief account we can clearly see that there is a trend away from the syncretism they followed earlier towards the more popular Hindu deities, such as Siddhi Vinayak and Mahalakshmi. It is also true that in present times no one is allowed to ask the caste of a person entering a temple, so all these shrines that were previously inaccessible to the untouchables are now accessed by them. However, within the area of their residence, the dhobis still do not enter the Hindu temples, but they are able to do so in the anonymity of another city. The Sai Baba cult is an open and all-encompassing one, one that is supposed to transcend the divisions of religion and caste and that therefore has universal appeal. The denial of going to the *dargah* at Nizamuddin is a clear indication of the separation of Hindu dhobi identity from the Muslims, though in practice most of them still do go there, especially for the critical moments. To some extent the dhobis have assumed a frontstage, backstage, everyday practice as a strategy to overcome their experience of ostracization over the years. Even while the dhobi I was talking to was lamenting that their area (the lane where I was sitting) was fast turning into a Muslim-dominated neighbourhood, he entered into a very cordial conversation with a Muslim person who came to chat with him. It has already been mentioned that a dhobi man or woman standing in a lane or at the corner of the neighbourhood acts as a nodal point for community conversation as well as an information centre. The elderly Muslim man lamented the breakdown of close community living and the primary group relations that were things of the past: 'Earlier no one put locks on their doors, the people just walked in and out of people's houses.' I agreed with him totally, having also been a witness to such times. Keeping doors closed was an unknown concept in the neighbourhoods of Delhi. The gods too were more accessible, sitting outside on the lanes and under trees. Today massive temples enclose them in most places, complete with guards and security.

The dhobis, however, in their pursuit of a definitive identity have not stopped at accepting upper-caste Hindu practices; they have also created their own pantheon, along with their history, relevance, and a culture of practices. Unlike the process of Sanskritization, in which a lower caste seeks to merge into or claim a higher-caste status, the dhobis wish to be accepted and elevated as dhobis, and as nothing else. In this they are influenced by the democratic, equalitarian principles of the market and globalization that surround them and in which they are embedded. Their religious activities, especially the public ones, are a narrative of claims and rights and are certainly not limited to the realm of devotion. To this end they have also constructed their very own deity, whom they refer to by the Hindu terms Kuldevta or Isht Devta.[16] Identifying caste-specific deities outside the upper-caste Hindu pantheon, or using a sacred symbol (a deity or holy person) to assert a place in society to claim moral superiority, have been seen among other marginal groups, especially untouchables, like the Satnampanth of the Chamars of Chhatisgarh under the leadership of Guru Ghasiram (Dube 1998), and Iyothee Thassar of Tamil Nadu in the early twentieth century (Aloysius 2013).

The One that Belongs to Them

The Sheheri dhobi *biradari* considers Nagar Sain Baba to be their presiding deity, and in September 2015 I was able to participate in the Shobha Yatra (Procession of Glory) of this deity, which is held as a big show in Old Delhi, near the Town Hall. This particular divinity is completely unknown in the Hindu pantheon, but considered as the *kuldevta* of the dhobis.[17] There was no mention of this deity in the 1970s, but with other transformations during the nineties an emergent religious assertion began to be manifested. Narayan (2021: 39) has described the desire of many marginal communities to have temples or places of worship dedicated to their own deities as part of their efforts towards social rehabilitation as well as assertion of a dignified personhood. The communities in Uttar Pradesh mentioned by him include the most deprived ones such as Dusadhs, Nats, Sapera, Sahariya, and Kabutara. They are still on the verge of starvation but, more than food, they desire their own deities and their own place of worship. The dhobis' journey towards having their very own *biradari* deity and being able to organize his worship on a large scale expresses this same urge for identity assertion on the part of a hitherto neglected and marginalized community. As described by Bishanlal, Nagar Sain was a dhobi who was born in Morena in Madhya Pradesh, several hundred years back. There is very little mythology surrounding Nagar Sain, as according to my observations he has appeared on the scene fairly recently. The kind of Shobha Yatra I had witnessed in 2015 had begun only about five years prior to that date, around 2010. When I was doing work among them in the seventies and eighties and even in the nineties, I never heard of Baba Nagar Sain. Furthermore, when I asked Bishanlal about him, he said, '*Woh garib dhukhi ka khyal rakhte the. Who chahate the ki dhobi log padh likh kar age barhe. Woh hamari unnati chahate the*' ('He looked after the poor. He wanted the dhobis to get educated and he wanted progress for our community').

On 21 September 2015, the ceremony was organized at the Kachcha Bag Community Centre, near the Town Hallin Chandni Chowk in the heart of Old Delhi, and now very close to the metro station. I was asked to arrive at 6 p.m., and coming out from the metro station at around that time, I saw the band playing and a huge crowd, with people holding up many placards announcing the event as the 'Shobha Yatra of Baba Nagar Sain' (Sacred Procession of Baba Nagar Sain), organized by Dhobi Samaj (Regd). I had never seen such a large congregation of persons from the dhobi *biradari* in one place; there were nearly a thousand people. There were open trucks carrying large painted clay images of various Hindu deities such as Ganesha, Ram and Sita, Radha, Krishna, and Hanuman. There were also children in the trucks dressed up as various deities, similar to the ones whose images were being carried. These children were mostly boys, with a few very young girls of less than 7or 8years of age. They all seemed to be enjoying themselves hugely. Along with the crowd, displaying an air of importance, were large numbers of young men, about fifty or sixty, who were wearing volunteer badges made of green, yellow, and orange ribbons, with either Jai Baba Nagar Sain or Dhobi Samaj (Regd) written on them in Hindi. The badges were quite shiny and fairly large in size—about 4inches across. They were made to look decorative with silver streaks and golden fringes. The volunteers (all young boys) also had saffron scarves around their necks with the same inscriptions. I was told that the procession had begun at 2 p.m. near the cycle market that was about 2kilometres away. They had taken nearly four hours to take a round of the Town Hall and reach the Community Centre.

I walked along with the procession to enter the community centre, which appeared even more impressive than the procession. Inside, there was a massive open space, the size of a football field, decorated with large statues of Hindu gods and goddesses such as Rama, Sita, Hanuman, and so on, and a large statue of Sai Baba was also prominently displayed. There was a huge signboard declaring a Bhajan Sandhya (an evening of devotional songs) by the Dhobi Samaj and another equally large sign declaring that the then Deputy Chief Minister of Delhi, Manish Sisodia, was going to attend the function, along with his photograph.

On entering there was a large hall just adjacent to the field, up a flight of stairs, and this too was choked full of people—more women and children, though many men were also present. The upstairs hall was the main venue, but it gave me a sense of throwback to earlier times, as there were hardly any chairs in the hall. Almost everyone, men and women dressed in their very best clothes, was sitting or squatting on the ground, which did not look very clean. But the people were quite indifferent to the muddiness of the floor and sat around happily, chatting among themselves. The dresses of the women displayed a great deal of variety and were showy and shiny according to the fashion of the day. While the married women of all ages wore sarees, the younger women were in all kinds of dresses, Indian as well as Western. This was a complete changeover from the 1970s, when wearing Western dress was taboo for dhobi girls and only very young girls wore frocks. But now even some married young women wear trousers and tops at home, although in public they wear an Indian dress even if they are not wearing the formal saree. But the unmarried are given free rein to wear what they wish and many choose to dress according to the latest trends.

The entire place was buzzing with conversation and children playing around. There were many people outside and in the ground-floor hall adjacent to the grounds. A large area had been cordoned off, where large ovens had been lit, and several cooks were busy making huge quantities of delicacies. Most persons looked similar in terms of their dress and their manner of speaking and greeting each other. Many were sitting down on the floor in the traditional Indian fashion. But it did not seem that everyone knew everyone, as not everyone was greeting or talking to everyone else. Some women looked askance at me, but no one came up to talk. This was another indication that the *biradari* had grown beyond the absolutely face-to-face intimacy it had till about the eighties. At that time any stranger, like me, would definitely have stood out and been asked about her credentials. But now people were not sure as to the identity of everyone, and they assumed that I was also one of them. Some women were looking more sophisticated than others, with well-dressed hair, wearing sandals, and carrying handbags; again, quite a change from the typical look of wearing flip-flops and tucking their money down the front of their blouses. Most dhobi women have long and thick hair, which they usually tied in plaits. Making a bun or otherwise styling hair, even for a ceremony, was not common practice. In fact, in the seventies and right up to the nineties, most people had no sense of dressing up for any festivity. The dhobis attended weddings and other ceremonies in their workaday clothes. Most people had perhaps one spare set of clothes and, as already mentioned, most wore the clothes that had come for washing. Clothes and appearance were values that had crept in after the 1990s, mostly be-cause of the liberalization of markets and other factors already discussed.

Yet the women maintained the same distance and etiquette, there was no mixing of young boys and girls, and men and women only talked to each other if they were kin, especially if older. One middle-aged man was furiously working at signing some certificates, sitting at the only table in the hall. I was told he was making certificates to be given to those dhobi children who had done well in their studies at school and college. However, all the certificates were made out for schoolchildren of primary classes. The person signing the letters was a dhobi who was a Class 1 of-ficer in the government. The children were to be given shields along with the certificates. Bishanlal, who had arrived by then with his wife and who at that time was the Sarpanch (Head of Panchayat) of the Sheheri dhobis, informed me that they were spending about 100,000 rupees on the food alone. There were two sweet dishes, in addition to the *prasad* (offering to the Gods), which consisted of fried *puries* (deep-fried wheat pancakes) and a special potato curry made in the culinary style of Old Delhi without onions or garlic. This type of cuisine is considered a regional speciality of this area, where there is a predominance of persons of the Baniya caste groups and also of Jains, who are all vegetarians, which means they do not eat onion or garlic as well as any kind of meat. Although the dhobis are not vegetarian, rather preferential meat eaters, for their rituals they seem to follow the upper-caste norms. This is also done so that no one from the upper castes, if they attend the function at all, can accuse them of being inappropriate in their conduct.

Bishanlal's wife had served me *prasad* on a disposable plate that contained fried *puries*, some potato curry and *halwa*, a sweet made with semolina, sugar, and pure ghee (clarified butter). The *prasad* was identical to that served at the ritual functions of all caste groups in North India, and especially in Old Delhi. Huge cauldrons were filled with this food, and young men with volunteer badges were serving it to everyone; most were sitting on the floor and eating, the older ones sitting on their haunches in the traditional manner and the younger ones with their legs tucked under them. Here it must be mentioned that all lower castes are used to sitting on the floor to eat, as from ancient times they were never allowed to sit on chairs or on any kind of elevation and they carry on this practice as a matter of habit, which also explains why the venue was bereft of chairs. In public places the lower castes not only sat on the floor but also were segregated, being made to sit separately from the upper castes, a norm extended to all of inferior status at most public functions. With the abolition of untouchability, these rules have attained the status of etiquette rather than enforced norms, but they are practised nevertheless. The function was disrupted by torrential rain, but the young men managed to drain the grounds by using buckets, demonstrating the qualities of hard work and perseverance that they have acquired as a community. No one showed any panic, and things were taken as a matter of course, with one woman even commenting that the rains were because the birth date of the deity was wrongly identified. It took only about an hour to flush out tonnes of water that had reached knee-high.

It was easy to recognize people around the venue. Bishanlal's wife took her grandson to meet a young man dressed as Hanuman, a Hindu deity, and I recognized him as the younger son of my earliest informant and friend, Omi Pehlwan, who was a well-known wrestler and bonesetter of his time. His older son, Shiv Kumar, is a recognized bodybuilder and wrestler. This was before the COVID-19 pandemic, and the major topic of conversation was about dengue, a mosquito-borne disease that had taken the form of an epidemic at that time. People living in narrow lanes and bylanes, as in the dhobi *katras*, with their open drains are very vulnerable to all kinds of airborne, vector-borne and waterborne diseases. I heard a woman describe another person who had dengue but was working till she was almost dropping dead.

The man writing the certificates had after some time finished his task and come over to talk to me, as Bishan had introduced me to him as a 'professor'. He came to get some advice about his son, who wished to do either French language or Chinese, preferably the latter, at the Department of East Asian Studies at Delhi University. Although it was an overtly religious meet, at the level of the *biradari* I found that education was an important topic of engagement, from discussing the education of their children to the giving of certificates to encourage more children to do well in school. This was a significant change from earlier times, when most persons did not recognize education as something of importance for the *biradari* members.

A *biradari* gathering like this is also focused on identifying and upholding high-achieving individuals from the community, who, as they say in Hindi, make the face of the community shine (*'Biradari ka muh roshan karenge'*), or in a similar vein will raise the head of the biradari (*'Biradari ka sar ooncha karenge'*). This kind of collective pride in community achievements was not there in earlier times. The reason is simple: till the nineties, the dhobis were resigned to the fact that they were always to be second-class citizens and could never assert their equality in society as 'dhobis'. But from the nineties, as the economy of the country was pushed forward by neoliberal policies, the economy boomed and brought its rewards for the dhobis, who found they were able to earn much more and thus transform their lifestyle. I have already mentioned the changes in their homes, in lifestyle and dress. In addition, their sense of elevation to middle-class status has infused a sense of pride and achievement that did not exist earlier. I too was given a badge and was told that the dhobi *biradari* was proud of me as I had written a book about them. Many of them have known me since I was a young student doing my PhD and feel good about my continuing association with them.

I met an elderly person at this function, sporting a long white beard, and he told me that he had retired as a guard from the Indian Railways and all his children were highly educated and had moved away from the *biradari.* His granddaughter had taken admission in AIIMS (the All India Institute of Medical Sciences), the most prestigious medical college in the country. Yet he continues to attend all the *biradari* events, like this one, and takes a lot of interest in *biradari* matters. For such persons, the theatre and sense of opulence created by the collective celebrations of certain rituals are a way of asserting the self-esteem of individuals as well as elevation of the collective identity.

From *Biradari* to *Samaj*: a Social Transformation

After that event, the Shobha Yatra was celebrated a few more times, but then it was discontinued for two years because of COVID-19. One took place on 18 April 2023. The place was the same as before, and the assembly took place at the cycle market and proceeded towards the community centre, reaching it at about 7 p.m. This time large colourful cards had been printed with the legend, 'Jai Baba Nagar Sain Janamotsav Samiti **Dhobi Samaj (Regd) (S/50363)** *ki or se* (on behalf of) **Dhobi Samaj** *ke Istdevta ki 19 vi* (the patron deity of the community's nineteenth celebration) **Vishal Shobha Yatra va Dharmik Sanskritik Karyakram** (huge procession and religious cultural programme)'. This legend clarifies the legal status of the Dhobi Samaj by giving its registration number; it specifies that Nagar Sain is their specific community deity (Isht Devta) and also informs us that this one is the nineteenth of such celebrations. Taking out the two years of COVID, it then puts the date of the first celebration as in the year 2002.

Among those invited as guests of honour, and listed on the card, were the following: The representative of the Scheduled Castes (SC) and Scheduled Tribes (ST) of the Delhi Government; MLA (Member Legislative Assembly) Chandni Chowk; Municipal member Chandni Chowk; Municipal member Delhi Gate; President of the Bisa Aggarwal Badi Panchayat (reg.) (Nigambodh Ghat); The Chief Minister Badi Panchayat Bisa Aggarwal (reg.) (Nigambodh Ghat); The priest of the Hanuman Mandir at the Cremation Grounds (Nigambodh Ghat).

After this there was a list of thirteen executive members in charge of various functions, and then a list of donors, which was organized area-wise (listing by name donors from various parts of Delhi that have dhobi clusters). These areas were Hailey Road, Lakshmi Nagar, Mandavali, Chander Nagar, Seelampur, Jheel and Gita Colony, Shashtri Park, Bhajan pura, Shahdara, Ghonda, and Karwalnagar. From this list one gets a comprehensive picture of the spread of the dhobis outside of Old Delhi. On the back of the card was printed the Facebook address of the organization—jaibabanagarsenjanmotsavsamiti—and in addition the names and phone numbers of seven persons were given as contacts, who obviously were the main office-bearers.

Those listed as guests of honour did not actually grace the occasion. But it is interesting to note that the names listed included two of the main functionaries at the Hindu cremation ground at the river Yamuna, the Nigambodh Ghat. This is the oldest and most holy of all the cremation grounds in Delhi and all important persons of Delhi are cremated there. This invitation followed the installing of the image of Baba Nagar Sain inside the Nigambodh Ghat, seen as a matter of great pride by the dhobi community. Most of the persons who attended and were given important-ance were men of the community itself. They were all conspicuous by the wearing of dazzling white shirts and *kurtas* (Indian-type shirts), and all wore the badge of the Dhobi Samaj. Women were more or less kept in the background, indicating that the dhobi *biradari*, which was to a large extent gender-neutral and egalitarian, is now evolving into the Dhobi Samaj, which is more patriarchal and hierarchical. The change of refer-ence from *biradari* to *samaj* also indicates a subtle change of values. The term *biradari* had the connotation of kinship and primary-group rela-tions, whereas the word *samaj* (society) is connotative of a more formal organization, and here the notions of patriarchy and hierarchy raise their heads. The dhobis who are now having aspirations towards a general ac-ceptance tend to use the term *samaj* to refer to themselves collectively. I had not heard this word spoken earlier, but only from 2020 onwards. Most upper castes use the term *samaj* to refer to their collective identity, such as Gujerati Samaj, Aggarwal Samaj, and so on. The use by the dhobis of this word is a signifier of a different mindset emerging among them.

This proliferation of deities and number of ritual occasions are on a huge upward trend among all sections of Hindus across India due to ex-posure to the media and the images and reporting about various events, mythology, and different forms of worship that are disseminated through television serials. Hindu mythologies, like most mythology, is full of drama and is conducive to the making of spectacular visuals, just like the cinema versions of the Bible and Greek mythology. The first mega Hindi serial based on the Hindu epics Ramayana and then Mahabharata had captivated and fascinated audiences all across India. The dhobis too have been influenced by these images and information coming from the virtual world.

Another reason for the rising popularity of various religious icons and deities has been the state propaganda that has turned towards the promulgation of a Hindu nation as against the former ideology of secularism followed by postcolonial Indian politicians. Although secularism in India has seen the acceptance of multiple forms of worship and of all religions, there was never public participation by prominent politicians in religious rituals, as is the case now. The active involvement of state agencies in perpetuating and encouraging religious activities has also led to a steep rise in the number of people taking part in them. The elderly dhobi women I engaged in conversation with on various occasions were also of the opinion that even a few decades back the people of Delhi had not heard of the Kanwariyas, people who carry the water of the Ganga from different places to the Himalayas. They also recognized that, in spite of all these increased religious activities involving the sacred rivers, they were being destroyed. Another woman from the same family said that she was from Farash Khana, and her family would go to the Minto Road ghats for washing clothes. She also said that they had shifted their clientele from being mostly Muslim to predominantly Hindu, as there were hardly any Muslim clients left in the Old Delhi area, and she attributed the proliferation of Hindu deities to this shift. The elderly woman continued her conversation to tell me about the *katra* life in the seventies and before, when they used to cook in open *chullhas*, everyone had face-to-face contact, there were no locks on doors. The most frequent lament that I heard from the elderly was that there were locks on doors in present times, a feature that was unheard of till the nineties. An associated factor could be the relative prosperity after the nineties when their houses acquired some objects worth stealing.

Certain definite changes in values have also crept in even, though slowly. The dhobi women in the seventies would defend their alcohol drinking by saying that it was necessary for them to keep their bodies 'hot', as they were working in water most of the time. One middle-aged woman retorted rather angrily at the upper-caste women's derogatory attitude towards alcohol drinking by saying, 'Let them come and lead the kind of life we lead for a day, then they will know why we drink. They live in comfort and pass judgement on us.' This criticism of upper-caste/class attitudes and moralizing was very common in the seventies, when there was a clear and insurmountable gap between the dhobis pursuing their caste occupation and those who were getting their clothes washed by them. On another occasion, a woman spat out, '*They (woh log)* think that only those who have a car under their buttocks [using a very derogatory colloquial Hindi word] are human.'

However, by the 1990s, with a new generation growing up, attitudes began to change. Most of the younger generation did not consider alcohol drinking as a normal part of day-to-day behaviour. The women in particular began to move away from it, so that there is practically no young woman in the generation of the 2020s who considers it morally correct to drink alcohol, and the men do it far more discreetly, if at all. A function that I attended in January 2017, in a big public park in East Delhi, demonstrates my point. The occasion was a *jagrata* (night-long vigil) organized by Ram Chander, the head of a religious organization known as Balaji Kirtan Samiti, as already mentioned. The event was well announced, with posters put up all over the vicinity, large display boards, and the distribution of invitation cards. However, when I went to the venue, the people nearby—the vendors and neighbours—told me that it was a 'dhobi function'. The arrangements were very conspicuous, lavish and elaborate with a large enclosure, heavily decorated with lights, *shamianas*,[18] carpets on the floors, and an elaborately constructed framework for the deities—what is known in Hindi as a *mandap*, which is a kind of stage arrangement that serves as a temporary site for worship, a replacement for a regular temple or shrine. What was interesting was the medley of prominent Hindu deities, who had all been represented by their well-crafted idols (*murti*). Although the central image was that of Balaji, he was surmounted by the images of Ram and Sita at a much higher level behind him. On the right of this central piece were the images of the Hindu Trinity—Brahma, Vishnu, and Mahesh—and on the left were the images of the three major female deities—Kali, Lakshmi, and Saraswati. In front were other forms of Balaji or Hanuman, the Five-headed Hanuman or Panchmukhi Hanuman, and there were idols of Radha and Krishna on the far left and Vaishno Devi on the far right. In other words, most of the deities popularly worshipped in this part of India were represented, irrespective of the eclectic nature of the mix.

More interestingly, a large facial representation of a deity was placed on the left side of Balaji but almost centre stage. It was a kinglike image with a crown and a moustache, who I was told was Sham Khatu, whom I described earlier. There was a large stage to complement the display of the deities, and there was plenty of activity on that stage, mostly by the dhobi person who was the chief organizer, and he was being assisted by a few other men. One of them was the father-in-law of his elder son, a person known in Hindi as a *samdhi*. Among the upper castes a *samdhi* is treated as a distant and avoidable relative, but here the two behaved like they were good friends. When his wife arrived, she took me close to the stage and I could see huge quantities of sweets in boxes. There was not less than 100 kilograms of sweets that were kept as offerings to the gods, along with plenty of fruits and other paraphernalia of worship like joss sticks, garlands, and various ritual items. But there was no priest, and only the dhobi men were presiding over whatever was going to be done.

At the same time some young men below the stage were strumming Western musical instruments like guitars, beating drums, and adjusting the very modern sound system. At the back of the huge enclosure there were arrangements for a very elaborate dinner, with large vessels full of cooked food, and many children were hovering around expectantly, eyeing the sumptuous quantities of richly spiced and oiled foods, such as were customarily served during wedding feasts and parties in Northern India. As time went on there was increasing noise, more and more people, and loud mechanized music. The *bhajan* singers arrived much later and sang, but there were no rituals other than what had been performed by the person who organized the entire function. He made some offerings to the deities, in the same way as people do simple rituals at home. However, the large amount of sweets, fruits, and other items were to be distributed as *prasad* to all those who had made contributions towards this function, and to all relatives and friends, who incidentally were all part of the *biradari*. In my long experience, I have found that since very few marriages have occurred outside of the Sheheri dhobi *biradari*, even in a large gathering most people can still trace their relationship to most others.

In large displays and highly visible public functions like this, the dhobis are not proving that their identity has changed; rather, they are just trying to show the world that dhobis are no less than anyone else, in the sense that they are emulating the way of life of the middle classes only to indicate their class but not their caste mobility, where class denotes both money and education. The changes are also fairly superficial. The homes of the most prosperous dhobis have not undergone any fundamental changes in culture, basic ways of life, or values. People still sit on the floor to eat at a public function. They still eat the same kind of food. The younger people wear different clothes, more modern as they think, but they are certainly not aware of the 'contemporary' fashions or come anywhere near to emulating the lifestyle of the upper middle classes. Yet what has changed is their self-confidence, the assurance with which they conduct public functions and perform rituals in which they are installing their own caste-based deities among the highest Hindu deities, a phenomenon that would not have been possible a few decades back, or in many other parts of India. Printing the names of prominent citizens on the cards celebrating their community events is another indicator of their claims to democratic equality. I would like to counter Srinivas by saying that what the untouchables and marginal castes and classes are staking a claim to is not a higher ritual identity or even a higher caste identity but their place in Indian democracy as equal citizens. With education and exposure via the media, the young generation are more aware of their rights, even their rights to the city as per Lefebvre (1996). The transition from *biradari* to *samaj* indicates this shift, from caste and community to being a citizen of a democratic country. In Weberian terminology, a legal and rational, rather than a traditional, claim to equality.

The next chapter discusses the dilemmas of identity transformation, the manner in which dhobis are envisioning their place in society, their relations with those in power, and their own negotiations for a place in the sun.

Notes

1. These elements are local, cultural, and specific to certain jati groups, and in spite of having the appearance of being Islamic, they may differ significantly from conservative and

hardcore Islamic practices, which of course even the low-caste Muslims are hardly known as practising.

2. This *puja* was never part of Brahmanical Hindu rituals but was introduced into Maharashtra during the struggle for freedom from colonial rule by Bal Gangadhar Tilak, as a symbol of Hindu Indian identity and as a way to bring the masses together.

3. The Old Fort is an archaeological site where there are many layers of the earlier cities that preceded Delhi, the earliest layer being Indraprastha, the city believed to be built by the Pandava brothers of the Mahabharata. Excavations are continuing at this site, which also houses a museum.

4. Hidimba, the demoness, finds a significant space in the narratives of the marginal. We also find her in the myth of Sham Bhatu, another popular deity of the dhobis.

5. Daksha is Shiva's father-in-law, the father of his wife Uma, who is Parvati in another birth. Daksha is arrogant and insults Shiva as a pauper and a person not deserving of his daughter, the daughter of a king. Uma, the faithful wife, is unable to tolerate the way her father berates her husband and gives up her life. An enraged Shiva takes her body on his shoulder and begins a dance of destruction (*tandava*) and, fearing that the entire universe will be destroyed, Vishnu, the preserver, cuts Uma's body into pieces; Hindus worship those spots as Shakti Peeth. Wherever a piece of her body fell is marked as a holy spot in the Hindu sacred landscape. Shiva, the destroyer, is accompanied by a variety of minor demons and devils who live with him in the cremation ground, help destroy evil, and help victims of injustice. Uma is reborn as Parvati and becomes Shiva's consort forever.

6. This is the same logic used by the upper castes to oppress the lower castes and legitimize their actions.

7. The deity called Sham Khatu by the dhobis is known as Khatu Shyam in Rajasthan and has considerable local following, but he is not a known or popular Hindu deity. The legend about him is almost the same as that told to me by Bishanlal.

8. These are a genre of devotional songs usually sung in a group, but they can have a lead singer or may also be sung alone. They are recognized by the musical accompaniments as well as by their tone; the singing of 'Hare Krishna, Hare Rama' is an example of *kirtan*.

9. *Aarti* is a specific form of Hindu worship that involves propitiating the deity with lamps and incense along with other objects.

10. Pallath (1995) has described the Theyyam myths and their expression in the ritual dances as embodied protest by the low-caste Pulayas of the Malabar region of South India. The Pulayas protest against the legitimacy of the Brahmins, the sexual exploitation of their women, and other forms of injustice meted out to their caste group.

11. The demolition of ghats began during Congress rule and under the chief-ministership of Sheila Dikshit, who made many aesthetic changes in the landscape of Delhi, building numerous flyovers, roads, and landscaped, manicured gardens following what Baviskar (2002) has labelled 'bourgeoisie environmentalism'. She had a mission to beautify Delhi, especially the banks of the river Yamuna, which were converted to a green belt. The memorials made to Indira Gandhi and her son Rajiv Gandhi on the riverbanks were marked by dense tree plantations. Sheila Dikshit is, however, known—or, rather, got a negative reputation—for the transformation of Delhi for the 2010 Commonwealth Games, for which many projects that were overtly detrimental to the environment were undertaken. The environment of Delhi has been declining over the years, as most of these changes were ornamental and, although somewhat pleasing to the eye, actually contributed to the deterioration of Delhi's air, which finally gave it the status of being one of the most polluted cities in the world. The dhobis are well aware of this, and they make it a point to describe how much the Yamuna is polluted in spite of the removal of dhobi ghats from its banks.

12. Jangam (2017: 6) has also mentioned, with respect to South India, that 'Dalit activists, under the influence of Hindu Brahmanical ideals, urged untouchables to refrain from eating meat, particularly beef, drinking alcohol and smoking, and to develop habits of hygiene'.

13. Sudhir Kakar (1991), the psychoanalyst, has done a detailed ethnographic study of this particular shrine.

14. Although, having almost exclusively Hindu followers, it would be difficult to call Sai Baba a Hindu deity.

15. *Samosa* is a popular Indian savoury of fried dough stuffed with spicy potatoes.

16. Both the terms Kuldevta and Ishtdevta refer among the upper castes to the patrilineal lineage groups (*Kul*) usually embodied in the joint family. Interestingly, the dhobis use the same terms for their *biradari* as for them; the *biradari* is the core unit of continuity and identity just as the *Kul* (lineage) is for the upper castes.

17. Kuldevta, or lineage god, is a concept variously understood in different parts of India. In some places it refers to the family deity, and in other places to the lineage deity; for the dhobis it seems to refer to the *biradari* deity.

18. *Shamianas* are integral to most Indian ceremonies that involve congregation in a public place. They comprise thick cotton or mixed-fibre sheets put together to make highly decorative awnings. Decoration of a *shamiana* is a specialized art that is sometimes highly innovative and attains great aesthetic standards. Most of them take on the appearance of a large well-lit and decorated hall.

6

The Political Realm

Why Dhobis Shun the Dalit Label

It is well recognized that the lower castes and untouchables in India have adopted the Dalit label as a political move towards both protest and emancipation, yet, as rightly pointed out by Deliège (1999: xi) and on the basis of my own observations, it is not a universally accepted label for all those who belong to the lowest rung of the jati hierarchy. Not all untouchables are even interested in protest or in taking up a militant attitude towards the jati/Varna system like the Dalit Panthers. Rather than taking the militant Dalit movement as a generalization, it is a more reasonable intellectual exercise to examine why the Dalit label became acceptable to some communities and in a similar way to examine why it has been rejected or ignored by others who belong to the same socio-economic level.

Although in my earlier writings I too have subsumed the dhobis under a Dalit identity (Channa 2001, 2005, 2013b), the dhobis themselves do not subscribe to it. I had put them in this category because of their marginality and untouchable status, but Dalit is a self-ascribed identity and cannot be imposed from the outside. The dhobis as a group are situated in a disadvantaged position, a position from where they hope to get little social advantage, although there are economic possibilities. Their mode of protest or contestation of their ascribed lowly ritual and social position is in the form of covert strategies and manipulations and not in terms of overt militancy. It is absolutely true that they do not accept their inferior position and have absolute belief in their dignity and humanity, a point emphasized by several scholars (Jangam 2017). As pointed out by Sarkar (1997: 10), the Brahmanical prescriptions for the ideal moral order in the Kaliyuga were in imposition of patriarchy and caste rules, a prescription that the collectives at the bottom of Hindu society hardly conceded to. In their version of history, the dhobis had said to me in a very early part of my association with them, 'the dhobis were created before the Brahmins'.

Dhobis of Delhi. Subhadra Mitra Channa, Oxford University Press. © Subhadra Mitra Channa 2024.
DOI: 10.1093/9780198926238.003.0007

This remark was in answer to my question as to why the Brahmin did not preside over dhobi weddings. The Brahmin's answer to that question would have been in terms of the dhobis and other jatis of similar rank not being *dwija*, or twice-born. Therefore the dhobis, as others like them, have 'an alternative worldview set against the unequal and oppressive Brahmanical Hinduism' (Jangam 2017: 5). At the same time they are governed by logic and rationality to seek maximum benefits that they can derive from their environment and conditions of existence, and dhobis that I have known often set aside emotion for reason.

In Chapter 3, details about the dhobis' relationship with their clients made it clear that they show overt deference to their clients, not because they actually feel that way, but because it makes good business sense. It is the viability of their jati-based occupation and the occupational logic of compliance towards their clients that make the dhobis conservative rather than rebellious in their attitude towards the upper castes and towards society in general. Their politics cannot be seen as separate from their economy. Several politically inclined men among the dhobis clearly stated to me that they did not subscribe to the Dalit movement and thought that it was a movement only for South India and Maharashtra. Few dhobis are even aware of the name of B. R. Ambedkar, unless they have been taught in school and college, and they do not recognize him as their own leader.

Although I too have been academically classifying the dhobis among the Dalits (Channa 2005, Channa and Mencher 2013), at this point I have been introspecting and am convinced that if the dhobis are not subscribing to this term, it will not be ethical to label them as such. They are more in tune with the names of Mayawati and Kanshi Ram as leaders of the untouchables.[1] The term that these two leaders have coined for the untouchables and lower castes is 'bahujan', meaning the masses or 'common people'. As far as the Sheheri dhobis are concerned, they are simply that, 'Sheheri dhobis', and seek no further political identity for themselves. This reluctance to be viewed as rebellious is linked to the logic of their everyday existence, as they are dependent on the upper castes and classes for their livelihood, in direct personalized relations. In this sense their dependency is somewhat different, say, from the dependency of the sweepers on their upper-caste supervisors in a formal organizational setting, namely that of the Municipal Corporation of Delhi as described by Prashad (2000). The dhobis are in personalized one-to-one relations with their clients, outside of the formal structure of organization that binds the sweeper to the supervisor. There is far more scope for manipulation and negotiation in the dhobi–client relationship than the one that the sweepers have with the rule-bound municipal corporation that is their employer. Although the dhobis at times have dealt with certain issues collectively, their daily sustenance and income come from individual clients whom they meet and interact with on an intimate non-political platform. There is a difference between having a 'job' and having a relation that is multifaceted with components of dominance/subservience, kinship/family, ritual dependence, and even friendship thrown in.

Since the sweeper's work was attached to a public institution, namely the municipal corporation, they could develop a sense of being a labour class, like the industrial labour from which the Dalit identity could evolve. 'The sweepers developed a sense of class in 1926 when the communists and socialists organized the sweepers union and forged a strike in Batala, Punjab' (Prashad 2000: 130). The dhobis have never evolved from a community to a class, never developed a collective political identity that is oppositional, which is essential for class formation. Their identity vis-à-vis the dominant castes has always been notionally complementary, even while it remains unequal in real terms. Their political actions are mobilized at the level of community, which is a cultural and not a class entity.

I have often been told by dhobi men and women that the traditional occupation leaves them with no time to spare. They never seem to have time for political action or preparations for the same. Although the *biradari* physically gets together on occasions, these are rare and never more than once or twice a year. Their lives are fragmentary, revolving around their time-consuming, labour-intensive work and *biradari/* family life within the overarching cultural relations that give them a sense of belongingness but not the goal-based collective interest motivation required for aggressive politicization. The process of 'culturalization of caste' (Natarajan 2012) is analogous to my own analysis of the dhobi *biradari* as a cultural construct, socially reproduced (Channa 1985). The desire to maintain internal divisions among the dhobis, as I described in Chapter 2, delimits the size of the unit that can act effectively as a political entity. The Sheheri *biradari* or *samaj*, as they now prefer to call it, maintains its differences with other similar dhobi units as it gets together for various purposes—panchayats, rituals, and weddings—and sees itself as a unified identity validated by cultural practices such as the Shobha Yatra described in Chapter 2. Keeping their *biradari* small has the advantage of reproducing its close-knit nature but dilutes its effectiveness as a political body. Yet in the present times they are engaging in some forms of negotiation that are effective without being conflictual, for example the magnified ritual enactments like the Shobha Yatra. These overtly non-aggressive practices have the political agenda of assertion and negotiation, as can be seen in their success in getting a space for their *biradari* deity at the cremation ground.

An additional factor for the dhobis' lack of military politicization like that of the Dalits is the steady nature of their association with the city of Delhi. For at least a couple of centuries and several generations, they have not suffered any displacement and have not been forced into a new setup. The traumas suffered by the city of Delhi—the various invasions and the Partition after independence—did affect them in emotional and economic terms, but never took away their livelihood. Somehow, they have been able to maintain their livelihood through all forms of disasters, and that has proved to be their resilience for recovery and for maintaining a semblance of stability. But this resilience and viability require a steady continuity of relationship with their clients, a dependency that will break if they were to exhibit any kind of rebellious action, no matter what they thought in private. In the practical consideration of their client–server relationship, the dhobis remain politically passive, expressing their discontent within the framework of acceptable social norms.

To understand the lack of emergence of Dalit identity among the dhobis, let us compare them with the historical/political context of the emergence of a Dalit identity, described and analysed by Omvedt (1994), which needs to be understood against the background of a narrative of contestation in which the untouchable leaders such as Jyotirao Phule and B. R. Ambedkar had critiqued the upper-caste-based nationalism that began in the colonial period but has taken a definite shape as Hindu nationalism in the present days. The lower-caste leaders had demanded social equity and erosion of caste hierarchy as an integral aspect of 'nationalism' and a democratic ideal that was essential for gaining true freedom. In their perspective, nationalism was not only a freedom from an external enemy but also a reform of the internal feudal caste-based society of India. Jangam (2017: 6) claims that the nationalism of the Dalits in the colonial period was a continuity of their critical perspective on Brahmanical society from precolonial times. In other words, it was not a product of colonial education or thoughts but an indigenous and original perspective. During the colonial period, the Dalit nationalism was present but overridden by the upper-caste nationalism of the major Indian leaders, who also harked back to the 'glorious Hindu past', the seeds of which have come to flower in present-day Hindu supremacist ideology. In contrast to it, the Nehruvian secularism considered caste-based inequalities as unacceptable and not legitimate in independent India, and the Indian constitution was drafted with a major contribution by Ambedkar into a document that overruled divisions based on caste, religion, ethnicity, and other forms of discrimination. But these 'empty' laws did not become pervasive in Indian civil society, as did the persistence of social inequalities and divisions that were getting more and more dominant and pervasive over time. However, at the level of policymaking, caste was ignored or pretended to be non-existent except for reservation or positive discrimination, a point of view that has come to shadow present-day policies that ignore all claims made on the basis of occupational and cultural rights of the various caste groups, especially of those at the bottom. It is not legitimate to claim any concessions founded on the 'difference' based on caste as a cultural entity (Natarajan 2012).

Here it is also relevant to mention that Mahatma Gandhi, in his more pragmatic approach, had recognized that the division of labour had some potential and that caste as 'difference' was not quite as negative as caste as hierarchy, and he specifically condemned untouchability as inhuman. For his views on caste, he has often been blamed as a conservative Hindu, yet he had an intuitive understanding that control over a specific skill, as provided by the caste-based occupation system, did have potential for social security and could be a resource for some. One can understand this perspective by the persistence of caste among those religious groups that do not subscribe to the ritual view of caste, such as the Muslims, and more interestingly, in the formation of new occupation-based caste groups such as the Muslim Zardoz of Delhi (Gupta and Channa 1996), who have been studied by Gupta (1996). A combination of endogamy and a household-based occupation involves women in work and also gives rise to a feeling of horizontal solidarity. The equal participation of women ensures a tendency towards, in fact a need for, endogamy, as having a skilled wife is essential for the running of the household. However, if the community did not have any specific specialization and were village servants like the Mahars, or if their occupation lost its significance in the contemporary capitalist economy, then they would look for a non-caste-based identity and greater political and economic choices.

There are two factors to which I would attribute the rise of the Dalit movement. Firstly, as Omvedt (1994) has analysed, it was the industrialization of Western India, especially of Bombay, Ahmadabad, and other cities, which opened up a space for absorption of the unskilled labourers of the village, who were earlier treated as village servants. The strength of the Dalit movement among such castes as the Mahars, who made the transition to industrial labour with ease, lay in this transition. Industrial labour is open to and conducive to organized political activity. Industrial workers are in an impersonal client relationship, can communicate with other workers, and are not bound by any inherited norms and values. Although, as I have shown in my work, dhobis also transition to other kinds of work but they are located in a different kind of economic field. Industrial labour, in the early phases of industrialization, was also subjected to a kind of clustering, where a large number of factory workers would be living in close proximity to each other. The Mahar Mohallas, for example, described by Moon (2001) in his autobiography, indicate that many persons of the untouchable castes lived together in clusters, but they did not have any particular caste-based occupation like the dhobis. They could use their proximity to engage in political action, unlike the dhobis, who use their community primarily for economic cooperation.

The second factor is the absence of an Ambedkar. Brass (1994: 26) has written that 'It is a recurring feature of Indian political history that only a charismatic leader with a simple appeal can unite the sub-continent or any of its larger people for a political purpose'. A Dalit leader in Pune belonging to the Maang caste group told me that at present the Mahars are dominating in local politics as well as in the national arena because of Ambedkar. He was an exceptional leader who rose from among the working class at a time when most other leaders in India belonged to the upper castes and classes. Along with Jyotirao Phule and Savitribai Phule, he provided leadership to the most downtrodden of Indian society. But it is important to remember that Ambedkar was a labour leader, leading factory workers in a newly industrializing region. An industry and factory environment brings men and women together on a common platform where they can be led easily under a strong and charismatic leadership like that of Ambedkar. The dhobi work is household-based, and a dhobi works with the cooperation of his wife, family, and other community members. Also, unlike in a factory, where workers have a usually formal and mostly hostile relationship with management, the dhobis maintain a personalized relationship with their clients. Although the degree of personalization is being diluted, it is not yet fully gone, and in the more conservative parts of the city it continues more or less as before. Even in recent times in my visit to the Old City, I have found clients sitting and chatting with the dhobi while he is ironing their shirt. The dhobis still get personal favours from the clients, and, more importantly, they still have expectations of their clients that go beyond a purely professional relationship; or, in other words, they still feel bound by moral ties rather than purely economic ones.

A very important aspect of Ambedkar's philosophy was his criticism of the caste system and of the practice of untouchability. While dhobis were always critical of the fact of being untouchables, I have not seen any of them being critical of the caste system itself. In fact, in the 1970s, many of them practised it themselves. I remember one woman telling me that they do not wash the clothes of those they consider as lower castes than themselves. So, I asked her, how will they know the caste of people who come to live in a hotel or eat at a restaurant, as they often wash clothes of establishments such as hospitals, hostels, and hotels? Her reply was that if they do not come to know, then it is alright, but she will not knowingly wash the clothes of a sweeper or leatherworker, 'aankhon dekhi makkhi nigli nahi jati' ('I cannot swallow a fly if I see it'). Although one would have expected that such a remark made at the end of the last century would rarely be heard now, it would be difficult to assess the persistence of such sentiments, as by now a majority of people are careful not to talk about such things, even if deep within they do believe in them. Blunt (1931) remarked that 'untouchability is such a deeply ingrained practice that it is respected by the untouchables themselves' (cf. Deliège 1999: 31).

From the perspective of the dhobis, as their livelihood lies *within the caste system* and not outside of it, they cannot criticize it from the inside, at least not beyond a point. The very viability of their caste-based occupation prevents them from becoming strong critics of the system. A very interesting comparison of the dhobis can be made with the Balmikis, or sweeper castes, studied by Prashad (2000), who makes the statement that the Balmiki community turned to the Hindutva movement and 'linked its destiny to the political agencies of the established order' (Prashad 2000: x). The Balmikis therefore present an opposed category to those who claim the identity of Dalits, but the dhobis are neither Dalits nor prone to 'linking their destiny' to the established order. What makes the work of those assigned to the sweeper caste groups different from most other untouchable caste groups is that their work is an essential service in the public domain. As Prashad has shown in his social history of the Balmikis, they were absorbed, almost forcefully, into the Delhi Municipal Corporation (DMC) as workers for the state, because it was realized that their bodies and labour needed to be controlled in the interest of the city at large. Their labour was deemed essential to the health and hygiene of the city in totality, and therefore control over them became as essential aspect of governance. The sweepers, it seems, did not give in easily, as they had a guild-like control over their clients from individual households. They went on strike in 1873 and 1876, but by 1884 the DMC enforced its rights over the 'nightsoil and sweepings'(Prashad 2000: 8)of the city, and subsequently the sweepers were forced to become employees of the DMC and lost their independent relations to their clients, exactly the kind of relations the dhobis still maintain. The DMC appointed ward-wide contractors to supervise the sweepers in 1887, who as indicated by the archives were 'middle class Ashraf Muslims and Hindus' (Prashad 2000: 12). Then, to make the system more controlled, the DMC appointed jamadars as overall managers who had absolute control over the hiring and firing of the sweepers. These Jamadars, who were mostly upper-caste, took undue advantage of the sweepers, including 'extra-economic favours' (Prashad 2000: 14) such as sexual favours from their women. 'The power of these Hindu and Muslim jamadars over Dalit sweepers was twice as strong, for not only did the jamadar exert the authority of his office, but he was able to exert the ritualized authority of his caste' (Prashad 2000: 16).

Post independence, the Balmikis were made to believe that their sufferings were related to their Muslim affinities, and they began to change their religious affiliations which, like the dhobis, were leaning towards

Sufism. Their earlier affiliation to Lal Beg, a deity that was neither Hindu nor Muslim but had its own identity with its own priesthood, was given up. Although the Arya Samaj had shunned the untouchables, by the early twentieth century the Hindu Sudhar Sabha began to admit the Dalits and allowed them to wear the sacred thread (*janue*). The Delhi Mehtars and Churhas (later named Balmikis) buried their dead with the chant of '*Allah ke supurd*' ('In the hands of Allah') and offered lamps at the shrine of Pir Bala Shah (Prashad 2000: 95). But later in the 1920s the shrine was transformed into the Balmiki temple, with a constructed myth of antiquity. At present the Balmiki colony exists near the Balmiki temple. The dependency of the sweepers on their upper-caste supervisors for all their life cycle problems led them to be part of anti-Muslim violence and also to turn towards a Hindutva ideology.

A somewhat tangential condition, but one that cannot be ignored, is the role played by a literary tradition in consolidating and taking forward the Dalit identity, as the works of many talented Dalit writers show. As pointed out by Jangam (2017: 3), 'Dalit intellectual arguments and political agitation in the public sphere brought the issues of untouchability, social exclusion and marginalization to the forefront of the nationalist imagination.' In South India, Dalits or untouchables seem to have taken an early lead in education, as reported by Jangam (2017: 24): 'As early as 1856, non-Brahman representation in schools increased considerably and was reported in the annual reports of the education department.' Dhobis have yet to develop an intellectual or literary mode of criticism, although they have amply used the ritual and symbolic domain to do so. Unlike the Quarashis described by Ahmad (2018: 45), whose 'writings express a biradari in search of its own historical narration', they have not yet shown any interest in penning their history, in using the written mode to demarginalize themselves (Narayan 2001). Their lives and central concerns are with the present and not with the past, although with the emergence of Nagar Sain one may discern a movement towards that process.

Difference and Discrimination

All differences do not necessarily translate into discrimination, although most do. Differences have their own function and the primary of these is that they facilitate exchange. According to Lévi-Strauss (1967) and other exchange theorists, if there were no differences then there would be no exchange and no social life. However, as societies become more complex, the differences assume hierarchical characters for purposes of extraction and exploitation of human bodies and other resources. Because of its discriminatory and hierarchical nature and the dehumanization brought about by the practice of untouchability, the caste system has been universally condemned and rightly so. Not just academics and social activists, even many religious leaders and spiritual personalities have condemned caste discrimination. The nineteenth-century Bengali saint Ramakrishna Paramahamsa is said to have cast away the sacred thread he wore as a Brahmin, saying that he would never reach his deity, his object of devotion, if he continued to wear it. But at the same time there are two aspects of jati-based differences that have a positive impact, although divisive: caste-based occupational monopolies and the caste-based community solidarities.

Several scholars, such as Gupta (1991), have also emphasized the 'difference' aspect of the caste system in addition to its other attributes. There were two points of view here: the 'organic solidarity' perspective of functionalists like Leach (1960), and the oppositional perspective of those, like Dumont (1970), who highlighted the inequality of the system. But all this was thought out from the outside, and it was only the path-breaking work of Mencher(1974) that opened up another viewpoint—that of looking at the system from the eyes of those at the bottom. Channa and Mencher (2013) have made an attempt to include as many voices from the untouchable communities as possible in their compilation of Dalit lives. In the present work, however, while making out the entire argument from the perspective of the dhobis, I stumbled upon the realization that the dhobis do not think in the perspective of the Dalit discourse at all. Their mind is oriented towards their day-to-day existence and the vagaries of a hard life of labour, but they also think only within the framework of the jati organization and do not have a perspective outside of it. They also do not have any oppositional or confrontational ideology like the Dalit activists. Their perspective indicates that the Dalit ideology may be limited to either the organized labour sector of the untouchables or their elite. For most others, it is the problems of daily existence that are of foremost concern and, like the dhobis, if the caste identity is conducive to a survival strategy, they are not averse to it. Not one dhobi, man or woman, I know has ever expressed a desire to transcend or disown their jati identity, at least among those who still live within the *biradari* organization. Only those who have a strong resource base and have attained a high level of economic and social security would opt for a jati-less identity. But it is equally difficult for some kinds of high achievers, especially those who have entered institutions of higher education like a medical or engineering college under positive discrimination rules, to deny their original caste identity. They may transcend the cultural aspects of their identity and opt for or assume a more cosmopolitan lifestyle, but a majority are still bound to their jati identity for their livelihood and social support.

To some extent this reinvention of jati identity is tied to the transformed economy and the introduction of a capitalist market system that has played a key role in giving economic viability and strength to some traditional occupations outside of their ritual and caste-based relevance (Gill 2010, Ahmad 2018, Kapoor 2018). The lower castes had been assigned to certain tasks because of their unpleasantness and perceived pollution for the upper castes, but the market economy has had a serendipitous effect for the some of the lower castes, who have found that the perceived polluting and degrading tasks that they were following took on a renewed vigour in the open capitalist market. The first study of this kind was conducted by Owen Lynch (1969) among the Jatavs of Agra, who belong to the Chamar community associated with leatherwork. The higher-caste Hindus shunned any contact with leather as highly polluting and would have nothing to do with it, even when shoemaking and -selling became an industry, and a highly lucrative one at that. The consequent transition of the Chamars to become Jatavs and their entry into politics and claims to a place within Indian democracy have been described by several anthropologists, including one belonging to the same community (Nandu 2013), as well as in the classic work by Lynch (1969) and more recent work by Kapoor (2018). Mayawati, the most powerful untouchable leader to emerge in recent times, is a Jatav.

I came in contact with a community of leatherworkers in a village in the Garhwal region, where a similar situation had prevailed. With the integration of the local and the global market, the skin and bones of animal carcasses were items that gained significantly in value. Whenever an animal died, the owner would auction the carcass, but the local community of traditional leatherworkers blocked anyone from outside the community bidding for them. Most local people would not do it anyway for fear of social ostracization, as an animal carcass is considered highly polluting for upper castes, but even if someone tried to bid, they would be faced with great hostility from the leatherworker community, which acted like one in these matters. Here too I was told that the *biradari* ties were strong and the people knew how to use them to their advantage. The very work that had kept them on the margins of society was now leading them to prosperity and economic gains that they were not ready to forsake.

Another instance of a caste-based occupation giving economic viability to a community is from my fieldwork done in Pachmarhi in 1973 as a Master's student of anthropology. There I had come across a community of 'Bhangis' (scavengers) who were becoming prosperous as they raised pigs. Earlier these were only raised for meat for eating by the lower castes (upper castes of Hindus do not eat pork). But by the late 1960s, again with the integration of local and wider markets, pig hair had assumed commercial importance as it was used for making paintbrushes. The monopolistic advantage that the community had and its highly polluting status within the caste hierarchy gave an economic advantage to the caste group and, like the Jatavs, it too used the horizontal community ties to maintain the monopoly gaining both economic and political status in the local region. Gill's (2010) work on the Khatiks and their monopoly of the plastic recycling industry is a recent and key example of the way a caste identity can turn into a market advantage.

The identity transition of the leatherworkers was captured beautifully by a woman with whom I had a conversation while visiting the Jatav neighbourhoods in Agra, on a visit in the 1980s. She said, 'First we were Chamars, then Mahatma Gandhi told us we were Harijans, now we have become Scheduled Castes.' When I pointed to a picture of Ambedkar on her walls and asked her who he was, she said, 'He was a great man, he has done a lot for us, he is like *bhagwan* [god] for the poor people like us.' But she did not mention the term Dalit, and in the course of my fieldwork I have not found this term being used by anyone in North India who is not an academic. The ordinary people on the ground do not associate with this term, although in some communities that are highly politicized, like the Jatavs, Ambedkar's name is familiar to many. This woman had also pointed to a spinning wheel (*charkha*) lying in a corner of her house and told me that when they were Harijans, she used to spin, but '*Ab hum schedule caste hain aur charkha nahi kat te hain*' ('Now we are scheduled castes and do not spin the spinning wheel anymore'). Many persons of other castes also told me, in whispers, 'Those who call themselves Jatavs now are actually Chamars.' I was told that because they have progressed on the economic ladder, they have changed their social identity. Some of them who have attained higher status, especially as activists and academics, also proudly flaunt their original identity of being Chamars. But for non-political ordinary persons like the woman I was talking to, these identities are assumed and external to their selves. The core identity is always around the *biradari*, the circle of kin and affines, and consists of the people they can call their own. But for all of them the economic viability and livelihood options are important.

The dhobis too have undergone perceived transformations in their collective identity, as I could assess from my multiple conversations with them. The young people I meet today are much less, in fact almost negligibly, burdened by their untouchable identity. Those, like Sheetal and her husband, who hold fairly respectable jobs in the formal sector have never complained about discrimination in the workplace such as I used to hear in the 1970s and 1980s. In the seventies, there was still a very significant amount of consciousness about their untouchable status, and it was openly verbalized by them. I was often looked at askance, especially by the elderly, as to why I was not averse to eating and drinking water in the dhobi households. Some even asked me if I was a Christian. Most households where I had not already been interacting would ask me whether I would accept water and food from them.

Parents would tell me how their children were humiliated at school by teachers who often refused to teach them. They would be told to go back home and wash clothes and iron like their parents. Things began to change slowly but not until near the end of the twentieth century. At present almost every dhobi child goes to school, wherever they may live, and many are studying in college. They dress well and mingle well with the other young people in their setting, and also there are now many children from the marginal and underprivileged who are going to school and college. In India, higher education is highly subsidized and almost free for all. While primary education is also free in the government-run schools, the standard of infrastructure in these schools is usually very poor and the education imparted is much below the standard of expensive privately run schools[2]. Needless to say, such a stratified schooling system has maintained the gap between the lower and higher castes/classes, and even though there is reservation at the highest level, such as medical and engineering colleges, it remains a difficult proposition for any child who was brought up in the dhobi *katra* of the seventies, or, for that matter, for those who are still living there, to qualify for these competitive examinations. In my long association with the dhobis, in which I have seen a generation or two growing up, I have come across extremely few young men and women making it to a higher white-collar job on a government reservation. But over time, what has changed is the social attitude towards them. While children from the lower strata were unwelcome and even rejected by the school system earlier, they have felt much less the burden of jati-based stigma during the past couple of decades. A sense of dignity and pride in their identity has also entered into the mindset of the present generation. One cannot say that all feelings of discrimination have disappeared, but they have certainly been diluted, at least in overt interactions.

Among the earlier generation there was a higher level of aspiration and lesser motivation to pursue the work of a dhobi than there is today. One major reason is a transformation in the concepts of ritual pollution that are now extremely diluted in the urban setting. The concept of jati that existed as an exclusionary mark, stamping people as untouchable, is no longer seen as acceptable within the social world of the megapolis. People still identify caste for purposes of marriage, as a political factor, and even as an occupational category, but few urban children have been brought up to actually practise untouchability.

Untouchability and Occupation

The two major negative marks against the jati/Varna system have been its seeming immobility and the practice of untouchability. The former assumption has come under much criticism by historians who have shown that the system was never as rigid as it had been supposed. Even Dumont (1970) pointed out that only the topmost and the bottom-most had their positions fixed but the middle orders always had the option to challenge their positions. This internal flux of the jati order, where different jatis have always contested and negotiated their positions vis-à-vis each other, is an inherent aspect of this system till the present day, when both economic and political power play a key role in this process of negotiation and contestation. The Varna orders that controlled the fluid power of politics and economy have always shown the maximum aptitude for contestation. Even in the earliest known historical periods, rulers from lower castes founded dynasties like the Nanda Dynasty. As pointed out by historians like O'Hanlon and others, the Ksatriya Varna has always made space for those who gained in power to acquire social privileges. The lowest and untouchable castes have been most constrained by the system, for they were always kept as dependants with no space or resources for manipulation. Within the village economy and society, the service caste groups provided service only in lieu of bare maintenance. Dalit literature abounds in such narratives that indicate the inhuman torture heaped upon those at the bottom of the jati hierarchy and those who were harnessed to the system for providing unpaid labour (Hazari 1951, Valmiki 2001, Dangle 2009, Bama 2005).

The urban milieu provided an alternative and more empowering environment for these marginal caste groups. The market economy and capitalist intrusion have directly benefited these groups in two ways. Firstly, as in the case of the Mahars, who were freed from bondage to enter the industrial economy as workers, to come out of the jati/Varna system altogether. The Dalit ideology that evolved from the factories and industries of Western India visualizes an emancipation that frees the individual from the bondage of jati-based servility altogether. But even in this situation we find that the community-based, horizontal solidarities survive, even when the community gives up on its traditional occupation and even religion. The original identities survive among even those who convert to Buddhism and Christianity (Dube 1998, Robinson and Clarke 2003). The second impact of the capitalist market system has been to free some of these occupations from caste bondage and give them commercial value as skills that have a fiscal potential, such as haircutting, washing of clothes, and stringing beads, among others. No doubt many skills have fallen by the wayside, especially those that did not fit in with the changing social and economic needs. Paradoxically, it was the skill and knowledge of the upper castes that became redundant rather than those of the lowest, because they had always performed the most basic functions of the fulfilment of everyday needs. While the knowledge of Sanskrit texts and the performance of daily rituals declined in value, the barbers, washermen, cleaners, and potters are finding that their skills still have potential in the modern market set-up. There were skills like fortune telling that completely lost their validity, as shown by the Rangswamis of Rajasthan who have become more impoverished than the lowest jati in their village (Channa 2019a). This is not to say that most of these tasks have gained considerably in social value, as they are still marginalized in social terms, but they do have the viability to enable the communities to survive. They also provided an alternative to those who would find it difficult to compete with the upper castes for the same occupational avenues with the limited resources that they have. Most importantly, their members realize that they have strength in terms of unity. Even in the seventies a young man told me, 'We dhobis have strength in our unity. If one person is in trouble, from our *biradari*, he just has to raise a voice and a dozen will gather to help him.' Nearly forty years later, another young man, a prosperous entrepreneur dealing in antiques in the Old Delhi market, told me nearly the same thing. He said, 'I am not involved in the traditional occupation of being a dhobi but I too realize that our *biradari* is our strength. I personally contribute to and organize activities that will bring the *biradari* together.' He told me that they have community activities at certain times of the year that bring them all together. Some of these are ritual, but there are other activities, like sports, that are more attractive for the younger and more educated generation.

In the seventies, the younger generation would often express negative views regarding their occupation. They told me that dhobi work was very labour-intensive and required exposure and discomfort, as they were mostly on the banks of the Yamuna River: 'Sometimes we are in the sun, and sometimes we are hanging onto our clothes that are getting blown away by the wind.' Another young man told me that they became unfit for other kinds of jobs, especially those that required them to sit on chairs, as their posture is distorted by standing and beating down on clothes: 'Our backs get bent in a certain way and we can no longer sit on chairs.' It is true that almost up to the nineties I rarely saw a dhobi man or woman sit in a chair, or even have chairs in their houses. However, at present most houses have chairs and sofas. The changing technologies and also the complete erasure of washing clothes on the Yamuna riverbank (at least for this community) have made the work conditions quite different for them. The ghats are now enclosed areas with cemented tubs for holding water. The water comes through pipes pumped by machines. Most of the clothes are washed in large commercial washing machines, with only the finer touches being given by hand. However, the easy camaraderie and cooperation still exist make for a different milieu at these modern dhobi *ghats*, where men wash the clothes and sometimes one sees women helping, in close proximity to each other. In fact the process of sharing common goods, the ghat, the washing machines, and the drying area has increased their sense of companionship.

The Yamuna riverbank was more dispersed, with family units acting as cooperating units—the women and children helping out in spreading and drying clothes, women bringing food and otherwise cooperating with their husband. The contemporary ghat scene is far more of a masculine domain, with mostly men running the water and machinery and forming units of work-help groups. Women, mostly older, are seen in small numbers helping in the drying of clothes, and children are totally absent. The slow transfer of dhobi work from a family work unit to a more masculine working culture is becoming clearly evident. The delivery and collection of clothes are mostly done by the younger men on motorcycles; gone are the days of the donkey carts, and only the older people still use cycles. Within the old city, the women may still collect clothes, going from house to house, but this is limited to household clothes only. Most commercial cloth washing has taken a more urban—and in the cognition of the dhobis, a more 'respectable'—turn. The elimination of women from the workplace seems also to be part of the process of respectability. From a family-based household form of labour, laundry is now assuming more of a commercial, market-based work aura dominated by men. They no longer feel any stigma when they are carrying the clothes on their motorcycles and washing them in washing machines at the cemented, commercialized ghats. To them it is like any other activity in the urban market arena. Clothes are still dried in the sun and the energy-consuming, expensive driers are only used in emergency situations, like if it is continuously raining or if a client is in a great hurry. To dry their clothes, they use any public space that is available to them. One can see clothes drying on flyover bridges, by the roadside, on dividers between busy roads, and in public parks, among other available spaces. Since there is no overt or written law or rule against the drying of clothes by the dhobis, no one says anything. Most Indians take the presence of the dhobi in the metropolis as a given, as something that has been a ubiquitous part of the city landscape.

By taking any available space to dry their clothes, the dhobis also stake a claim to the city—a city to which they feel they belong. The shift to the use of machines from manual labour has brought about a sea change in their perception of their own identity. Earlier they felt they were designated a lower position in society because they were doing manual labour, but as they have transitioned to the use of machines for most of their work, they feel they have climbed a step on the ladder of respectability. Even in their own houses, most dhobis wash clothes in a domestic washing machine, and many school- and college-going young people wash clothes at home in these machines. However, they still retain the heavy metal iron for ironing clothes, as the use of these is the trademark of the dhobi. No one can iron like a dhobi, as they use these irons for pressing the most difficult of clothes. It is for this reason that in the urban areas, while most people use a machine at home for washing clothes, they are still given to the dhobi for ironing. Only emergency or light ironing is done at home. The need for so much ironing is also linked to the Indian way of clothing, which uses a lot of cotton material, sarees and dhotis, long shirts and large scarves, that need heavy ironing. Giving clothes to the dhobi to be ironed has now become a daily routine of most urban households, even though only the more conservative give clothes to be washed, and they are getting fewer in number. However, with this trend the work of the dhobi remains useful and necessary, and most residential complexes have their share of dhobis who use whatever spot is available to them to set up their ironing spaces. These take on a semi-permanent character so that the dhobis keep their clothes, ironing tables, and other paraphernalia within the complex, and quite often clothes are also left in bundles, on trust that they will not be disturbed. Such dhobis also become part of the community of residents and may be helped by the residents when in need. So even in the more conservative milieu of the Old City, where the dhobi–client relationships were part of the moral universe that transcended purely commercial relations—even in the very modern, sophisticated urban gated communities, which have been referred to as 'luxotopias'—the dhobi is still regarded as someone who is part of the community of residents.

However, a significant change has been in terms of gender division of labour. In the seventies, the work of ironing was left primarily to the women, but now, as washing is declining in importance, in many households the men have also taken to ironing, if they are not otherwise employed. This has also led to more dhobi women living a middle-class life, taking care of their appearance, taking the children to school and back, cooking, and spending more time doing daily *puja* at the shrines that many of them have put up at home. To many dhobis, these transitions have, again, led them up the social ladder, where the dhobi woman is no longer a harried figure running from home to the river or standing by the roadside ironing clothes. While many women still do iron, more and more men have taken to ironing.

Opportunities and Choices in the Neoliberal Era

When education and non-caste-based occupations entered Indian society, primarily as a result of Western colonization, the advantages went almost entirely to the upper castes and classes who grabbed all opportunities of education and economic expansion. As of now this advantage continues, as the marginal castes are still struggling to find a foothold in the modern educational and occupational system, in spite of reservation.[3] Only a few have had the chance to make good, and many of them come from second- or third-generation advantaged families. In my forty years of association with the dhobis, I have seen a minimal impact of reservation on them. While in the seventies a few young men got government and bank jobs on the basis of reservations, the situation has not progressed. A young woman who has been serving as an assistant professor in a college in Delhi University for the past ten years finally had her job regularized in January 2024. This is not just a reflection on the policies of reservation but on the changing policies of the government at the centre, which is moving towards a system of contractual employment as contrasted with the 'secure' government jobs that were the norm in the first decades of the Indian governance and administration systems.

In a detailed cover story in *India Today* in March 2022, Kaushik Deka has provided facts and figures as to just how scarce and near impossible it is to get a government job in the present day. Most jobs that require a middle-level qualification draw aspirants that massively outnumber the posts available. The situation has become so dire that large-scale unemployment riots have begun to take place, and there are many destructive avenues that the unemployed youth are having recourse to. Gill (2010: 173) also shows through data that jobs in the formal sector have shrunk since the economic liberalization of the 1990s, and those available at the higher end are still monopolized by the upper castes/classes, and only lower-end menial and low-status jobs in the informal sector are available for the masses. At the same time smaller numbers of young people from the upper castes aspire to a secure government position, as was the norm earlier, and are moving towards being independent entrepreneurs or work in the non-governmental sector, as can be seen by the proliferation of start-ups and government support and encouragement for these.

This has left young people in marginal communities such as the dhobis with little choice. They mostly lack the opportunities to work in the private sector, as they do not have access to the kind of education or sophistication that is required for a respectable job in the non-governmental sector that also does not have any reservations. Whenever they get some work outside, it is mostly at a lower rung, and there are many who do work as clerks, salesmen, bookbinders, and servants in business establishments. Some of the more enterprising young men have found work in the developing information technology (IT) sectors, but they are still few. As of now, any household that has a good clientele for its traditional work of washing clothes is passing it down to the younger generation; or we may say that the younger generation, even if fairly adequately educated, still finds the washing of clothes a fairly attractive option. The reasons for this lie in several associated factors.

First and foremost is the changed attitude towards caste and the practice of untouchability that is considerably diluted in an urban setting like that of Delhi, although it may still be widely prevalent in the interior and rural areas of the country. Delhi has now assumed the nature of a cosmopolitan megapolis, with enough urban concentration to make the practice of untouchability a difficult proposition. Crowded subways and buses make touch prohibitions an impossibility, and busy young couples are happy to eat out or order food in without bothering about the caste or religion of the person delivering the food. At the dhobi ghats, young men have often been introduced to me as 'friends' who are of different castes, even Baniyas or Brahmins. The young men and women who are now working in offices do not complain of caste discrimination as much as those who were working in similar places used to complain in the seventies. Since they do not suffer from caste discrimination as much as they did before, the present generation is less averse to continuing with their occupation than they were in the seventies. At the same time it must be remembered that the dhobi status is still not high or very acceptable, but in a crowded environment, where there are many poorer and more deprived categories, the dhobis, who have roots in the city and fairly thriving source of income, do not feel as marginalized as they felt earlier when they were confined to the Walled City and bore the full brunt of caste discrimination against them. They also feel that they have an advantage over the poor migrants to the city, who occupy the lowest social rung, being rootless, propertyless, and very poor. As many of them have moved to more mixed neighbourhoods, and are no longer confined to the marked *katras*, they feel freer and more in tune with modern living. The dhobi households that I have visited outside of *katra* life show a middle-class lifestyle, but one that is not completely cut off from the past—where a daughter is going to college, while her mother is still ironing clothes. I visited a young couple, both of whom are educated and have white-collar jobs. They have a 'modern' set-up with computers and all the gadgets, yet they prefer to live in the old part of the city, near their family members.

How the Dhobis Visualize Themselves

Most of the comprehensive analysis of the caste system had been done when India was considered a 'holistic' and conservative society. Most, including the much-quoted ones such as Srinivas (1952), Dumont (1986), Moffatt (1979), and others, were done with ethnography from rural and smaller societies. The ones done in urban areas also focused on the conservative parts of the city and were done before the great economic transformation of the 1990s, when the Indian economy expanded and entered the 'liberal' phase. The market and the technological resources are greatly transformed in the urban sector. Society too is liberalizing, with a much higher rate of physical and social mobility, input from the electronic media, and rapid communication channels. The dhobis are now living in a changed world like anyone else. How they are negotiating their identity and, more importantly, making choices in this new world is something that may not have been recorded before. There do exist some commendable works on comparable caste groups—Ahmad (2018), Gill (2010), Prashad (2000), Kapoor (2018), and Natarajan (2012)—which I have discussed at various point in this book, but the discourses about caste in academia and outside of it are still focused on the works of 'classical' authors such as Dumont and Srinivas. Some of these recent works have clearly indicated the emerging identities that keenly perceive the advantages of a caste-based community, a *biradari* or *samaj* and the viabilities of 'blood'-based skills or at least the imagining of them.

In a recent essay (Channa 2023a), I have described how the present-day urban planning has no place for traditional occupations like that of the dhobis. The political stigmatization of 'caste' in totality (in spite of its recognized political viability) gives a policy of deliberate misrecognition to the social reality of caste. The blind adoption of a modern (read Western) model of development and the ignoring of all indigenous institutions as regressive have created more economic pressure and put an unfair burden on the state that is expected to provide jobs for everyone in a densely populated country. Even in the West, as pointed out by Chatterjee (2011: 24), while normative equality exists at the level of abstraction, at the actual level 'differentiated citizenship has, in some form or the other, become normal practice in the empirical sense in most Western countries'. It means that citizens are regularly perceived, as well as given differential treatment, on the basis of race, ethnicity, gender, and other such markers. As Van Dijk (2017: 23) points out, the policymakers are themselves entrenched in the same subjectivities that they profess to get rid of. In visualizing a 'modern' city, they are weighed down by the 'symbolic register', the vision and construction of reality within the schema that one is born in; for India, it is the caste/class conjunction. What appear as aesthetic sores in the eyes of the policymakers and the visionaries of the modern city are the traditional pockets, the persistence of caste-based occupations, the dhobi ghats and the abattoir (Ahmad 2018), the slums of the garbage collectors (Gill 2010), and all those vibrant examples of thriving and struggling in the city, whose viability and significance escape their jaundiced vision.

The dhobis as well as other marginal groups, however, are not blinded by a borrowed vision of development, but more by the exigencies of daily life and a pragmatic approach to making a livelihood and to survival in the city. They are therefore very cognizant of the failure of those in power to take care of their interests. They are to a large extent aware of the potential of maintaining, in fact nurturing, a caste-based identity that they have now translated into *samaj* from the earlier used *jat-biradari* or simply *biradari*. Here it is pertinent to bring in Austin's (1962) argument that an utterance can be seen as a social act and have a meaning that is embedded in the context of its use. The now almost persistent use of the term *samaj*, something I had not heard about a few years back, indicates a political awareness about the community that was not present earlier. Till about 2000, the kinship and horizontal solidarity aspects were mostly emphasized, and the *biradari* was seen as a kinship and occupational group. At present the community at the level of the *biradari* has the same structure (endogamous largely), but its visualization has transcended the kinship base to the possibilities of a pressure group. The magnification of collective performances such as the Shobha Yatra and the flaunting of political connections (even if symbolically) are indicative of the emerging identity of the Sheheri dhobis as a political entity. *Samaj* is a sanitized and formal expression; it exudes respectability and has a formal connotation that relates it to the larger society and does not limit it to an internal cohesion, as in the case of *biradari*. It seems time that the dhobis finally move out of their *katra* into the world at large.

Notes

1. Kanshiram was from a low caste and founded the Bahujan Samaj Party (BSP), giving the label Bahujan (common people) to the marginalized as opposed to all other previously used labels. He mentored Mayawati, an educated woman from a lowly caste, as his successor to the party, and at present she holds the position of the most powerful woman from the low castes in Northern India, and is the leader of the BSP.

2. The popularity of the Kejriwal-led Aam Aadmi Party (AAP) is a great deal influenced by the commendable work done by them to improve the standards of the government-run schools in the National Capital Region under their jurisdiction. In 2022 the AAP dislodged the BJP's fifteen-year rule over the Delhi Municipal Corporation, and the first statement they issued was about improvement of infrastructure in the Municipality-run schools.

3. For a detailed account of the implications and reflections on the reservation system in present times, see Madsen (2023).

7

Conclusion

Surviving in a Discriminatory World and the Future of the City

In this last chapter I will summarize the way in which the dhobis have lived and survived in the city. The life of the dhobis can be seen as a small mirror for the city as it is growing and proliferating into an unwieldy and unmanageable megacity, fraught with tensions, as is the character of most global cities with their unrealistic urbanization. The dhobis have survived in this city that evolved from a pre-industrial, premodern city built by an emperor in the seventeenth century to its present-day incarnation as a megacity, the seat of power of a democratic republic, and now fast evolving further into a global city, part of the World City Network (Sassen 1991). The core of Delhi, the Walled City or Old Delhi, is an orthogenetically evolved city (Sjoberg 1960). What we see today had its foundations laid in the past, and, in spite of many upheavals, one can still see and experience the remnants.

The Old City and the Dhobis

At the time when the city was built and for a long period after that, there was designated space in the city for the service castes, as the performance of their occupations was a necessary component of the social functioning of the city. As Bayly (1999: 227) has pointed out, caste was an essential aspect of the new urbanity of India when the peasant castes began to populate the city, to the extent that the presence of the service castes in the city was more marked than it was in rural areas. The urban was not merely a space for the discharge of the instrumental and pragmatic aspects of life; there was also a moral universe, a collective sentimentality of value, that

Dhobis of Delhi. Subhadra Mitra Channa, Oxford University Press. © Subhadra Mitra Channa 2024.
DOI: 10.1093/9780198926238.003.0008

imagined the city as a place where jati/Varna identities were invented, consolidated, and legitimized. Robinson (2006) has identified all cities as having something special, something that is in their character that connects them to others, and one can safely point to the jati system as underlying most South Asian cities. These relations are connective as well as clustering.

In earlier chapters I have described the designing of the city to accommodate the untouchables, the marginal, and the impure in ways that their services were available at all times, even if their presence was marked as invisible. The place of the dhobis in this city was almost at the bottom. No matter how the city evolved and changed, they have remained practically where they were in terms of jati ranking and social position. I do not have any narratives or material about how they were treated in the city of the past, but one can have a fairly good idea from what I learnt in the 1970s about being untouchable in the city. The presence of caste and other aspects of so-called 'Indian' traditions in the Indian cities points to their seamless continuity with the rural (Pocock 1960, Bayly 1999) or to their 'Indianness' (Chandavarkar 2009: 213), the city actually manifesting the social institutions such as caste, community, and joint family in their fullest form. The power-holders of the past were well aware of what Foucault has called the knowledge/power nexus, as certain kinds of knowledge were confined to the upper castes, especially the knowledge that gave them social and ritual superiority. The gradation of knowledge and skills, integral to the workings of the jati/Varna hierarchy, gave primacy to ritual knowledge, followed by that of warfare and governance (Raj Dharma), then the power of money and trade skills, and last came the primary skills essential to society—all the work that needs to be done for survival. All land and resources belonged to the higher Varna of priests, rulers, and traders, but all labour was provided by the last category. The work of the service-providing jatis, such as the launderer, barber, potter, ironsmith, leatherworker, butcher, or basket-maker, was polluting and extremely essential. And they were held in a kind of moral and material bind, where they were told that they must provide their services to the community as part of their dharma but what they received in return was a condescending gift (Raheja 1988), by the land-owning jatis.

The village-level *jajmani* system traditionally required the *jajmans* to take care of all the needs of the service providers, but it was entirely at their discretion to interpret at what level they perceived that these needs should be located. This is exactly the point at which the rosy pictures of the Indian village and the harmony of the *jajmani* system as painted by scholars like Hocart (1950), Srinivas (1952) and Leach (1960) may be faulted. They identified, perhaps rightly, that each caste had a ritual (Hocart 1950), social, and economic space in village society and each was indispensable, giving them a level of security for survival. But what they did not comment on was the interpretation of what 'survival' could mean. No doubt ideally there was an expectation that the lowest castes would be treated well, but at best it was a paternalistic expectation. What was critical to the system was the lack of agency of these service-providing castes; they were not free to choose their work, their way of living, their clothes, their food, or their aspirations. They were denied education, could not train in any other skill than the one into which they were born; they had to eat, wear, and consume only what was doled out to them. Even in the modified versions of *jajmani*, as evolved within the modern state and market system, the situation was hardly better. Prashad (2000) has shown that during the colonial period the absorption of the sweepers into the state system, namely their recruitment as municipal workers, made their situation even worse as they were then brought under the thumb of the supervisors of upper castes, who in addition to all other forms of exploitation expected that they should have free access to the women. One may note here how the secular system of the colonial governance colluded with the existing caste hierarchies and mechanisms of exploitation to create new forms of caste-based dominance.

Within the Hindu worldview, the hierarchy of gods parallels the hierarchy of humans, and those deities who are at the lower end of the scale are usually controlled by the lower castes, as described in Chapter 5. Those at the lower end are also the ones who control the negative forces of disease, snakebite, and misfortunes of various types. But even their control over the darker forces of the universe did not give the lower castes any special privileges; rather, it condemned them to a miserable existence. I remember a young woman in a Garhwal village telling me that 'the Jogis [the untouchables of that village] are healers; they save us from several diseases and prevent suffering, yet look what miserable lives they live'.

The control over their lives lay outside, and although not every anthropologist and sociologist has written about it, the lives of the untouchables have found poignant expression in literature (Bama 2005, Valmiki 2001).

Contemporary times have not evolved beyond the caste-based hierarchies and stereotypes. I have heard several privileged people say things like, 'Oh, *those* people do not need warm clothes in winter, *they* do not feel cold like us'; 'Those people can survive on any kind of food, *they* don't need to eat such expensive items'; 'They are used to walking barefoot, *they* don't need shoes.' Although, with the changing values of society as some Indians are becoming more cosmopolitan and getting exposed to egalitarian values,[1] such views are being reduced among some, a majority of Indians still hold them, as seen in the treatment meted out to lower-level workers in any organization and household helps. My mother once remarked, while driving through Delhi in the nineties, that she felt India has really developed after independence because so many persons, even the workers and poor people, were wearing shoes on the streets. In the early part of the century and even at the time India became a free country, she said, only the affluent wore shoes; a majority of the people on the street were seen barefoot, in summer or winter.

While the interpretation of 'needs' was greatly biased according to the rank of the person's jati, they were expected to feel extremely grateful for whatever was given to them. Some of these values and interactions have been immortalized in literature, such as Bandhu Madhav's *Poisoned Bread* written in Marathi in 1992 and published in English Dangle (1992). This superordinate–subordinate relationship was viewed and is often still viewed by the upper-caste patrons as justifiable, and makes legitimate the gratitude that is expected out of the lower castes for whatever little is doled out to them as favours.

My ethnographic journey was also one of discovering caste and inequality in the city. Being born into a fairly liberal family where caste was never a matter of discussion, I was clueless the first time I came across the harsh realities of caste discrimination. In the seventies, a couple living in the Hamilton Road *katra* near Kashmiri Gate told me that they opened a *dhaba* (small kiosk) selling tea and snacks, but soon people began to say, '*dhobi ki chai, dhobi ki chai*' ('it is dhobi's tea, it is dhobi's tea'), and they had to close down. Initially I was perplexed: 'What is the significance of *dhobi ki chai*?'. I was also not quite enlightened when some of my upper-caste teachers in the department of anthropology screwed up their noses in disgust: 'Why dhobis? Why not choose another community?' But a few months' interaction with the community began to make the situation clear. I slowly realized that the dhobis were regarded as untouchables. Everyday life for them was a negotiation of space and touch, a strategic game where they were dependent for their livelihood on the very people who shunned them.

Unlike what some scholars have written about the marginalized in the caste system (Dumont 1970, Moffat 1979), the dhobis, at least from the time I knew them, were resentful of the practice of discrimination in various forms that they faced every day of their lives. They also had no illusions that the upper castes were higher or better than them—quite the contrary—not in any way conceding their inferiority to anyone, what Jangam (2017: 6) calls as 'anti-caste egalitarian consciousness'. Pardo and Prato (2021: 8) support this observation for the dominated in most urban situations, saying, 'it is advisable for our analysis to steer away from the belief that ordinary people are basically powerless puppets who are unwittingly manipulated into ethical stances and actions which serve adverse interests and appreciate'. My very first group interview with young men on the roof of a house in a *katra* had made it clear that they had deep-seated emotions of injustice and a kind of contempt for those who looked down upon them. This attitude is widely prevalent among the marginal jatis, and has been recorded by many scholars, such as Mencher (1974, Kapadia 1995), among others. Mencher (1974), in her path-breaking essay, indicated that anthropological methodology that focuses only on the testimony of the upper caste fails to understand completely the real attitude and world view of those at the bottom. The perspective from the bottom can only be grasped through the narratives that originate from there and not from interpretations and understandings of those who are at the top. The ideology of those at the top serves to control the overall workings of the system and is an effective screen to stifle the thoughts and make invisible the covert practices of the dominated. The alternative discourse built up from below not only subverts the overall dominance of the higher strata but also restores dignity and self-respect to the dominated sections.

Foucault (1976: 94) has described power as something diffuse and pervasive and not localized or concentrated in one place. As explained, power creates its own critique; there is always power that comes from below, precluding any opposition between the ruler and the ruled but, rather, giving rise to a constant struggle, a process rather than any outcome. 'Where there is power there is resistance, and yet, or rather consequently, this resistance is never in a position of exteriority in relation to power' (Foucault 1976: 95).This precisely describes the caste system and its internal struggles. Both sides are engaged in strategies, and these take some predictable and ubiquitous forms, the most pervasive being the way their women are conceived of and treated (Chakravarty 2003, Channa 2001). As pointed out by Unnithan Kumar (1997), women's bodies are boundary markers, a point elaborated by Channa (2017). Gender relations and expressions of patriarchy are greatly influenced by how the group is situated within both the local power field and that of the larger social environment. Kapadia (1995), in her study of the untouchable Paliyans of Tamil Nadu, has shown clearly how the women, who have to fall back on their own kin and labour resource to take care of themselves and their children, hold their menfolk largely in contempt. The women realize their own worth as breadwinners for the family and the inability of the men to support them. These women are therefore both aggressive and independent. This is in complete contrast to the attitude of the upper-caste women, where the wives are supported by their husbands and have a completely dependent status. They have to remain subordinated as they cannot express their emotions and even their real potential as human beings. The more glorified the status of the husband, the more suppressed is that of the wife. By the norms of jati rules, the full status of a twice-born was attainable only by men, by the wearing of the sacred thread. Women, who could never wear the sacred thread and had no access to knowledge, were never considered full members of the jati/Varna society. They gained social status only through the men. In this sense the women, being always of impure bodies, were not very different from each other, irrespective of their jati/class status. This is also seen in the closer relationship that women across the class/caste barrier have with each other. The upper-strata women often develop intimate relations of empathy with their domestic helps, washerwomen, and others who may come to serve or entertain them. I have described the relations of the middle-class housewife with the dhoban in the Old City. Anathamurthy (2000: 44) has described with respect to his own household, that of a

Brahmin, how women would sororize in the backyard, drawing water from a well and gossiping: 'in the backyard, caste barriers among women were forgotten and they would confide in the secrets of their sexual life'. In this world of women, cutting across class and caste barriers, the female body is a central issue, especially as they all believe that men will never understand the pains and travails of being born a woman.

When we situate the dhobi men and women in comparison with the men and women of the upper castes, it is clear that the dhobi men are situated far below the status of upper-caste men in the social hierarchy and thereby are not too different from their own women. In other words, the inequality between a dhobi man and a dhobi woman is almost negligible. One can make comparisons with other marginalized and oppressed groups elsewhere in the world, such as African Americans, where men and women are often bound in solidarity rather than in opposition (Lorde 1992). Throughout my fieldwork, this relative equality was observed in many situations and has been described in the relevant chapters. As in the 1970s, even today most women treat their husbands as equals, and more like friends than as superiors. I have never come across any husband who holds an iota of power over his wife.

The Public and the Private

Here it would be interesting and illuminating to touch upon the public/private as it conditions the movements of men and women within the city. It has been generally agreed upon that women and men in most societies, especially where there is a clear-cut division between the public and the private domains, are located differentially in these two domains (Lamphere 1993). This location—men in the public and women in the private—also intersects with the division of social power, where it is also recognized that men and women hold more power in the domains in which they dominate or play crucial roles (Thornton 1991). Politics and economy, for example, are domains of masculine prominence, and reproduction and nurturance are domains of feminine excellence. In many societies, the division of labour follows, or at least followed, this ideological division. Importantly, when it came to the division of social space and the mapping of physical movements, the dichotomy of masculine and feminine domains superimposed itself on what space was appropriate for which gender. One reason for resentment at the non-heterosexual persons is that they do not fit into the social allocation of space and physicality.

But confusion often arises in comprehending that the definition of public and domestic may vary among communities and groups, according to their internal culture. Take, for example, urban India, or more specifically urban Delhi, where even in present times women find it difficult to negotiate public transport or public space (Channa 2004). But dhobi women and women of service castes, such as scavengers, vegetable sellers, and others who are seen as performing traditional work, have an easier time, as long as they conform to the norms of being appropriately located and dressed for their roles. For example, few people comment on or try to harass the women who are sweeping the streets, ironing clothes, or moving around the neighbourhood delivering and collecting clothes, like the dhobi women. Yet they would attract attention if they did not dress or appear like dhobi women. In other words, these performers of daily tasks tend to blend in with the background of the city, forming an integral part of its landscape. Compare them to the self-conscious young woman who is going to college, taking public transport, and wearing Western clothes. She almost invariably becomes a target of sexual harassment or 'eve-teasing' as it is known in India. The reason, as I have argued elsewhere (Channa 2004), is that some gender roles are yet to be absorbed and accepted in urban India, despite globalization and westernization to a large extent. Indian cities also differ in their cosmologies and reactions to such gender roles and the spatial distribution of the feminine and the masculine. The women of the service castes have been part of the city workforce for several centuries. So, one can surmise that service providers like dhobis, barbers, and scavengers were always an inseparable part of the city landscape. However, the phenomenon of women of respectable families traversing the public space is quite new and even now not familiar or acceptable to many men (Channa 2013c).

If one asked the dhobis about the work that the women do, they replied, 'ghar ka kaam', meaning quite simply 'domestic work'. Unlike the stereotypical concept of domestic work that it is confined to the precincts of the home, the dhobi work, even when it is designated as 'ghar ka kaam', takes the women to various locations, except that these are known and nearly fixed ones. In earlier times they would go to the riverbank, but now they go to the homes of their clients and also, if they iron, to some fixed location where they set up their shop every day. It does involve them being present in a public location in full view of anyone who is around. The dhoban is, in folk sayings, the eyes and ears of the neighbourhood, and anyone interested in knowing anything about the location will usually approach the dhobi or dhoban, if one is seen around. At the same time these women learn the body language and attitude for defence (Channa 2001, Searle-Chatterjee 1981). According to traditional jati norms, the bodies of lower-caste women were seen as 'available'; a fact highly resented by the community—both men and women. The most resented term among the dhobis is the address 'dhoban'. While men do not mind being addressed as 'dhobi', the women resent it and explicitly do not wish to be addressed as such. The term 'dhoban' brings to mind centuries of atrocities heaped on these women. As may be recalled from an earlier chapter, the only issue that brought all the dhobis from across the country together was to protest against the term 'dhoban' used in the title of a film.

The first step towards acquiring dignity and self-respect therefore centres on the bodies of women. Whenever possible, as soon as a household transcends the economic barrier towards relative prosperity, the immediate action involves the withdrawal of women from public spaces. A change in their occupation that has taken some of them towards fulltime ironing has seen men take up ironing, if there is no washing to be done. The earlier model was that of men washing clothes and women ironing them. In contemporary times, with washing machines and synthetic fibres, few clothes require washing by the dhobi, but most still need ironing. A change seen in most metropolitan cities is that dhobi men take up ironing inside apartment complexes, which sometimes even set some space aside for service providers like dhobis. When ironing is the only household occupation, is always done by men, who also collect and deliver the clothes. Within apartment complexes, the clients too may deliver the clothes to the dhobi. As was mentioned to me by some residents of South Indian cities like Bangalore, the dhobi women sometimes even wash the clothes of the households, which are then given for ironing to the dhobi men. Among the Sheheri dhobis, I have not seen such a transition; the women never go anywhere to wash clothes. They either do no dhobi work—just stay at home and do household work, now making the real transition to actual domesticity—or they iron clothes at home. At present only in more conservative areas of Delhi, mostly inside Old Delhi, one still finds dhobi women ironing clothes in the neighbourhood. The reason is again already explained: the Old Delhi area still retains the primary group type face-to-face relations in the local networks, and there is always the safety net of familiarity. In the unfamiliar and impersonal modern neighbourhoods the women do not venture outside to work. Ironing work requires the woman to be standing in one place for many hours and she needs to be absolutely sure of her personal safety and the security of her dignity. The contemporary view of urban space is one that is not just physical space but a space that is constructed out of experience (Cinar and Bender 2007), but collective experience is not universally alike. The way dhobis and dhobi women experience the city space is not the same as a middle-class woman travelling by car or an office-goer travelling by metro experiences it. A dhobi woman experiences the city from her position on the margins, both economically and socially, and in her case influenced by centuries of discriminatory jati hierarchies, especially the value system in which her body is made available (Chakravarty 2003, Channa 2013c). Till very recent times, the sexual exploitation of lower-caste women was not news; even now most such incidences in rural areas and hinterlands go unnoticed. In the city, always a 'site of inequality and struggle' (Hannigan and Richards 2017: 2), women's bodies, especially those of lower jati/class women, remain the most vulnerable; even as those of all women are at risk (Channa 2019b).

This is the summary of the dhobi life that is played out in the city of their residence, a city that has seen many changes in its landscape, its philosophy, and now in its very purpose.

The Changing City and the Dhobis

In an earlier essay (Channa 2018b) I described the different nature of urbanity in Delhi as compared to similar metropolises in other parts of the world. Delhi has a conservative core; also its culture differs from one neighbourhood to another. The newly built parts of the metropolis have a culture that is more cosmopolitan, and to some extent the formality of urban culture may be found here. But as mentioned at the very beginning of this book, 'urban' does not exist in the same form everywhere, a fact that has been recognized by most scholars of urbanism (Robinson 2006). In the orthogenetically evolved city like Old Delhi and even its adjunct, New Delhi, there has been a place for diverse ways of life to survive and sometimes even to thrive. The dhobis have not only survived but also made good in this modernizing and globalizing city, where they have a decent enough commercial foothold to be able to continue not only with their occupation but also with their community ties in the form of the *biradari*, as I have described at length throughout this work.

But in contemporary times the vision of the city—how it is imagined as an ideal place of dwelling—is varying according to the gaze of the collective that is located in differential power zones. Those at the apex of power, who play decision-making roles, are increasingly enamoured by the glamour of what they perceive as 'global cities', such as New York and Singapore. The nationalist regime at the centre, committed to restoring the 'lost glory' of India, are bent upon sanitizing the city of Delhi, which is seen as embarrassing to the eyes of the postmodern global vision, whether in the form of foreign dignitaries or tourists, or even as represented and broadcast in the media. As is to be expected, the dhobis are not aesthetically a part of the imagined modern utopia, but more like the 'real' (Zizek 1993) who cause irritation. To those with visions of an artificially created 'modern' city, they appear to blight the city's landscape with their rows of clothes hanging out to dry at the roadside, over bridges, and on the grass. The dhobi women look rustic, dressed traditionally and modestly. Even though they are urban, they appear to be more on the fringe in terms of their appearance. Such is not what has been imagined for the global city. The 'capacity for assertion in the public sphere, of making the presence of power within the visual narrative and landscape inescapable' Campos (2017: 236) lies only in the hands of the state, and maybe in the hands of the corporate powers that dictate the modern state, but it certainly does not lie in the hands of marginal and weak communities like the dhobis. Yet they retain the power of contestation and protest.

As recognized globally, a significant change in urban life and also in the nature of stratification has occurred as land became commercialized with the spread of the neoliberal economy. In India, and in Delhi, from 1992 onwards, a transformation has occurred in the manner in which even the state is handling urban land. As Shatkin and Vidyarthi (2014: 1) explain, the transition from a socialist ideology and Gandhian thinking to the 'hard driving utilitarianism of a globalizing business class' is creating tensions, as the daily lives of the urban poor tend to encroach upon the 'planned order' of the imagined city. Furthermore, the nation state built on real or imagined ideals of the nation (even if elite-driven) is giving way to what Kapferer and Taylor (2012: 5) refer to as the 'corporate state'. The state powers in this emerging situation are pushing corporate interests, which transcend the situated morality of communities and people towards an impersonal profit-driven motivation. The spiralling of land values, pressure of population, and scarcity of urban resources are systematically pushing out the poor and the marginal from the centre of the city to its periphery. I have described how one by one the dhobi ghats inside the city, especially those in what are considered 'prime locations' at present, are being demolished (Channa 2021). These are now making way for ornamental gardens and government buildings, including a very 'visible' headquarters of the Bharatiya Janata Party (BJP), in power since2014,whichneeded a spectacular presence in the capital city of Delhi.

Those at the helm of affairs imagine Delhi to be a global city, a part of the World City Network (Sassen 2002). The present regime of the BJP is not just aiming to make India a global superpower; it is also focused on its own version of nationalism (Channa 2021). While this project of making Delhi representative of national pride and a glorious past has led to renaming as well as transforming certain iconic spaces of the city in terms of their representational value, it is also envisaged that Delhi will be not just a heritage city but one that is located on the economic map of the world as a destination for transnational corporate organizations and global business. Towards this end, Delhi has increasingly been compartmentalized into zones of differentiation. While Old Delhi continues in its role as a marker of heritage and national identity, Lutyens' Delhi is the seat of power. The glitz and modernization are embodied in what used to be a rural suburb of Delhi, Gurgaon, renamed Gurugram as *gaon*, meaning 'village', fits ill with a part of the city that is closest, at least in outward appearance, to 'world cities' like Singapore.

While the Old City and Lutyens' Delhi have their historical and cultural value, Gurgaon is just an urban economic 'modern' satellite city and, as any Old Delhi person will tell you, has no soul. The soul of Delhi resides in the Old City, with its narrow lanes and bylanes and the presence of people and ways of life that have continued from the days of the past. It has the stories, the ghosts, and the jinns (Darympole 1993);one newspaper, *The Statesman*, used to run a regular column, 'Quaint Corner', depicting people and events that were part of what is still known as 'Delhi culture'. Efforts are being made, even as the rest of Delhi is being elevated to the status of a world city, to renovate and reinvent this Delhi culture. But this is being done mostly as a commercial venture, as a 'tourist attraction', in a manner that will complement the growth and gentrification of the rest of the city.

Singh (2022: 5), in an article published in the daily newspaper *Hindustan Times*, has reported that two key heritage sites within Old Delhi are to be revamped and restored: the Town Hall and the Lahori Gate heritage *haveli*. While the former is a British-built structure dating to the time they occupied the city after 1857, the latter was a private residence, built in 1929, which is planned to be made into the Shahjahanabad Museum, featuring the old city in its original name. Earlier, the central government has created an Indian National Army (INA) museum within the Red Fort. The Red Fort was the residence of Emperor Shah Jehan and his family, and was known as Qila-e-Mubarak. It then became the barracks of the British army, who destroyed almost three quarters of the internal structures of the Fort, including its fountains, gardens, and residential palaces. Towards the end of the colonial period, it became the site of the INA trials, a major event of the nationalist struggle, which brought together all the Indian political parties including the Muslim League. Three officers of the INA—Major-General Shah Nawaz Khan, Lieutenant Colonel Prem Sahgal and Colonel G. S. Dhillon—were put on trial in November 1945, provoking nationwide protests. A battery of senior Indian lawyers, under the leadership of Bhulabhai Desai, defended the three and the case was won, soon before India became independent on 15 August 1947. The INA was a standing army created by Subhas Chandra Bose popularly known as Netaji, a revered figure representing India's fight for freedom. By making this museum, the ruling regime is attempting to focus attention on nationalism rather than the Islamic past of the Fort. However, it also represents the last Mughal emperor, Bahadur Shah Zafar, whose poetry remains inspirational even till present times.

In their attempts to create a 'modern' as well as historical and heritage city out of Delhi, the policymakers have left a major segment of Delhi out of their reckoning: its people. I have mentioned earlier how the project of beautifying the banks of the river Yamuna has deprived many people of their livelihoods, some of which were age-old, such as divers, boatmen, and of course the dhobis, who had to relocate. The dhobis have suffered relocation in the past, yet those in power had recognized their utilitarian value and replaced the loss of the river with artificially constructed cemented ghats with proper water connections. Such ghats were even part of Lutyens' Delhi, and the luxury bungalows so characteristic of this zone often housed dhobis in the servant quarters. The restructuring of space in New Delhi, visualized and imagined in the light of Singapore and other similar urban cities, is being done with no heed to its past culture, especially that of the marginal communities. If any heritage at all is visualized, it is of the elite and of the renowned—for example, the restoration of Ghalib's *haveli*[2] in Old Delhi and now the proposal to make a Shahjahanabad museum. But what about the Nai, dhobis, Khatiks, Kumhar, and others who have thronged its lanes and bylanes for centuries and provided essential services? One reason why such communities have been overlooked or even deliberately ignored is that their identities are rooted in the jati/Varna system, a system that right from the framing of the Indian constitution has found disfavour with the makers of modern India. The formal legal and constitutional framework considered the jati/Varna system to be redundant and regressive, something like racism that needs to be done away with as soon as possible. It is another story that these identities have survived and are still thriving, even controlling the political scenario in modern India. Yet, at another level, it is not possible to officially acknowledge their presence and even less to make any policies towards their preservation. The Congress government's efforts to provide the dhobis with ghats in the resettlement colonies were a reflection of their socialist commitments. They were interested in the preservation of livelihoods of the poor people. But such commitment does not find any resonance in the modern corporate state.

It is paradoxical that the Indian constitution in its efforts to visualize unity and equality has overlooked differences. Although it is often professed that India stands for unity in diversity, the diversity is understood in various ways, such as cultural and ethnic, but the jati system with its division of labour stands condemned. There is no provision for persuasion of traditional occupations within the jati system. If any activities at all are encouraged, it is the arts and crafts, but not essential services. Contrary to encouraging their earlier ways of life, such communities are being overtly encouraged to go for formal education, give up their jati-based occupations, which are seen as retrogressive, and opt for a 'modern' existence.

The policymakers, the elite, are scarcely in touch with reality, or even if they are aware, are committed to preserving their power base. It is also true for most parts of the world that those who actually experience the city, who walk on its roads and use its resources at the very basic level, have little say in how their lives are governed. In the path to so-called 'modernization', the trope of 'development' is used to create a false hope that all that is unwanted and undesirable will be replaced. As Tara van Djik (2017) has pointed to the visualization of two Indias: one backward, ridden with redundant cultural baggage, mostly rural or urban poor; and the other 'Shining India', the would-be global power, the India of the rich, the talented, the entrepreneurs, the scientists, and the urban elite with unlimited buying power. As she observes critically, most people blame the persistence of poverty and ignorance and practices such as female feticide to the persistence of ancient values and a culture lag; they feel that if one can get rid of the inherited cultural traits and replace them with modern cosmopolitan values, things will change, they will become better. But this is where the fallacy lies. The problems of today are rooted in the present; they are not a leftover from the past. The two Indias are not different but divergent faces of the same India. It is not possible to wipe the slate to put India on the path to progress.

As was amply proved during the pandemic of COVID-19 and when hundreds of thousands of poor, marginalized migrant labour were forced out onto the streets, the shining India was being built on the sweat and blood of those bodies that were hidden behind the shining surfaces and glittering lights of the huge highways, flyovers, and mega-hotels of the city. These people are the real builders of modern India. The capitalist economy exploits these people, who are available as cheap labour because of certain conditions that push them to accept a life of risk and uncertainty, to accept whatever wages are given to them and whatever condition of life is made available. These are the poorest of the poor, the 'infrastructural labour' (Gidwani and Maringanti 2016). But then there are layers of poverty and marginalization.

The dhobis in that sense are not absolutely at the bottom, at least not the Sheheri *biradari* that I am describing here. Chatterjee (2011) sees a dichotomy between 'political society' and 'civil society', the former being people with no legal rights, with no resources and no social position, people who may have to resort to violence in order to exert their rights and to survive—like the migrants, the racially marked, the ones on the fringes of the economy. The latter, civil society comprises people with legal and social standing, who can assert legitimately their rights and possessions, who have a voice. Chatterjee assigns the former to what he refers to as the non-corporate survival economy. But in my mind this distinction is too stark; it does not take care of people who fall in between categories. All those who do not belong to the formal sector of the economy are not quite marginal, for there are tradition-based rights that may not be absolutely legal but which belong to the moral universe of which a community is part. The jati-based economic relationships may be seen in this manner. For example, there is no legal basis that only a Brahmin can perform certain rituals like a Hindu marriage, but convention and norms ensure that it always happens. Similarly, the age-old occupational specializations are not legally protected, yet society ensures that only they are entrusted with these tasks, high or low.

The dhobis, and most such communities which derive legitimacy from cultural institutions such as the jati system, cannot be classified in terms that are a derivative of the modern capitalist system. Nor are they part of the modern, sophisticated, Western-influenced upwardly mobile middle classes; nor are they poor migrants from the rural areas who form the majority of slum dwellers and homeless in the city. They do not consider themselves to be Dalits, for they have not yet escaped from the hereditary occupational relations. They also do not wish to exit the system as long as they are assured of a level of survival that they are not sure of finding outside their traditional occupation.

The Sheheri dhobis consider themselves to be the original, or at least very old, residents of the city of Delhi. They feel they have a claim to the city and that the city power-holders should legitimately listen to their voices and also fulfil their needs. They have always been citizens with their designated though poor dwellings and, most importantly, part of thriving social networks with the upper castes and gentry. The extent of their legitimate place within the city is exhibited in the protests that they have launched from time to time; these have all been done in a non-violent and approved manner, like any other civil society member would do. Till very recent times, urban policies have recognized both the existence and the importance of these groups, making a legitimate place for them within the city, for both their residence and their livelihood. The British characteristically formalized the presence of the dhobis, making numbered ghats for them in key areas of the city. Even during the Congress regime, they were accommodated within the changing landscape.

Brugmann (2009: 274) argues forcefully against the 'corporate city models' and in favour of what he terms the 'development of local urbanisms' that take care of the communities and their culturally informed local needs. He advocates a process of 'co-creation with communities, users, and local urbanists' (2009: 276). However, if communities continue to be represented by the elite, then the tensions as envisaged by Shatkin and Vidyarthi (2014: 1) are not solved. Even the most liberal and democratic societies have their prejudices and their exclusionary practices directed towards some or other category of persons. It has been forcefully argued with respect to the most modern urban society that the ideals of urban equality and social justice are never attained. However, while most authors write about 'contestations' in their visible, antagonistic forms, 'identity politics of negotiations' (Chatterjee 2014: 151), there are communities like the dhobis who do not have the numbers or the collective power or even desire for confrontation. It is the last sentiment that is most notable as the work of the dhobi and their identity are intrinsically linked to their compliance with the system and not in contesting it. The dhobis have had the advantage of the viability of their occupation within the capitalist growth of the city (Channa 2021). The dhobi is still a ubiquitous person in every part of the city, even in what Teresa Kuldova (2017) calls 'luxotopias'.

However, the dhobis remain hidden from both the sight and the mind of the power-holders and those who make decisions. The potential of the dhobi as a dhobi to make good in the expanding capitalist sector goes unnoticed primarily because people still do not recognize that even as the system is hitched onto a global market and technologies and communications are both globalized and follow a Western pattern, the heart of the system is still anchored in the persisting value systems of jati/ Varna and the moral order of the community.

The problem with such praxis is that they are almost ubiquitous and, in being so, are invisible, in the nature of what Bourdieu has called 'doxa'. Most persons, when asked, will find it quite preposterous that there is anything unusual in a dhobi doing laundry. Most will say, 'Well that is what they do.' No one will see the incongruence of such a jati-based occupation persisting in a capitalist market economy. But not just the dhobis but many other such occupations thrive; for example, Bapat (2024) has reported that the hair trade, done by a community that specializes in it, actually feeds a million-dollar global industry. So in an economy which still retains many pre-capitalist roots, where the remnants of a moral-based economy still condition pragmatic market relationships, jati-based occupations still have a place and, more importantly, still remain an important source of livelihood for many.

Some occupations have died out. The *kathputli wala* (puppeteer), the *bhisti wala* (the man with a leather container of drinking water), the *bio-scope wala* (the man with a box playing music and showing images to children): all are gone with the times, but this is not the case for some other occupations that have found a renewed viability in the modern sector. The more the city expands its capital sector, the more the chances for the dhobi to get more work. But they have never quite developed as a 'political society' in Chatterjee's terms. On the contrary, in my association with the dhobis for almost the past four decades, I have observed that they have always harboured an ambition to be good citizens, but on their own terms. They wish to be accepted as respectable and reliable. They are also perfectly cognizant of the fact that there is an immense opportunity for them to thrive in the expanding economy. In this way, they do not demand that policymakers indulge in any deviation from legitimate norms, but that their demands should be part of the legitimate lawful architecture of the city, and for this they always showcase the space that they had been assigned not only in the precolonial but also during the British period. To the dhobis, their ghats and their way of life are in the nature of 'an engram' (Wolf 1982), 'a shared, remembered and somehow practiced basic script of potential common claim making' (Kalb and Mollona 2018: 12). The dhobis consider their 'forever' presence in the city to be a strong basis for their claim for conditions favourable to their livelihood, but they have not been able to emerge as a strong political class, as their claims are based on functional and instrumental needs rooted in actual life conditions. What they want can be put in simple language but does not contribute towards raising any catchy slogans. Their needs and goals cannot fit into the category of what Ernesto Laclau (1977) has termed empty signifiers that drive populist movements, like 'corruption', 'state', and 'environment'. The power of such signifiers is that they can draw a diverse group of people together and sometimes cut across class and other diversities. The dhobis are essentially limited and specific in their demand that is too closely centred on their unique livelihood. Moreover, they cannot be anti-establishment like the homeless and marginal poor, because their livelihood is not disjoined from the capitalist economy but is actually thriving as a result of its spread. But at the same time they are in danger of being ousted not by the actual economy, but by its 'imagined' vision held by the policymakers.

Thus, while the dhobis consider their livelihood as having fairly good prospects as the city grows, the city planners do not see the situation in quite the same way. In their myopic vision and zeal to emulate borrowed models of cityscapes, they regard the dhobi settlements as equivalent to slums. In their distorted vision that has very little touch with reality, they visualize a city with slick laundromats and no embarrassing dhobi ghats and hanging clothes. But this is an unrealistic vision given the onto-logical situation where the existing symbolic register is already tuned to the dhobi as the launderer. From the point of view of the dhobis, they also understand that they are set to gain from being more inclined towards civil society than political society, as their livelihood is linked to a healthy social relationship with the middle class and upper middleclass as well as businesses. At the same time, if pushed too far, they can also take up the role of a political society, as when they went on strike for several days, camping in the Town Hall and demanding more ghats and facilities to ply their trade.

In an orthogenetically evolved city like Delhi, there are rights that are vested in places and people that may not follow the formal legal pattern that was imposed on a country like India with colonial rule. In the primordial system of the jati organization (see Inden 1976), there was a place and a privilege for everyone, however basic it might have been.

The evolving market system also provides new opportunities and fresh avenues for communities like the dhobi, but it seems the contemporary political regime wishes to turn a blind eye to these facts.

What needs to be emphasized is the lack of political will and vision that ignores and overlooks an indigenous model of development. As Rajnarayan Chandavarkar (2009) has written about Bombay, the policy-makers are strongly influenced by their vision of modernity, but filtered through their own version of caste/class. Elsewhere, I have mentioned how the definition of urbanism is itself a biased one, coloured by Western theory, with little attention paid to the historical and cultural realities of non-Western cities (see Channa 2018a). The dhobis I have studied over forty years still find the pursuit of their traditional occupation viable, yet receive no official encouragement to continue with their work. By encouraging the continuity of informal sectors of the economy, the policymakers will help take the pressure off the need to provide jobs for everyone. As Brugmann (2009) suggests, it is prudent to have local versions of urbanism with active participation from local communities.

However, policymakers in the developing countries are following a distorted vision of the Western model of development that has also accepted differentiated citizenship, where not everyone is even expected to have the same or equal rights (Chatterjee 2011: 24). The homeless and destitute line the most fashionable streets in the richest parts of the world, such as New York, London, and Paris. The power-holders of a global first-class city have no option but to turn a blind eye to the blight on the city's aesthetics. Yet, confident in their First World position, they also do not care if their legitimate citizens do not conform to the ideological fantasies that the world holds about them. It is the developing countries of the South that are so concerned about their 'image'. Even while they make policies towards a futuristic city, they are influenced by values of caste and class that put a veil of obscurity over the ontological. The very non-recognition of the value of the dhobi way of life is rooted in what van Dijk has analysed as the non-separation of the 'modern' and the 'traditional' in India. Even as the policymakers profess their goal as 'modern', they themselves lack the qualities of being modern or urban that are free from subjectivity and the baggage of 'symbolic register' (van Djik 2017: 23), the meanings and constructed vision of reality that one is born with. Convinced that a low and marginal community like the dhobis have no

place in the modern space of a global city, they are blind to the possibilities of creating an indigenous version of development that has the
potential to merge and reinvent a new and locally appropriate model of
urbanism.

At the end one may round up the argument by bringing in the concepts
of political and police as envisaged by Rancière (1999). He conceptual-
izes the 'police' as 'an order of bodies that defines the allocation of ways
of doing, ways of being, and ways of saying, and sees that those bodies
are assigned by name to a particular place and task' (Rancière 1999: 29).
Within the caste system this order was almost perfected in terms of occupations, ranks, and entitlements. When caste became inscribed within
the democratic set-up and superimposed on the concept of citizenship,
that assumes an 'equality' that being non-existent opens up the possibility of the political coming into existence, where 'political' is the coming
together of the two heterogeneous processes of 'police' as defined above
and that of equality (Rancière 1999: 30). With democracy, the possibility
of equality as citizens rather than being a silenced and voiceless part of
the city has opened the possibility of the political process of a claim to a
voice and to even ask for a right to 'speech', as against the silence that was
assigned to the marginal groups within the older system of jati ranking.
It is significant that the vernacular term for 'noise' is identical in meaning
and connotation when those in power refer to the protests of the fringe
or 'silenced' groups as 'shor' (noise) rather than speech or 'awaz'. They
would often refer to the verbal protests by those who are not 'part' of
those expected to speak or have a voice as 'woh shor machete hain' ('those
people make noise'), which also means that there is no need to pay heed
to what is just noise and not speech. What the dhobis today are inching
towards is the right to have the *possibility of speech,* even if they are not
being heard.

Notes

1. Indians who have travelled or lived abroad in more egalitarian set-ups like the USA may develop more liberal ideologies or may be influenced by their education and reading.
2. Mirza Ghalib was one of the most popular poets (*shayar*) of Old Delhi in the nineteenth century, whose couplets are extremely popular even to this day. His *haveli* (place of residence)
was, however, lying in a neglected state until the Delhi government's plans to restore it as a
heritage site.

Bibliography

Abraham, Janaki 2017 'The Lives of Others: The Production and Influence of Neighbourhood Cultures in Urban India' in I Pardo and G Prato (eds.) *The Palgrave Handbook of Urban Ethnography*, Cham: Palgrave Macmillan, pp 95–111.

Abu-Lughod, Lila 1991 'Writing Against Culture' in Richard G Fox (ed.) *Recapturing Anthropology: Working in the Present* , Santa Fe: School of American Research Press, pp 137–54, 161–2.

Ahmad, Zarin 2018 *Delhi's Meatscapes: Muslim Butchers in a Transforming Mega-City*, New Delhi: Oxford University Press.

Allen, Charles 2012 *Ashoka: The Search for India's Lost Emperor*, London: Abacus.

Aloysius, G 1997 *Nationalism without a Nation in India*, New Delhi: Oxford University Press.

Aloysius, G 2013 'Rediscovering God: Iyothee Thassar and Emancipatory Buddhism' in S M Channa and J Mencher (eds.) *Life as a Dalit: Views from the Bottom on Caste In India,* New Delhi: Sage, pp 208–24.

Anathamurthy, U R 2000 'Towards the Concept of a New Nationhood, Languages and Literature in India' in Peter Ronald d'Souza (ed.) *Contemporary India—Transitions*, New Delhi: Fundacao Oritente and Sage, pp 37–48.

Appadurai, Arjun 1986 'Theory in Anthropology: Centre and Periphery' *Comparative Studies in Society and History* 28(2): 356–61.

Atkinson, Paul 2017 *Thinking Ethnographically*, London: Sage.

Austin, John 1962 *How to Do Things with Words*, 2nd ed., Cambridge, MA: Harvard University Press.

Axel, Brian Keith 2002 'Introduction: Historical Anthropology and Its Vicissitudes' in Brian Keith Axel (ed.) *From the Margins: Historical Anthropology and Its Futures*, Durham and London: Duke University Press, pp 1–42.

Bapat, Dipti 2024 'Moving with Rags: India's Second Hand Clothes Recycling trade' *South Asian History and Culture* 15(1): 111–30.

Bama 2005 *Sangati: Events*, tr. from Tamil by Lakshmi Holmström, New Delhi: Oxford University Press.

Bandhumadhav 2009 'The Poisoned Bread' in Arjun Dangle (ed.) *Poisoned Bread, Translations from Modern Marathi Dalit Literature*, New Delhi: Orient Black Swan.

Basham, A L 1967 [1954] *The Wonder that Was India; A Survey of the History and Culture of the Indian Sub-Continent before the Coming of the Muslims*, London: Fontana Collins.

Bayly, Susan 1999 *Caste, Society and Politics in India from the Eighteenth Century to the Modern Age*, Cambridge: Cambridge University Press.

Baviskar, Amita 2002 'Between Violence and desire: Space, Power and Identity in the making of Metropolitan Delhi' *International Social Science Journal* 55: 89–98.

Béteille, André 1969 'The Decline of Inequality?' in André Béteille (ed.) *Social Inequality* , Harmondsworth: Penguin Books, pp 362–80.

Béteille, André 2012 [1965] *Caste, Class and Power: Changing Patterns of Stratification in a Tanjore Village* (Oxford India Perennials), 3rd ed., Delhi: Oxford University Press.

Bernier, Francis 1916 *Travels in the Mogul Empire, A.D., 1656–1668*, Oxford: Oxford University Press.

Bhatty, Zarina 2016 *Purdah to Piccadilly: A Muslim Woman's Struggle for Identity*, New Delhi: Sage.

Blunt, Edward Arthur Henry 1931 *The Caste System of Northern India: With Special Reference to the United Provinces of Agra and Oudh*, London: Oxford University Press.

Bourdieu, Pierre 1996 [1984] *Distinction: A Social Critique of the Judgement of Taste*, tr. Richard Nice, Cambridge, MA: Harvard University Press.

Brass, Paul 1994 [1990] *The Politics of India Since Independence* (Cambridge History Series) Cambridge: Cambridge University Press.

Brugmann, Jeb 2009 *Welcome to the Urban Revolution: How Cities Are Changing the World*, India: HarperCollins.

Campos, Ricardo 2017 'On Urban (In)Visibilities' in John Hannigan and Greg Richards (eds.) *The Sage Handbook of New Urban Studies*, New Delhi: Sage, pp 232–49.

Carstaris, Morris G 1967 *The Twice Born* , Bloomington: Indiana University Press.

Certeau, Michel de 1984 *The Practice of Everyday Life*, tr. Steven Randall, Berkeley: University of California Press.

Chakrabarty, Uma 2003 *Gendering Caste through a Feminist Lens*, Calcutta: Stree.

Chandavarkar, Rajnarayan 2009a *History, Culture and the Indian City*, Cambridge: Cambridge University Press.

Chandavarkar, Rajnarayan 2009b 'Urban History and Urban Anthropology in South Asia' in *History, Culture and the Indian City: Essays by Rajnarayan Chandavarkar* , Cambridge: Cambridge University Press, pp 206–35.

Channa, Subhadra Mitra 1985 *Tradition and Rationality in Economic Behaviour*, New Delhi: Cosmo.

Channa, Subhadra Mitra 2001 'The Right to Selfhood: The Paradox of Being a Dalit Woman' *Social Action* ·51(4): 337–52.

Channa, Subhadra Mitra 2003 'The Crafting of Human Bodies and the Racialization of Caste in India' *Ambedkar Journal of Social Development and Justice* XI: 35–49.

Channa, Subhadra Mitra 2004 'Globalization and Modernity in India: A Gendered Critique' *Urban Anthropology* 33(1): 37–73.

Channa, Subhadra Mitra 2005a 'Metaphors of Race and Caste-Based Discriminations against Dalits and Dalit Women in India' in Faye V Harrison (ed.) *Resisting Racism and Xenophobia: Global Perspectives on Race, Gender, and Human Rights*, Walnut Creek, CA: AltaMira Press, pp 49–66.

Channa, Subhadra Mitra 2005b 'The "Descent of the Pandavas": Ritual and Cosmology of the Jad of Garwhal' *European Bulletin of Himalayan Research* 28: 67–89.

Channa, Subhadra Mitra 2011 'Global Economy and Constructed Social Imagination: Intersection of Aesthetics, Race, Gender and Caste in South Asia in Peter Nas, Hao Shiyuan, and Zhang Xiaomin (eds.) *Keynotes in Anthropology*, China, pp 84–100.

Channa, Subhadra Mitra 2013a 'A Reading of "Untouchable: The Autobiography of an Indian Outcaste"' in Channa and Mencher (eds.) *Life as a Dalit* , New Delhi: Sage, pp 72–80.

Channa, Subhadra Mitra 2013b 'Becoming a Dhobi' in Channa and Mencher (eds.) *Life as a Dalit*, New Delhi: Sage, pp 171–86.

Channa, Subhadra Mitra 2013c *Gender in South Asia: Social Imagination and Constructed Realities*, Cambridge: Cambridge University Press.

Channa, Subhadra Mitra 2013d *The Inner and Outer Selves: Gender, Cosmology and Ecology on the Himalayan Borders*, Delhi: Oxford University Press.

Channa, Subhadra Mitra 2017a 'Hinduism and Jainism' in Hilary Calan (ed.) *The International Encyclopedia of Anthropology*, Hoboken, NJ: Wiley Blackwell, 1558.Channa, Subhadra Mitra 2017b 'Selves and Codified Bodies' in Simon Coleman,

Susan B Hyatt, and Ann Kingsolver (eds.) *The Routledge Companion to Contemporary Anthropology*, London and New York: Routledge, pp 219–33.

Channa, Subhadra Mitra 2018a 'Understanding Caste through an Anthropological Lens' in Dilip K Chakrabarty (ed.) *History of Ancient India VI: Social, Political and Judicial Ideas, Institutions and Practices*, Delhi: Vivekananda International Foundation and Aryan Book Depot, pp 1–42.

Channa, Subhadra Mitra 2018b 'Being Urban in the Context of Global Urbanization: The Case of India' *Diogenes* 63(3–4): 123–30.

Channa, Subhadra Mitra 2019a 'The Thirsty Village' *Social Change* 49(4): 590–604.

Channa, Subhadra Mitra 2019b 'Negotiating Gendered Violence in the Public Spaces of Indian Cities: Globalization and Urbanization in Contemporary India' in Mehrangiz Najafizadeh and Linda L Lindsay (eds.) *Women of Asia: Globalization, Development and Gender Equity*, New York: Routledge, pp 307–19.

Channa, Subahdra Mitra 2021 'Negotiating Hierarchies through Symbolic Praxis' in Biswajit Das and Debendra Prasad Majhi (eds.) *Caste, Communication and Power* , New Delhi: Sage, pp 101–20.

Channa, Subhadra Mitra 2023a 'Development Policies and Marginal Groups: Case Study of Dhobis in Delhi' in Rahul Choragudi, Soni Pellissery, and N. Jayaram (eds.) *Caste Matters in Public Policy: Issues and Perspectives*, London and New York: Routledge, pp 152–64.

Channa, Subhadra Mitra 2023b 'Discarded at Birth, Neglected if Alive: The Girl Child in India' in R Biakady et al. (eds.) *The Palgrave Handbook of Social Change*, Cham: Palgrave Macmillan, pp 1–17.

Channa, Subhadra Mitra, and Joan P Mencher (eds.) 2013 *Life as a Dalit: Views from the Bottom on Caste in Indian Society*, New Delhi: Sage.

Channa, Vardesh Chander 1979 *Caste Identity and Continuity*, Delhi: B.R. Publications.

Chatterjee, Ipsita 2013 'Social Conflict and the Neoliberal City: A Case of Hindu–Muslim Violence in India' in Gavin Shatkin (ed.) *Contesting the Indian City: Global Visions and the Politics of the Local*, John Wiley & Sons, pp 145–75.

Chatterjee, Partha 2011 *Lineages of Political Society: Studies in Postcolonial Democracy*, New Delhi: Permanent Black.

Chowdhry, Prem 2004 [1996] *The Veiled Women: Shifting Gender Equations in Rural Haryana*, New Delhi: Oxford University Press.

Cinar, Alev, and Thomas Bender (eds.) 2007 *Urban Imaginaries: Locating the Modern City*, Minneapolis: University of Minnesota Press.

Clifford, James 1990a 'Introduction: Partial Truths' in James Clifford and George E Marcus (eds.) *Writing Culture: The Poetics and Politics of Ethnography*, Delhi: Oxford University Press, pp 1–26.

Clifford, James 1990b 'On Ethnographic Allegory' in James Clifford and George E Marcus (eds.) *Writing Culture: The Poetics and Politics of Ethnography*, Delhi: Oxford University Press, pp 98–121.

Cook, Scott 1966 'The Obsolete Anti-Market Mentality: A Critique of the Substantive Approach in Economic Anthropology' *American Anthropologist* 63: 1–25.

Cook, Scott 1973 'Economic Anthropology: Problems in Theory, Method and Analysis' in John J Honnigman (ed.) *Handbook of Social and Cultural Anthropology*, London: Rand McNally.

Cooley, Charles Horton 1902 *Human Nature and the Social Order*, New York: C. Scribner's Sons.

Cooley, Charles Horton 1998 *On Self and Social Organization,* ed. Hans-Joachim Schubert, Chicago: University of Chicago Press.

Dalmia, Vasudha 2017 *Fiction as History*, New Delhi: Permanent Black.

Dalrymple, William 1993 *City of Djinns*, London: Penguin Books.

Dangle, Arjun 1992 *Poisoned Bread: Translations from Modern Marathi Dalit Literature*, Bombay: Orient Longman.

Dehlvi, Sadia 2010 *Sufism: The Heart of Islam*, New Delhi: HarperCollins.

Deka, Kaushik 2022 'Government Jobs: The Hunger and the Mess' *India Today* 28: pp 22–30.

Deliège, Robert 1999 *The Untouchables of India*, tr. from the French by Nora Scott, Oxford: Berg.

Derrida, Jacques 1974 *Of Grammatology*, Baltimore: Johns Hopkins University Press.

Dirks, Nicholas B 2001 *Castes of Mind: Colonialism and the Making of Modern India*, Princeton, NJ: Princeton University Press.

Dube, Saurabh 1998 *Untouchable Pasts: Religion, Identity and Power among a Central Indian Community, 1780–1950*, Albany, NY: State University of New York Press.

Dumont, Louis 1970 *Homo Hierarchicus: The Caste System and Its Implications*, Chicago: University of Chicago Press.

Dumont, Louis 1986 [1957] *A South Indian Subcaste: Social Organization and Religion of the Pramalai Kallar*, Delhi: Oxford University Press.

Eliade, Mircea 1959 *The Sacred and the Profane: The Nature of Religion*, tr. Willard R Trask, New York: Harcourt, Brace & World.

Engebretsen, Elisabeth Lund 2012 'On Urban Anthropology in Contemporary China' in Italo Pardo and Giuliana B Prato (eds.) *Anthropology in the City: Methodology and Theory*, Farnham: Ashgate, pp 191–214.

Folke, C 2006 'Resilience: the Emergence of a Perspective for Social-Ecological Systems Analysis' *Global Environmental Change* 16: 253–67.

Foucault, Michel 1976 *History of Sexuality: 1, The Will to Knowledge*, London: Penguin Books.

Fox, Richard 1977 *Urban Anthropology*, Englewood Cliffs, NJ: Prentice Hall.

Freeman, James M 1979 *Untouchable: An Indian Life History*, London: George Allen & Unwin.

Fuller, Christopher J 1987 'The Hindu Pantheon and the Legitimation of Hierarchy' *Manns* 23(1): 19–39.

Geertz, Clifford 1973 *The Interpretation of Cultures*, New York: Basic Books.

Gidwani, Vinay, and Anant Maringati 2016 'The Waste-Value Dialectic: Lumpen Urbanization in Contemporary India' *Comparative Studies of South Asia, Africa and the Middle East* 36(1): 112–33

Gill, Kaveri 2010 *Of Poverty and Plastic: Scavenging and Scrap Trading Entrepreneurs in India's Urban Informal Economy* , New Delhi: Oxford University Press.

Godelier, Maurice 1972 *Rationality and Irrationality in Economics*, London: New Left Books.Goffman, Erving 1956 [1971] *The Presentation of Self in Everyday Life*, Edinburgh: University of Edinburgh Social Science Research Centre.

Goody, Jack 1973 *Bridewealth and Dowry*, Cambridge: Cambridge University Press.

Goodfriend, D 1983 'Changing Concepts of Caste and Status among Old Delhi Muslims in India' in Imtiaz Ahmad (ed.) *Modernization and Social Change among Muslims in India*, Delhi: Manohar Publications, pp 119–52.

Gotham, Kevin Fox, and Bradford Powers 2017 'Constructing and Contesting Resilience in Post-Disaster Urban communities' in John Hannigan and Greg Richards (eds.) *The Sage Handbook of New Urban Studies*, New Delhi: Sage, pp 139–54.

Gould, Harold A 1965 'Lucknow Rickshawallas: The Social Organization of an Occupational Category' *International Journal of Comparative Sociology* 6(1): 24–47.

Grove, Jairus Victor 2019 *Savage Ecology: War and Geopolitics at the End of the World*, Durham and London: Duke University Press.

Guha, Ranajit 2009a 'A Colonial City and its Time(s)' in Partha Chatterjee (ed.) *The Small Voice of History: Ranajit Guha, Collected Essays*, New Delhi: Permanent Black, pp 409–34.

Guha, Ranajit 2009b 'Writing the Past: Where Generations Meet' in Partha Chatterjee (ed.) *The Small Voice of History: Ranajit Guha, Collected Essays*, New Delhi: Permanent Black, pp 333–45.

Gupta, Charu 2018 *The Gender of Caste: Representing Dalits in the Present*, Washington: University of Washington Press.

ikGupta, Charu Smita 1996 *Zardozi: Glittering Gold Embroidery*, New Delhi: Shakti Malik Abhinav Publications.

Gupta, Charu Smita, and Subhadra Mitra Channa 1996 'Caste among the Muslim Zardoz of Delhi: A Study of Occupational Culture and Sub-Group Identity' *Man in India* 76(2): 103–13.

Gupta, Dipankar, 1991 'Continuous Hierarchies and Discrete Castes' in Dipankar Gupta (ed.) *Social Stratification*, Delhi: Oxford University Press, pp 110–45.

Gupta, Narayani 1981 *Delhi between Two Empires, 1803–1931: Society, Government and Urban Growth*, New Delhi: Oxford University Press.

Gusterson, Hugh 1997 'Studying Up Revisited' *Political and Legal Anthropology Review* 20(1): 114–19.

Habib, Irfan 2007 [1995] *Essays in Indian History: Towards a Marxist Perception*, New Delhi: Tulika Books.

Hannarez, Ulf 2010 *Anthropology's World: Life in a Twenty-First Century Discipline*, London: Pluto Press.

Hannigan, John, and Greg Richards 2017 'Introduction' in John Hannigan and Greg Richards (eds.) *The SAGE Handbook of Urban Studies*, New Delhi: Sage, pp 1–14.

Harraway, Donna J 1999 'Situated Knowledge: The Science Question in Feminism and the Privilege of Partial Perspective' in Anthony Elliott (ed.) *The Blackwell Reader in Contemporary Social Theory*, London: Blackwell, pp 287–95.

Hart, K 1973 'Informal Income Opportunities and Urban Employment in Ghana' *Journal of Modern African Studies* 11(1): 61–89.

Hazari 1951 *An Indian Outcaste: The Autobiography on an Untouchable*, London: Bannisdale Press (repr. 1969, New York: Praeger Publications).

Hearn, Gordon Risley 1905 *Seven Cities of Delhi*, Calcutta and Shimla: Thacker, Spink & Co.

Hocart, A M 1950 *Caste: A Comparative Study*, London: Methuen.

Hosbey, Justin 2016 'I Looked with All the Eyes I Had: Black Women's Vision and the Stakes of Heritage in Nicodemus, Kansas' *Urban Anthropology* 45(3–4): 303–47.

Inden, Ronald B 1976 *Marriage and Rank in Bengali Culture: A History of Caste and Clan in Middle Period Bengal*, Berkeley: University of California Press.

Jackson, Antoinette T 2009 'Conducting Heritage Research and Practicing Heritage Resource Management on a Community Level—Negotiating Contested Historicity' *Practicing Anthropology* 31(3): 5–10.

Jangam, Chinnaiah 2017 *Dalits and the Making of Modern India*, New York: Oxford University Press.

Kakar, Sudhir 1991 *Shamans, Mystics and Doctors: A Psychological Inquiry into India and its Healing Traditions*, Chicago Illinois: University of Chicago Press.

Kalb, Don, and Massimiliano Mollona 2018 'Introductory Thoughts on Anthropology and Urban Insurrection' in Don Kalb and Massimiliano Mollona (eds.) *Worldwide Mobilizations: Class Struggle and Urban Commoning*, New York and Oxford: Berghahn Books, pp 1–30.

Kapadia, Karin 1995 *Siva and her Sisters*, Boulder, CO: Westview Press.

Kapferer, Bruce, and Christine C Taylor 2012 'Introduction: Forces in the Production of the State' in Angela Hobart and Bruce Kapferer (eds.) *Contesting the State: The Dynamics of Resistance and Control,* Canon Pyon: Sean Kingston Publishing, pp 1–20.

Kapoor, Shivani 2018 'The Search for "Tanner's Blood": Caste and Technical Education in Colonial Uttar Pradesh' *Review of Development and Change* 23(2): 118–38.

Khare, R S 1985 *The Untouchable as Himself: Ideology, Identity and Pragmatism among the Lucknow Chamars,* Cambridge: Cambridge University Press.

King, Loren Antony 2018 'Henri Lefebvre and the Right to the City' in Sharon M Meagher, Samantha Noll, and Joseph S Biehl (eds.) *The Routledge Handbook of Philosophy of the City,* London and New York: Routledge, pp 76–86.

Kothari, Rajni 1995 [1970] *Caste in Indian Politics,* New Delhi: Orient Longman.

Kuldova, Tereza 2017 'Guarded Luxotopias and Expulsions in New Delhi: Aesthetics and Ideology of Outer and Inner Spaces of an Urban Utopia' in Tereza Kuldova and Mathew A Varghese (eds.) *Urban Utopias: Excess and Expulsion in Neoliberal South Asia ,* London: Palgrave Macmillan, pp 37–52.

Kuldova, Tereza, and Mathew A Varghese 2017 'Introduction' in Tereza Kuldova and Mathew A Varghese (eds.) *Urban Utopias: Excess and Expulsion in Neoliberal South Asia ,* London: Palgrave Macmillan, pp 1–16.

Kumar, N 1988 *The Artisans of Benaras: Popular Culture and Identity, 1880–1986 ,* Princeton, NJ: Princeton University Press.

Laclau, Ernesto 1977 *Politics and Ideology in Marxist Theory: Capitalism, Fascism, Populism,* London: Verso.

Lamphere, Louise 1993 'The Domestic Sphere of Women and the Public World of Men: The Strengths and Limitations of an Anthropological Dichotomy' in Caroline B Brettell and Carolyn F Sargent (eds.) *Gender in Cross-Cultural Perspective ,* Englewood Cliffs, NJ: Prentice Hall.

Leach, E R 1960 'Introduction: What Should We Mean by Caste?' in E R Leach (ed.) *Aspects of Caste in South India, Ceylon and North-West Pakistan,* Cambridge: Cambridge University Press.

Leacock, Eleanor, and Richard Lee 1982 'Inroduction' in Eleanor Leacock and Richard Lee (eds.) *Politics and History in Band Societies,* Cambridge: Cambridge University Press.

LeClair, Edward E, and Harold K Schneider 1968 *Economic Anthropology: Readings in Theory and Analysis,* New York: Holt, Rinehart & Winston.

Lefebvre, Henri 1996 *Writing on Cities,* tr. by Eleanor Kofman and Elizabeth Lebas, Oxford: Blackwell Publishing.

Lévi-Strauss, Claude 1967 *The Elementary Structures of Kinship,* London: Eyre & Spottiswood.

Liddle, Swapna 2017 *Chandni Chowk: The Mughal City of Old Delhi,* New Delhi: Speaking Tiger.

Lorde, Audre 1992 'Age, Race, Class and Sex: Women Redefining Difference' in Helen Crowly and Susan Himmelweit (eds.) *Knowing Women: Feminism and Knowledge,* Cambridge: Polity Press in association with Open University, pp 47–57.

Lynch, Owen 1969 *The Politics of Untouchability: Social Mobility and Social Change in a City of India,* New York: Columbia University Press.

Madsen, Stig Toft 2023 'Caste In and Out of Place: State, Market and Culture' in R Choragudi, S Pellissery, and N Jayaram (eds.) *Caste Matters in Public Policy: Issues and Perspectives,* London and New York: Routledge, pp 25–46.

Marcus, George E 1990 'Contemporary Problems of Ethnography in the Modern World System' in James Clifford and George E Marcus (eds.) *Writing Culture: The Poetics and Politics of Ethnography,* New Delhi: Oxford University Press, pp 165–93.

Marshall, John H 1931 *Mohenjo Daro and the Indus Civilization,* London: Arthur Probsthain.

Mathur, Nayanika 2016 *Paper Tiger: Law, Bureaucracy and the Developmental State in Himalayan India,* Cambridge: Cambridge University Press.

Mayer, Adrian C 1960 *Caste and Kinship in Central India: A Village and Its Region,* London: Routledge & Kegan Paul.

Mead, Margaret 1949 *Coming of Age in Samoa,* New York: Mentor Books.

Meillassoux, Claude 1981 *Maidens, Meal and Money: Capitalism and the Domestic Community,* Cambridge: Cambridge University Press.

Mencher, Joan 1974 'The Caste System Upside Down or The Not-So-Mysterious East', *Current Anthropology* 15(4): 469–93.

Mendelsohn, Oliver, and Marika Vicziany 1998 *The Untouchables: Subordination, Poverty and the State in Modern India,* Cambridge: Cambridge University Press.

Mines, Diana 2002 'The Hindu Gods in a South Indian Village' in Diane M Mines and Sarah Lamb (eds.) *Everyday Life in South Asia,* Bloomington: Indiana University Press.

Moffat, Michael 1979 *An Untouchable Community in South India: Structure and Consensus,* Princeton, NJ: Princeton University Press.

Mohan, Sanal and Joel, Lee 2022 'Dalit Religion' *Religion Compass,* https://doi.org/10.111/rec3.12429.

Mohanty M 2006 'Social Inequality, Labour Market Dynamics and Reservation' *Economic and Political Weekly* XLI(35): 3777–89.

Monge, Fernando 2012 'Urban Anthropological Research: Urban Spaces and New Ways of Liv Ming' in Italo Pardo and Giuliana B Prato (eds.) *Anthropology in the City: Methodology and Theory,* Farnham: Ashgate, pp 215–24.

Moon, Vasant K 2001 *Growing Up Untouchable in India: A Dalit Autobiography,* tr. from Marathi by Gail Omvedt, New Delhi: Vistaar Publications.

Mumford, Lewis 1961 *The City in History,* New York: Harcourt, Brace & World.

Narayan, Badri 2001 *Documenting Dissent: Contesting Fables, Contested Memories and Dalit Political Discourse,* Shimla: Indian Institute of Advanced Studies.

Narayan, Badri 2021 *Republic of Hindutva: How the Sangh is Reshaping Indian Democracy,* India: Viking Penguin.

Narula, Smita 1999 *Broken People: Caste Violence against India's 'Untouchables',* New Delhi: Human Rights Watch.

Natarajan, Balmurali 2012 *The Culturalization of Caste In India: Identity and Inequality in a Multicultural Age,* Abingdon: Routledge.

Obama, Barack 1995 *Dreams from My Father,* New York: Three Rivers Press.

O'Hanlon, Rosalind 1985 *Caste, Conflict and Ideology: Mahatma Jotirao Phule and Low Caste Protest in Nineteenth-Century Western India,* Cambridge: Cambridge University Press.

Oldenburg, Veena Talwar 1984 *The Making of Colonial Lucknow 1856–1877,* Princeton, NJ: Princeton University Press.

Omvedt, Gail 1994 *Dalits and the Democratic Revolution: Dr. Ambedkar and the Dalit Movement in Colonial India,* New Delhi: Sage.

Otto, Rudolph 1923 *The Idea of the Holy,* London: Oxford University Press (tr., pub. 1917 in German).

Pallath, J J 1995 *Theyyam: An Analytical Study of the Folk Culture, Wisdom and Personality,* New Delhi: Indian Social Institute.

Pardo, Italo 1996 *Managing Existence in Naples: Morality, Action and Structure,* Cambridge: Cambridge University Press.

Pardo, Italo 2018 'Corrupt, Abusive and Legal: Italian Breaches of the Democratic Contract' *Current Anthropology* 59(S18): 60–71.

Pardo, Italo, and Giuliana B Prato 2012 'Introduction: The Contemporary Significance of Anthropology in the City' in Italo Pardo and Giuliana Prato (eds.) *Anthropology in the City: Methodology and Theory*, Farnham: Ashgate, pp 1–28.

Pardo, Italo, and Giuliana B Prato 2021 'Querying Urban Inequalities' in Italo Pardo and Giuliana B Prato (eds.) *Urban Inequalities: Ethnographically Informed Reflections*, Cham: Palgrave MacMillan, pp 1–24.

Parry, Jonathan 2012 'Comparative Reflections on Fieldwork in Urban India: A Personal Account' in Italo Pardo and Giuliana B Prato (eds.) *Anthropology in the City: Methodology and Theory*, Farnham: Ashgate, pp 29–52.

Pettigrew, Joyce J M 1975 *A Study of the Political System of the Sikh Jat*, London: Routledge & Kegan Paul.

Picket, S T A, M L Cadenaso, and J M Grove 2004 'Resilient Cities, Meanings, Models, and Metaphor for Integrating the Ecological, Socio-Economic and Planning Realms' *Landscape and Urban Planning* 69: 369–84.

Pike, A, S Dawley, and J Tomaney 2010 'Resilience, Adaptation and Adaptability' *Cambridge Journal of Religion, Economy and Society* 3: 59–70.

Pocock, David E 1960 'Sociologies: Urban and Rural' *Contributions to Indian Sociology* 4: 63–81.

Prashad, Vijay 2000 *Untouchable Freedom: A Social History of a Dalit Community*, New Delhi: Oxford University Press.

Raheja, Gloria Goodwin 1988 *The Poison in the Gift: Ritual, Prestation and the Dominant Caste in a North Indian Village*, Chicago: University of Chicago Press.

Ram, Nandu 2008 *Dalits in Contemporary India: Discrimination and Discontent*, Delhi: Siddhant Publications.

Ram, Nandu 2013 'Atrocities and Segregation in an Urban Social Structure' in Subhadra Mitra Channa and Joan P Mencher (ed.) *Life as a Dalit: Views from the Bottom on Caste in India*, New Delhi: Sage, pp 35–52.

Rancière, Jacques 1999 *Disagreement: Politics and Philosophy*, Minneapolis: University of Minnesota Press.

Rao, Anupama 2003 'Introduction' in Anupama Rao (ed.) *Gender and Caste*, New Delhi: Kali for Women, pp 1–47.

Redfield, Robert 1955 'The Social Organization of Tradition' *Far Eastern Quarterly* 15(1): 13–25.

Redfield, Robert 1956 *Peasant Society and Culture*, Chicago: University of Chicago Press.

Redfield, Robert, and Milton B Singer 1954 'The Cultural Role of Cities' *Economic Development and Cultural Change* 3: 53–73.

Redman, C L 2005 'Resilience Theory in Archaeology' *American Anthropologist* 107: 70–7.

Risley, Herbert H 1891 *The Tribes and Castes of Bengal: Anthropometric Data*, New Delhi: Rupa & Co. (repr. ed.).

Robinson, Jennifer 2006 *Ordinary Cities: Between Modernity and Development*, London: Routledge

Robinson, Rowena, and Sathianathan Clarke 2003 *Religious Conversion in India: Modes, Motivations and Meanings*, New Delhi: Oxford University Press.

Rosaldo, Renato 1997 'Grief and a Head Hunter's Rage' in Terence Bunk, Suzanne Diamon, Priscilla Perkins, and Ken Smith (eds.) *Literacies*, New York: W.W. Norton & Co., pp 469–87.

Roy, Ash Narain 2022 'We the Republic?' *The Statesman* 12: p 6.

Safvi, Rana 2019 *Shahjahanabad: The 'Living' City of Old Delhi*, India: Harper Collins.

Sahlins, Marshall 1972 *Stone Age Economics*, London and New York: Routledge.

Sahni, Bhisham 2008[1972] *Tamas*, Delhi: Penguin India.

Sarkar, Sumit 1997 *Writing Social History*, New Delhi: Oxford University Press.

Sassen, Saskia 1991 *The Global City*, Princeton, NJ: Princeton University Press.

Sassen, Saskia 2002 'Locating Cities on Global Circuits' *Environment and Urbanization* 14(1): 13–30.

Sax, William 2009 *God of Justice: Ritual Healing and Social Justice in the Central Himalayas*, Oxford: Oxford University Press.

Schneider, David 1968 *American Kinship: A Cultural Account*, Englewood Cliffs, NJ: Prentice Hall.

Scott, James C 1985 *Weapons of the Weak: Everyday Forms of Peasant Resistance*, New Haven: Yale University Press.

Searle-Chatterjee, Mary 1981 *Reversible Sex Roles: The Special Case of Benaras Sweepers*, Oxford: Pergamon Press.

Sen, K M 1961 *Hinduism*, Penguin Books.

Seneviratne, H L (ed.) 1997 *Identity, Consciousness and the Past: Forging of Caste and Community in India and Sri Lanka*, Delhi: Oxford University Press.

Shah, A M 1998 *The Family in India: Critical Essays*, New Delhi: Orient Longman.

Shatkin, Gavin, and Sanjeev Vidyarthi 2014 'Introduction: Contesting the Indian City: Global Visions and the Politics of the Local' in Gavin Shatkin (ed.) *Contesting the Indian City, Global Visions and the Politics of the Local*, Chichester: Wiley Blackwell, pp 1–38.

Simmel, Georg 1903 *The Metropolis and Mental Life*, New York: Free Press (repr. 1976).

Singh, Khushwant 1956 *Train to Pakistan*, Penguin Books.

Singh, K S 1993 *The Scheduled Castes*, Delhi: Oxford University Press.

Singh, Paras 2022 'Two Key Walled City Heritage Sites in Delhi's Revamp Plans' *Hindustan Times*, 25: p 5.

Sjoberg, Gideon 1960 *The Pre-Industrial City: Past and Present*, Glencoe, IL: Free Press.

Smith, Brian K 1994 *Classifying the Universe: The Ancient Indian Varna System and the Origins of Caste*, New York: Oxford University Press.

Spiro, Melford E 1967 *Burmese Supernaturalism: A Study in the Explanation and Reduction of Suffering*, Englewood Cliffs, NJ: Prentice Hall.

Srinivas, M N 1952 *Religion and Society among the Coorgs of South India*, New Delhi: Oxford University Press.

Srinivas, M N 1959 'The Dominant Caste in Rampura' *American Anthropologist* 61: 1–16.

Srinivas, M N 1962 *Caste in Modern India and Other Essays*, Bombay: Asia Publishing House.

Srinivas, M N 1966 *Social Change in Modern India*, Berkeley, CA: University of California Press.

Srivastava, Kumkum 2009 *The Wandering Sufis: Qalandars and their Path*, New Delhi: Aryan Books International.

Stevenson, Deborah 2003 *Cities and Urban Cultures*, Maidenhead: Open University Press, McGraw Hill.

Tambiah, S J 1973 'From Varna to Caste through Mixed Unions' in Jack Goody (ed.) *The Character of Kinship* , Cambridge: Cambridge University Press, pp 191–230.

Tambs-Lyche, Harald 2017 *Transaction and Hierarchy: Elements for a Theory of Caste*, Delhi: Manohar.

Tambs-Lyche, Harald 2021 'Caste: History and the Present' *Academia Letters* June 2021: 1–3.

Thapar, Romilla 1992 *Interpreting Early India*, New Delhi: Oxford University Press.

The Managing Committee, Central Hindu College Benaras 1916 *Sanatana Dharma: An Elementary Text Book*, Benaras: Pandya Gulab Shankar at Tara Printing House.

Thiessen, Ilka 2012 'Skopje as a Research Site: Issues of Methodology and Representation' in Italo Pardo and Giuliana Prato (ed.) *Anthropology in the City: Methodology and Theory*, Farnham: Ashgate, pp 101–17.

Thornton, Margaret 1991 'The Public/Private Dichotomy: Gendered and Discriminatory' *Journal of Law and Society* 18(4): 448–63.

Trautmann, Thomas R 1997 *Aryans and the British in India*, Berkeley: University of California Press.

Unnithan-Kumar, Maya 1997 *Identity, Gender and Poverty: New Perspectives on Caste and Tribe in Rajasthan*, Oxford: Berghahn Books.

Valmiki, Omprakash 2001 *Joothan: An Untouchable's Life*, New York: Columbia University Press.

Van Dijk, Tara 2017 'The Impossibility of World Class Slum Free Indian Cities and the Fantasy of "Two Indias"' in Tereza Kuldova and Mathew A Varghese (eds.) Urban Utopias: Excess and Expulsion in Neoliberal South Asia, London: Palgrave MacMillan, pp 19–36.

Walsh, Judith E 2011 *A Brief History of India*, New York: Facts on File.

West, Condance and Don H Zimmerman 1987 'Doing Gender' gendered. *Society* 5(1): 125–51.

Williams, Raymond 1973 *The Country and the City*, London: Chatto & Windus and Spokesman Books.

Wirth, Louis 1964 *Urbanism as a Way of Life*, Chicago: University of Chicago Press.

Wiser, W H 1936 *The Hindu Jajmani System*, Lucknow: Lucknow Publishing House.

Wolf, Eric 1982 *Europe and the People without History*, Berkeley: University of California Press.

Yagi, Yoko 1999 'Rituals, Service Castes, and Women: Rites of Passage and the Conception of Auspiciousness and Inauspiciousness in Northern India' in Masakazu Tanaka and Musashi Tachikawa (eds.) *Living With Sakti: Gender, Sexuality and Religion in South Asia*, Osaka: National Museum of Ethnology, pp 243–81.

Yiftachel, Oren 2009 'Theoretical Notes on "Gray Cities": The Coming of Urban Apartheid?' *Planning Theory* 8(1): 88–100.

Zerubavel, Eviatar 2012 *Ancestors and Relatives: Genealogy, Identity, and Community* , Oxford: Oxford University Press.

Zizek, Slavoj 1993 *Tarrying with the Negative: Kant, Hegel and the Critique of Ideology*, Durham: Duke University Press.

Author Index

For the benefit of digital users, indexed terms that span two pages (e.g., 52–53) may, on occasion, appear on only one of those pages.

Abraham, Janaki 17–18
Abu-Lughod, Lila 125
Ahmad, Zarin 7, 14–15, 16–17, 22–23, 28–30, 36–38, 42–43, 64, 74–75, 201, 203, 213–14
Allen, Charles 27
Aloysius, G. 179
Anathamurthy, U. R. 220–22
Appadurai, Arjun 118
Atkinson, Paul 54
Austin, John 215
Axel, Brian Keith 9–10, 21–22

Bama 138, 206–7, 218–19
Bapat, Dipti 233
Basham, A. L. 46–47
Baviskar, Amita 40–41, 112–13
Bayly, Susan 42–43, 45–46, 216–17
Bender, Thomas 224–25
Beteille, André 17–18
Bhatty, Zarina 44–45, 56–57, 176
Blunt 199
Bourdieu, Pierre 3, 4, 233
Brass, Paul 60–61, 175, 198–99
Brugmann, Jeb 232, 235

Campos, Ricardo 226
Certeau, Michel de 2–3, 120, 157–58
Chakrabarty, Uma 137
Chandavarkar, Rajnarayan 217, 235
Channa, Subhadra Mitra 4, 7–8, 17–18, 20–21, 24–25, 28–30, 44, 48, 56, 59, 67, 70, 91, 94–95, 97, 99–100, 101–2, 103, 108, 114–16, 137, 154, 155–56, 158–59, 162–63, 193–96, 202–3, 207–8, 214, 220–22, 223–27, 232, 235
Chatterjee, Ipsita 231, 232, 233–34
Chatterjee, Partha 235–36
Chowdhry, Prem 65–66

Cinar, Alev 224–25
Clarke, Sathianathan 207–8
Clifford, James 6–7, 31–32
Cook, Scott 1–2, 3, 21–22, 23–24, 53, 97, 100, 101–2
Cooley, Charles 17–18

Dalmia, Vasudha 22–23, 30–31, 33–34, 37
Dangle, Arjun 206–7, 219
Das 28–30
Dehlvi, Sadia 160, 175–76
Deliege, Robert 6, 22–23, 193, 199
Derrida, Jacques 6–7, 101–2
Dirks, Nicholas B. 42–43
Dube, Saurabh 179, 207–8
Dumont, Louis 58–59, 62, 166–67, 206–7, 213–14, 220

Eliade, Mirce 170–71
Engebretsen, Elisabeth Lund 3
Ernesto Laclau 233–34

Folke, C. 25–26
Foucault, Michel 217, 220–22
Fox, Richard 9–10
François Bernier 22–23
Fuller, Christopher J. 166–67

Geertz, Clifford 163–64
Gidwani, Vinay 230–31
Gill, Kaveri 2–3, 7, 8–9, 14–15, 16–17, 24–25, 36–37, 40–41, 42–43, 64–65, 91, 131, 203, 204, 212, 214
Godelier, Maurice 20–21, 100
Goffman, Erving 103
Goody, Jack 142–43
Gotham, Kevin Fox 25–26
Grove, Jairus Victor 20, 31–32
Guha, Ranajit 20–22, 120

Gupta, Charu 16–17, 27, 28–30, 48–49
Gupta, Charu Smita, 42–43, 64, 197–98
Gupta, Dipankar 44, 202–3
Gupta, Narayani 4–5, 12–13, 14–15, 22–23,
 27–31, 33

Habib, Irfan 44
Hannarez, Ulf 5–6
Hannigan, John 224–25
Hazari 206–7
Hearn, Gordon Risley 27, 32–33
Hocart, A. M. 56, 218
Hosbey, Justin 31–32

Inden, Ronald B. 57–58, 234–35

Jackson, Antoinette T. 6–7
Jangam, Chinnaiah 193–94, 196–97,
 201, 220

Kakar, Sudhir 174–75
Kalb, Don 233–34
Kapadia, Karin 162, 170–71, 220
Kapferer, Bruce 220
Kapoor, Shivani 89–90, 91, 101–2,
 203, 213–14
Khare, R. S. 16–18
Kothari, Rajni 60–61
Kuldova, Tereza 12, 232–33

Lamphere, Louise 222–23
Leach, E. R. 202–3, 218
Leacock, Eleanor 20–21
LeClair, Edward 20–21
Lee, Joel 158–59, 162–63, 168–69
Lee, Richard 20–21
Lefebre, Henri 26, 190
Lévi-Strauss, Claude 201–2
Liddle, Swapna 27
Lorde, Audre 222–23
Lynch, Owen 16–17, 43, 203

Marcus, George E. 10–11, 19–20
Maringati, Anant 230–31
Mary Searle-Chatterjee 16–17
Mathur, Nayanika 157–58
Mayer, Adrian 142–43
Mead, Margaret 132
Mencher, Joan 20–21, 202–3, 220
Mendonsohn, Oliver 6
Mines, Diana 166–67

Moffat, Michae 213–14, 220
Mohan, Sanal 158–59, 162–63, 168–69
Mohanty, M. 131
Mollona, Massimiliano 233–34
Monge, Fernando 4
Moon, Vasant K. 198
Mumford, Lewis 11

Narayan, Badri 20–21, 36–37, 160–61, 173–
 74, 179–80, 201
Natarajan, Balmurali 16–17, 103, 195–
 97, 213–14

Obama, Barack 16–17
Oldenburg, Veena Talwar 30–31
Omvedt, Gail 196–97, 198
Otto, Rudolph 170–71

Pallath, J. J. 170–71
Pardo, Italo 5–6, 11, 17–18, 220
Parry, Jonathan 7–8, 9–10, 11–12
Pettigrew, Joyce J. M. 65–66
Picket, STA 25–26
Pike, A. 25–26
Pocock. David E. 17–18, 217
Prashad, Vijay 7, 15–17, 42–43, 102, 157–58,
 159–60, 194–95, 199–201
Prato, Giuliana 11, 220

Raheja, Gloria Goodwin 28–30, 217
Ram, Nandu 20–21
Ranciere, Jacques 236
Redfield, Robert 11–12, 162–63
Redman, C. L. 25–26
Richards, Greg 224–25
Robinson, Jennifer 7–8, 216–17, 225–26
Robinson, Rowena 207–8
Rosaldo, Renato 3
Roy, Ash Narain 155–56

Sahlins, Marshall 94–95, 143–44
Sarkar, Sumit 4–5
Sassen, Saskia 216, 227
Sax, William 3–4, 120, 166, 167, 168–69
Schneider, David 56–57
Schneider, Harold 20–21
Searle-Chatterjee, Mary 16–17, 67, 223–24
Seneviratne, H. L. 42–43
Shah, A. M. 71–72
Shatkin, Gavin 226–27, 232
Simmel, Georg 17–18

Singer, Milton 11–12
Singh, Khushwant 35–36
Singh, Paras 228
Sjoberg, Gideon 216–17
Smith, Brian K. 56
Spiro, Melford E. 158–59
Srinivas, M. N. 8–9, 56, 57–59, 94–95, 172–73, 175, 213–14, 218
Srivastava, Kumkum 162, 169–70

Tambs-Lyche, Harald 58–59
Taylor, Christine 220
Thapar, Romilla 171
Thiessen, Ilka 24–25
Thornton, Margaret 222–23
Trautmann, Thomas R. 63, 154

Valmiki, Omprakash 207–8, 218–19
Van Dijk, Tara 214
Vicziany, Marika 6
Vidyarthi, Sanjeev 226–27, 232

Walsh, Judith E. 175
Williams, Raymond 11–12
Wirth, Louis 17–18
Wiser, W. H. 89, 94–95
Wolf, Eric 233–34

Yagi, Yoko 28–30, 89–90
Yiftachel, Oren 6

Zerubavel, Eviata 56
Zizek, Slavoj 226

Subject Index

For the benefit of digital users, indexed terms that span two pages (e.g., 52–53) may, on occasion, appear on only one of those pages.

adaptability 7–8
age at marriage 147
Ala 158, 160–63, 164–65
alcohol/alcohol drinking 56–70, 71–72, 76, 144–46, 165–66, 172–73, 187–89
All India Dhobi Mahasabha 60–61
alternative worldview 193–94
Ambedkar 194, 196–97, 198–99, 204–5
ascribed identity 120, 193–94
auspiciousness 28–30

Balmikis 15–17, 42–43, 199–201
Baniyas 33–34, 45–46, 48–49, 212–13
Bhairav/Bhairon 159, 165–69, 178–79
Bhakti movement 60–61, 160
Bhakti tradition 160
Bharatiya Janata Party 52, 175, 226–27
bhatti 38–39, 40, 95–96, 101–2, 105–8, 109–12, 117
biradari 6–7, 14–15, 20–21, 25–26, 36–37, 43, 50, 54, 58–59, 60–61, 62, 63–68, 69–70, 71, 74, 76–80, 81–87, 89–90, 96, 102, 107–8, 109–10, 113–14, 116–18, 121–22, 123–24, 125, 135–36, 138–39, 143–44, 146–47, 150–51, 154, 155–56, 157–58, 160–61, 164, 170–71, 174–75, 177, 179–80, 181–82, 184–85, 186, 189, 195–96, 201, 202–5, 207–8, 213–14, 215
bodies of women 176, 224–25
bourgeois environmentalism 112–13
bride price 67–68, 142–43
bride-givers 66–68, 85
British 14–15, 22–23, 32–36, 37, 45–47, 48–49, 51–52, 62, 63, 95–96, 228, 231–32, 233–34

caste 5–6, 7–9, 11–12, 14–16, 18–19, 21–22, 28–30, 33–34, 40, 42–44, 45, 48–49, 56, 59, 60–61, 65–66, 67, 70–72, 88–89, 90–91, 94–95, 102–3, 120–21, 122–23, 138, 147, 150–51, 159, 164, 167, 183, 187–88, 193–94, 196–98, 207–8, 216–17, 218, 222
caste and inequality 219–20
caste as 'difference', 196–98, 202–3
caste as hierarchy 197–98
caste discrimination 60–61, 155–56, 171–72, 201–2, 212–13, 219–20
dominant caste 28–30, 57–58, 94–95, 195
caste-based community solidarities 201
caste-based occupational monopolies 201–2
caste-specific deities 179
Chamar 14–15, 16–17, 28–30, 42–43, 45, 89–90, 179, 203, 204–5
Chandni Chowk 27–28, 48–49, 53, 148–49, 164–65, 180–81, 185
childcare 74, 127
city 4, 6–8, 11, 12, 15–16, 17–18, 20–21, 24–25, 27, 32–33, 34, 37–38, 40–41, 42–43, 49, 51, 61–62, 71–72, 89, 92, 95, 98, 113, 121–22, 128, 166, 196, 209–10, 213–14, 216, 225, 227, 235–36
city space 33–34, 224–25
city's landscape 27, 48–49, 226
class 5–6, 8, 15–16, 35–36, 37, 67–68, 69–70, 79, 102–3, 113, 127, 148, 154–55, 166, 171–72, 175, 190, 195, 198–99, 220–22, 224–25, 233–34, 235
clustering 17–19, 198, 216–17
collective identity 86–87, 184–85, 186, 205
colonial period 34, 35, 42–43, 45–46, 49, 130, 154, 196–97, 218, 228
community 1, 4, 5–6, 7–8, 9–10, 12, 16–17, 19–20, 23–24, 32, 42–43, 54, 58–59, 60, 61–62, 67, 76, 79, 84–85, 86–87, 92, 114, 116–17, 125, 142–43, 147, 170, 178–79, 180–81, 184, 185, 186, 195, 198, 203–4, 215, 219–20, 231, 232–33
Congress government 40–41, 78–79, 108, 161–62, 229
Connaught Place 47–48, 51–52, 53–54, 177–78

cosmology 62, 158–59

Dalit 22–23, 158–59, 168–69, 193, 194–95,
  196, 199–200, 201, 202–3, 231
  Dalit identity 22–23, 193–94, 195, 196–
  97, 201
  Dalit ideology 95–96, 202–3, 207–8
  Dalit literature 206–7
  Dalit movement 8, 193, 194, 198
death rituals 97–98, 158–59
democracy 58–59, 60–61, 130–31, 171–72,
  175, 190, 203, 236
Devi Jagarans 158–59
dharma 39–40, 58–59, 60, 217
dhobi identity 84–85, 120–21, 154, 155–
  56, 178–79
dhobi panchayats 83
Dhobi Samaj 180–81, 185, 186
dhobi women 40, 67, 77, 98, 101–2, 103, 105,
  123, 127, 137, 138, 176, 181–82, 187–88,
  211, 223, 224–25, 226
dhobi–client relationship 153, 194–
  95, 210–11
discrimination 58–59, 60–61, 62, 76, 91,
  120–21, 124–25, 154–56, 171–72, 196–
  97, 201–3, 205, 206, 212–13, 219–20
domestic space 66–67
dowry 67–68, 85, 142–43

economic liberalization of the 1990s 212
economic viability 203, 204–5
endogamous 19–20, 42–43, 56–57, 63, 64–
  66, 76, 85, 121–22, 144–45, 215
ethnographies 1, 7, 16–17, 31–32
ethnohistory 1–2, 38–39
exogamous 57–58, 65–66

fictive kinship 77–78, 95, 96–97
First War of Independence in 1857, 30–31

gated communities 12, 111, 210–11
gender division of labour/gender
  roles 211, 223
gender inequity/hierarchy 66–67
gendered power hierarchy 65–66
generational transformation 69–70
gentrification 12–14, 50, 52–53, 227–28
ghats 36–37, 41–42, 49, 51, 52, 53–54,
  73–74, 78–79, 104–5, 106–9, 111–13,
  117, 123–24, 136, 140, 146, 149, 170–
  71, 175–77
global cities 18–19, 216, 226

global market network 20, 93–94
globalization 9–10, 24–25, 93–94, 179, 223

haveli 33–34, 46–47, 48–49, 228–29
heterodox sects 160
heterogenetic 11–12
Hindu/Hinduism 8–9, 16–17, 22–23, 27–30,
  33–34, 36–37, 40, 44–45, 46–47, 56–57,
  60–61, 64, 88–89, 94–95, 97–98, 99–100,
  121, 131, 158–63, 166–67, 170–71, 173–
  74, 175–211, 218–19, 231
Hindu Khatiks 36–37, 64
Hindu national identity 171
honour of women 138
horizontal solidarities of jati 63
hypergamy 150–51

identity 10–11, 14, 19–20, 22–23, 25–26,
  32, 35, 39–40, 45–46, 56–57, 59, 61–62,
  63–64, 71, 82, 84–85, 86–87, 91, 111–12,
  120–22, 125, 138, 159, 164, 170, 171–72,
  178–79, 186–87, 190, 193–95, 197–98,
  202–3, 204–5, 210–11, 215, 227, 232
ideological basis of caste 91
inauspiciousness 28–30
Indira Gandhi 39–40, 50–51, 112–13, 175
inequality 1–2, 6, 86–87, 91, 99–100, 103,
  137, 202–3, 219–20, 222, 224–25
informal economy/sector 6, 36, 64–65, 93–
  94, 114–16, 141–42, 152, 212, 235
internal hierarchy 147–48
ironing of clothes 72–74, 141–42, 150–51

jajmani system 28–30, 44, 89, 94–95, 97–
  98, 218
Jatavs 16–17, 203, 204–5
jati 8–9, 14–15, 17–18, 20, 22–23, 45, 54, 56–
  57, 58–59, 60, 63, 65–66, 82, 85, 86–87,
  92, 120–22, 130–31, 137, 138–39, 150–
  52, 154–55, 158–59, 164, 166–67, 177–
  78, 193–94, 199, 202–3, 206–8, 216–17,
  219, 225, 229–30, 231, 234–35
jati-based Economic Relationships 231
jati-based occupations 233
Jats 57–59, 65–66
joint families/households 4, 27–28, 40,
  46–48, 70–72, 76, 78–80, 88–89, 95,
  98, 100–1, 107–9, 111, 113, 122–23,
  128–29, 133–34, 139–40, 141–42,
  147–48, 149–50, 151–52, 170–71,
  173–74, 205, 211
Jyotiba Phule 198–99

katra 14–15, 36–37, 42, 48–49, 50, 71, 76, 78, 83, 104–5, 108, 114, 127, 128–29, 136–37, 138, 148, 153, 161–62, 164, 173–74, 176, 183–84, 215, 219–20

Khatiks 16–17, 24–25, 36–37, 42–43, 64, 91, 204

kinship 9–10, 16–17, 19–20, 21, 42–43, 45, 64, 77–79, 93, 95, 96–97, 100, 177–78, 186, 194–95, 215

kinship terminology 78

life cycle rituals 158–59, 164, 170–71

little traditions 162–63

lower-caste women 137, 223–24

Mahars 45, 197–99, 207–8

Mahatma Gandhi 27–28, 37–38, 58–59, 204–5

Mandal Commission 60–61

Manusmriti 58–59, 150–51

marginal 2–3, 4–5, 6, 7, 8, 13–14, 24–25, 34, 71–72, 74–75, 91, 123, 124–25, 158–59, 164–65, 167, 169–70, 179, 190, 205–6, 207–8, 211, 212, 215, 217, 226, 231, 233–34

marginalities 67, 74–75, 86–87

marginalized communities 58–59, 150–51

market economy 6, 94–95, 131, 134–35, 203, 207–8, 233

marriage network 64–65

marriage prestations 142–43

Mayawati 8, 194–95, 203

middle-class 17–18, 22–23, 24–25, 35–36, 67, 73–74, 77, 81, 127–28, 130–31, 138–39, 144–45, 147–48, 149–50, 151–52, 170–72, 184, 211, 212–13, 224–25

migrants 6, 36–37, 45, 64–65, 121–22, 147–48, 231

Minto Road 51–52, 53–54, 104–5, 108, 112–13, 123–24, 177–78, 187

moral economy 100

Mughal 27, 32–33, 35–36, 44–45, 62, 228

Muslim butchers/Muslim Qurashis 16–17, 36–37, 64

Muslim rule in India 44

Muslim Zardoz 64, 197–98

nationalism 196–97, 227, 228

neoliberalism 6

New Institutional Economics (NIE) 2–3

Nigambodh Ghat 37–38, 185–86

Nizamuddin shrine 162

non-Western cities 7–8, 235

occupational specialization 49, 86–87, 91, 231

Old Delhi 11–12, 14–16, 20, 27, 35–36, 39–40, 45, 49–50, 61–62, 63, 64, 71–72, 84, 88–89, 92, 98, 104–5, 111, 113–14, 122–23, 129–30, 138, 148–49, 164, 166, 177–78, 179–80, 183, 185–86, 207–8

oral traditions 6–7

other backward classes (OBC) 50, 58–59

partition/partition at the time of independence 23–24, 35–36, 88–89, 102

patriarchal joint family 71–72

patriarchy 67, 125, 140–41, 186, 220–22

political mobilization 43, 60–61

political movements 58–59

positionality 3, 4

postcolonial 7–8, 37, 49, 147, 187

post-liberalization period 131

process of stereotyping 154

protest movements 60–61

public/private 222–23

purdah 48, 81, 96–97, 139–40

purity and pollution 12–13, 17–18, 48, 66–67, 97–98, 176

Ramvilas Paswan 8

Red Fort 27, 33, 37–38, 39–40, 53, 95–96, 228

reinvention of jati identity 203

religion 9–10, 14, 17–19, 23–24, 60–61, 62, 63, 158–60, 169–72, 175, 178–79, 187, 207–8

religion of the oppressed 157–58

reservation 60–61, 116–17, 120–21, 131–32, 133–34, 154–55, 196–97, 205–6, 211, 212

resettlement colonies 50, 51, 111–13, 229

rise of the Dalit movement 198

riverbank 38–39, 40–42, 74, 82–83, 92, 105–8, 110–11, 124, 131–32, 140, 208–10

river Yamuna 7, 27–28, 30, 37–38, 49, 62, 82–83, 92–93, 104, 186

sacred symbols 84–85

Sai Baba 169–70, 177, 178–79, 181

Sanatana Dharma 58–59

Scheduled Castes 60–61, 116–17, 185, 204–5

self-construction of identity/self
    identity 124, 171–72
sexual exploitation 77, 224–25
Shahjahanabad 28–30, 33–34, 37–38, 42–43,
    46–47, 61–62, 228
Sheheri dhobis 6–7, 14, 19–20, 46, 71–72,
    95, 107–8, 123–24, 125, 177–78, 182–83,
    194–95, 215, 231–32
Shobha Yatra of Nagarsain baba 83–84, 179–
    81, 185, 195–96
social and political identity 63–64
social justice 6, 91, 232
social transformations 4
son preference 67, 70
Sufi shrines 27–28, 169–70
supernatural 166–67
survival 3–4, 6–7, 19, 20–21, 26, 74,
    88–90, 94–95, 202–3, 215,
    218, 231
symbolic register 214, 234, 235–36
system of reservation 131–32

technology 41–42, 100, 110–11, 212
traditional occupation 18–20, 21–22, 36–37,
    51, 60, 63–65, 82, 95–96, 114–16, 132,

139–40, 176, 177–78, 195–96, 203, 207–
    8, 214, 229–30, 231, 235
twice-born jatis 158–59

unequal gender relations 65–66
untouchable 6, 7, 16–17, 22–23, 34, 44, 45–
    46, 47–48, 59, 62, 91, 120–21, 124–25,
    146, 154–56, 158–59, 162, 170–71, 176,
    178–79, 190, 193–95, 196–97, 198, 199,
    200–1, 202–3, 205, 206, 217, 218–20
urban anthropology 11
urban landscape 30
urban research 4
urbanism 9–10, 11, 17–18, 21–22, 225–26,
    232, 235–36
urbanization 6, 7–8, 11, 39, 45, 216

Varna 8–9, 20, 56, 58–59, 94–95, 158–59,
    193, 206–8, 217, 229, 232–33

walled city 14–15, 27–30, 33–34, 49, 51, 62,
    71–72, 164, 212–13, 216
washermen 10–11, 20, 21–22, 28–30, 34
westernization 37, 223
worldview 193–94